PRAISE FOR E

"*Embodied* absolutely covers the whole body—spiritual, emotional, physical for healing trauma. Vicky's choice of exercises and fluid writing style invite the reader on a healing journey of embodiment that can be visited many times. *Embodied* will remain on your book shelf under "healing trauma" forever. It is cutting edge writing with a complete healing plan which you can refer to and embody always. My thanks to Vicky!"

—Myrtle Heery, PhD, author of *Unearthing the Moment* and *Awakening to Aging,* and director and psychological trainer at the International Institute for Humanistic Studies, www.human-studies.com.

"Vicky Roubekas has written an intelligent and very accessible treatise on trauma: its origins, manifestations, survival mechanisms and treatments. She weaves through a feminine lens, a deeply moving memoir of her own journey accompanied by cultural commentary and up-to-date science. I will recommend *Embodied* to students and clients."

—Lisa Herman, PhD, MFT, REAT, independent scholar, writer, actor.

"Vicky provides a unique holistic approach to trauma and becoming re-connected to our bodies. Shamanism and energy work meet modern psychology in this comprehensive healing plan. From setting healthy boundaries to identifying limiting beliefs, Vicky walks us through the empowering healing process of how to live a more authentic life and truly become EMBODIED."

—Stephanie Hrehirchuk, author of *Householder Yogini: Practices & Journaling Exercises for Women who Live at the Intersection of Spirituality & Family.*

"*Embodied* presents a comprehensive and holistic vision to healing trauma and reconnecting with ourselves. From dealing with thoughts and emotions to setting boundaries and connecting with spirit, this book has all the components we need to journey on the path towards wholeness."

—Ling Lam, PhD, Lecturer in Counseling Psychology, Santa Clara University.

"*Embodied* takes you on a journey of profound self-discovery—healing hearts, resolving old traumas and transforming negative beliefs that prevent you from being (or even seeing) who you really are. Only then can you reconnect with your true self to live deeply, love fully and embody your uniqueness."

—Olga Sheean, mastery coach and author of *The Alphabet of Powerful Existence.*

"When walking through the steps Vicky took in her life to become embodied, it is easy to reflect and question the way one has approached their own life. Each chapter takes you on a mental, emotional, and spiritual journey. You can pick and choose exercises to deal with aspects of yourself that you may find challenging, which often awakens a lost and forgotten trauma out of the depths of one's memory. It's the kind of book you can come back to over and over, when things are not going right in your life—each time taking the reader to the next level of reflection and discovery, then ultimately becoming embodied."

—Constadina Zarokostas-Vasiliades, editor, writer, Reiki master, and herbalist, healthybalancedworld.com.

Embodied

How to Connect to Your Body, Ignite Your Intuition, and Harness Universal Energy for Healing

Vicky Roubekas

Foreword by
Dr. Beth Hedva

VR Publications

Published by VR Publications
Edited by Maraya Loza-Koxahn

Cover Design by ER Canedo
Cover Image by Fona | Adobe Stock
Author Photograph by Jayme Amaral Photography
Illustrations by Maila Khan and Maria Sultana Mou

Paperback: 978-1-7778784-1-2
Hardback: 978-1-7778784-0-5
E-book: 978-1-7778784-2-9

Also available in audiobook.

The intent of this book is to provide accurate general information. The author of this book disclaims any liabilities for following any of the practices, exercises, and advice contained herein. The instructions and advice printed in this book are not intended as a substitute for medical treatment or counseling with a licensed physician, counselor, or healthcare provider.

Mention of specific organizations, authorities, or websites printed in this book are offered as a resource. They do not imply endorsement by the author, nor does mention of specific organizations, authorities, or websites imply that they endorse this book or its author. While the author has made every effort to provide accurate information at the time of publication, the author does not assume any responsibility for errors, or for changes that occur after publication, nor does the author assume responsibility for third-party websites, or vouch for the content of these sites for the life of this book.

Except for family members, names and identifying characteristics of individuals mentioned have been changed to protect their privacy.

To all my past, present, and future clients,
thank you for entrusting me to hold space
on your healing journey.
I am honored and humbled to bear witness
to your vulnerability, courage, and resiliency
as you dive deep into your wounds.
You are inspirational!

CONTENTS

FOREWORD

Unlike Western sciences, ancient Eastern sciences, as well as contemporary indigenous cultures, respond to pain and loss by recognizing the sacred within every experience in life—including our traumatic injuries. *Embodied* gives the reader tools to do just that through the lens of the author's personal experience of trauma, and her healing journey through exploration of Peruvian shamanic traditions, training as a psychologist, and on-going studies in trauma recovery.

Since the end of the 19th century, when the field of psychology was conceived, we have become experts at naming trauma. Family violence. Intergenerational trauma. Developmental trauma. The trauma of dysfunctional relationships. Substance abuse. Physical abuse. Emotional intimidation. Mental coercion. Sexual exploitation. Bullying. Work-politics and harassment. Social and economic injustice… and more. We have given voice to what violates our sense of humanity, and have permission to call out those behaviors that harm our personhood, or have injured our confidence and sense of personal worth.

In the wake of recognizing the truth of our natural human vulnerability, we also have been grappling with how to recover from the stress of living with the pain that follows from enduring personal injury and betrayal. At first, every traumatic injury magnifies the experience of separation from our sense of safety, love, support, or security.

With a focus on the development of energetic hygiene and healthy psychological boundaries, *Embodied* blends Western scientific insights with Eastern spiritual healing traditions together with ancient and indigenous teachings and 'energy medicine.' This book provides practical experiential exercises designed to guide the reader along a path of spiritual Self-discovery toward integrative healing.

Whether we are conscious of it or not, we are vibrational beings. Our bodies are receiving stations transmitting neurological signals between outer and inner experiences. We are wired to interpret the molecular vibration of chemicals as a sense of smell, waves of light that impact the retina of the eye as visual perception of our world, and sound waves that become language, as well as sensory nerve transmissions that we perceive as physical reality. Ancient traditions teach how these ordinary five senses are augmented by more extraordinary subtle senses—like our gut feelings, and inner 'clairvoyant' seeing, hearing, and non-local psychic awareness, among others.

In my clinical experience, which includes supervising and training helping professionals to use embodied awareness and inner psychic resources in their clinical practice, it is more important to be inclusive rather than exclusive. This is because stress, especially traumatic stress, impacts us physically and physiologically, cognitively and mentally, emotionally and socially, psychically and spiritually, as well as energetically. The synergy of all these pieces together creates awareness that is greater than any one part alone—and this is the kind of healing needed in our current day and age.

Embodied is the next generation of this pioneering work in transpersonal psychology and spiritually-directed therapy. It offers methods to use a variety of inner resources to help the reader design their own path toward healing, health, and wholeness. Herein, you will discover that recovery of well-being happens from gaining skill in energetic healing and the ability to intuitively sense when to activate Self-care: to relax your body at will; to deliberately steady your heart in the face of life's stressful events (whether generated from memory or current events); to consciously evolve your brain to be able to respond skillfully when natural, instinctive reactions emerge if you become triggered; and to intentionally return to embody your spirit as a personal 'practice.'

When the mind is clear and quiet, the body relaxed and calm, and the heart is open and light, awareness expands. Like a gentle breeze of fresh air, suddenly everything makes sense, and it is easy to understand the relationship between yourself and others, to feel your connection to the environment, the universe—and that deeper sense of unity with everyone and everything. Eastern cultures call this 'Enlightenment,' Nirvana, or Self-realization. I call this 'embodied awareness.' After injuries are healed and energetic obstructions are removed, embodied awareness is our natural state of being.

Embodied offers the reader impeccable tools to 'do the work' to heal and awaken.

Dr. Beth Hedva
Author of *Betrayal, Trust and Forgiveness:*
A Guide to Emotional Healing and Self-Renewal
Founder of Embodied Awareness Facilitator Certification

INTRODUCTION—
WHERE MY STORY BEGINS

*"Be an advocate for the people and causes important to you,
using the most powerful tool only you have—
your personal stories."*

John Capecci and Timothy Cage

My Disconnection

Disconnecting from my body wasn't a conscious decision. I didn't wake up one day and say, "Hey, my body sucks. It isn't safe, and I don't want anything to do with it." It resulted after many experiences over the years telling me my body wasn't okay or safe. Traumas, criticisms, objectification, comparisons, and self-hatred all played their part.

I can pinpoint the day I became aware my body was unsafe. It was summer—my favorite season. I was approximately four years old. For a child, summer is the time to have fun playing with friends outside. We were in the alley close to my home when a boy, the same age as me, pulled at the front of my bathing suit bottom and peered inside. Perhaps he was curious, as kids are at that age, or maybe he wondered if I had the same body parts as him. I remember feeling intense fear.

Survival kicked in, and I fled down the alley in the opposite direction of my house. I was unable to reason. I turned left at the end of the alley to make my way around the block back to my home. Halfway up the street, I realized I would have to pass the boy and the other kids now playing in the pool at the side of an apartment building. My heart raced in panic, but I managed to hold myself together and walk past.

———

Our brains are fascinating. Besides fear and panic, I also experienced shame. Why would I, as a four-year-old, feel shame? Why would I interpret the experience as indicating something wrong with me and my body? I'm curious about whether it was my first unsafe experience, or if I had others stored in my subconscious mind. I potentially had already received messages about my body and sexuality, whether directly or indirectly. I may have been predisposed to language around not letting other people touch my private parts. Sadly, this wasn't my only traumatic experience around my body.

Growing up, I felt different—that I didn't belong. I had few friends and often felt lonely. There were limitations on what I could do within my Greek culture. I grew up in a strict household. There was no room for discussion, and there was no back talk. As such, I was unable to speak up for myself, and had low self-worth. It was a challenge for me to connect with my Canadian friends, who were free to hang out wherever, whenever, and with whomever they wanted; I felt excluded.

From a young age, I got mixed messages about my body. I felt like my body wasn't mine. Other people got to choose what I was supposed to be, or how my body could satisfy their desires.

There was an expectation from my mom about how I should look. She commented on being concerned about my weight to another woman, even though I was only slightly chubby. My mom told me what to wear in order to be *presentable* at church. I was told how to act *properly* for a girl and not embarrass the family.

My body was hypersexualized. By the age of ten, I had breasts and curves, and started menstruating. Boys and men felt they had a right to touch me. I experienced several inappropriate and unwanted sexual touches, which left me feeling scared, ashamed, and confused.

On one hand, my body wasn't good enough, and on the other hand, men objectified it.

I struggled with my weight the majority of my life, and it left me feeling socially handicapped. I felt the sting of rejection, struggled with low self-esteem and low self-confidence, and felt judged and criticized. I hated my body, felt betrayed by it, and so, I disconnected from it. It was much easier to focus on my mind, and close off any emotions that would connect me to others—other than rage. I built a sturdy wall around myself.

Defining Moment

I'll never forget the moment I recognized how disconnected I was from my body. I thought I was so clever to disengage from it. That by doing so, it wouldn't exist for others either. I didn't realize my body was still visible to others, and expressed itself in ways that were not okay with me.

The defining moment occurred in my mid-20s when someone said to me, "Your face doesn't look angry anymore." My face looked angry? Wow, that was an eye-opener. I was wearing my rage like a garment for all to see and feel.

My Philosophy

What changed for me? Being detached from people was unacceptable. I wanted to connect, to be open, and to love.

As a voracious learner, I read and participated in several alternative healing practices and training:

- I became a Reiki Master.
- I became a Peruvian shamanic practitioner, and traveled to Peru to learn from shaman healers and participate in life-altering ceremonies.
- I participated in local indigenous teachings about the medicine wheel.
- I learned about Buddhism and other Eastern philosophies.
- I took several courses on plant medicine and the chakras.[1]

Why did I choose these alternative teachings? I was born and raised in Canada. However, I grew up in a strict, indoctrinated Greek Orthodox faith that left me feeling *apart from* instead of *a part of.* There was an undercurrent of shame about being a woman. We weren't allowed to take communion, or touch any of the icons, when we had our period because we were dirty. I felt *less than*, not only in the religion, but in a patriarchal Greek culture and home. I wasn't allowed to do the same things my brother did because I was a girl. It seemed unfair and made me feel like an outsider. As an adult, I recognize many of these beliefs didn't come from religion, but from generations of men who imbibed rules for women to subjugate them.

My spirituality and connection to God were nonetheless important to me. I believed (and still do) in a God of love and compassion, not punishment. As such, I sought out new spiritual experiences to find a meaningful connection. Through energy work, breathwork, meditation, visualization, ritual, ceremony, and a connection with nature and Mother Earth, I have transformed my relationship with my body. I have let go of things that no longer serve me. I feel more grounded and at peace. I accept and love my body.

———

God is inside us, not separate from us; we all have the Divine within. When you no longer ignore or disconnect from your body, and learn ways to become embodied, you connect with your Higher Self and your Divine nature. You intuitively listen to your body's needs and work with it to support, nurture, and heal.

If you don't connect with God, that's okay. Here are some other words that might resonate with you: Creator, Divine, Goddess, Higher Self, Mother Earth, Spirit, Source, or Universe. Your beliefs are yours. You get to decide if your belief is a traditional view of God, an alternative form, or neither. Whatever your belief system, the practices in this book will help you reconnect to your body in a deep, meaningful, and invaluable way.

Why I Wrote This Book

All of my experiences define who I am and the work I do. As a psychologist, I work with women to help them process their wounds and traumas to reconnect with their bodies, become embodied, and live their true authentic selves. When they become embodied, they feel confident, deserving, worthy, and capable. I feel honored to be a part of their healing journey and to hold space to witness their transformations. I want to assist women to know they are perfect just the way they are. As such, I felt called to write this book to bring my knowledge and experiences to help more women heal, grow, and transform their relationship with their body—to reconnect and become embodied.

Embodied

What does it mean to be embodied? When embodied, you can feel into your body using all your known senses and extrasensory perceptions to understand and be present in all your experiences and with your environment. You can feel where your emotions reside in your body, and permit yourself to feel both pleasant and uncomfortable emotions. You understand how other people and the environment influence you with their energy, which supports you to set and maintain healthy boundaries. By being embodied, you are open to receiving and interacting with others, which allows for deep, meaningful connections. You can trust your body's wisdom, engage with your body's innate intuition, and connect with your higher knowing and guidance.

How to Work Through this Book

Here are some guidelines for using this book, and what to notice:

- Take as much time as you need to ensure you feel safe and comfortable. There is no reason to rush. You are not in competition with anyone. Your journey is yours alone.
- Give yourself permission to support yourself and work on your personal growth.
- I've set up this book with several headers and brief sections, so you can read one part or as many as you like.
- Have a notebook and pen handy. After you read a section, or several sections, take time for self-reflection and ask yourself some of the following questions:

  - How does this relate to me, my story, or my relationship with my body?
  - What emotions are coming up in me now? Do I feel agitated, anxious, sad, scared, or something else? (If

you struggle with naming or feeling emotions, don't worry, I'll discuss how to do so in Chapter 4.)

- What body sensations am I experiencing, if any? Do I feel pain, tired, achy, or restless? (This may be difficult, hence, why you purchased this book. There are exercises throughout the book to help you feel into your body, and Chapter 7 will explore this in more detail.)
- Was I distracted? Did I check out? Did I leave my body?
- Did any memories come up? If you have time, and feel safe to explore or journal about any memories, feel free to do so.

• There is no right or wrong way to complete the exercises in this book. Put aside self-judgment, and all-or-nothing thinking, and begin.

• Read one section, several sections, or one chapter, then take time to absorb the material; choose one exercise or concept to work on for a week or more. As that becomes easier and habitual, add in another practice or idea. Take a slow and steady approach and feel comfortable as you incorporate the changes.

• I don't like rules, and I'm not a rule follower, primarily when adamantly enforced. Teenage Vicky shows up: stubborn and rebellious. However, I do suggest you read the book from start to finish at least once. There is information and exercises that build upon each other in each chapter. Feel free to go back to specific sections to re-read and repeat exercises. Do what works best for you.

Self-Care and Coping Strategies

As you read the chapters and engage in the exercises, your trauma(s), wounds, or other disturbing experiences may surface.

You may get emotionally triggered or flooded with unprocessed or unhealed memories. If this happens, engage in self-care and coping strategies to help soothe your body and support mental, emotional, and physical well-being. Below are some suggestions:

- Close your book or journal and put it away.
- Leave the room.
- Splash some cold water on your face or take a cold shower.
- Go outside for a breath of fresh air or a walk.
- Put your back up against a tree or sit on Mother Earth to ground yourself. (See more on grounding in Chapter 6.)
- Do some deep-breathing exercises.
- Eat something small and nourishing like a handful of nuts.
- Drink a glass of water or some herbal tea.
- Take a bath with a soothing essential oil like lavender.
- Listen to calming music or a guided meditation.
- Do something distracting: watch TV, do a puzzle, or play Sudoku.
- Call a friend or family member.
- See a counselor.

I don't know where you are in your healing journey. If you have experienced several traumas in your life, and have never seen a counselor to work through those experiences, I highly recommend you see a counselor first, or in conjunction with the exercises in this book. The intention of this book is to support your reconnection with your body and help you become embodied, not to re-traumatize you. If any exercise triggers or overwhelms you, stop immediately and seek support.

Embodied Exercise

Write out what you currently do for self-care and coping strategies. Also, write out your support systems and local resources, including family, friends, counselors, support groups, agencies, or a crisis line. Who can you call or see when you are struggling and need support? Keep this list handy, add to it, and use one or several of these each day as you work through the book.

Procrastination

Let's talk about procrastination. If you are procrastinating with reading this book, or engaging in a particular exercise, something may be holding you back. It may be a limiting belief. For example, "I am not strong enough to do this." Maybe a part of your brain believes it is protecting you, and thinks you are safe the way you are and don't need to change. Change is scary. Your brain wants to ensure your survival, but this is a false threat. Your life is not in danger. Bring in your rational mind. Thank your brain (or natural instincts) for trying to protect you. Let it know you are not in danger, and you are safe enough to read this book and engage in the exercises.

Embodied Exercise

If you are procrastinating, get out a pen and paper and ask yourself two questions:

- What is the worst thing that could happen if I read this book or engage in the exercises?
- What are some positive things that could happen if I read this book or engage in the exercises?

The benefits you will experience as you engage with the exercises and connect with your body will be rewarding. You have an innate right to a meaningful connection with your body; you deserve it. Imagine being able to connect, understand and feel good in your body, and engage with yourself and others with your whole being. It is possible!

Your body is where you will experience true healing. As you connect with your body, it will provide you with invaluable insight and deep self-knowing. As you become embodied, you will live a more fulfilled and authentic life.

Word Use

I have some experiential knowledge and course work in First Nations' teachings, and have more extensive knowledge of Peruvian shamanic teachings. As such, I use the terms Mother Earth and *Pachamama* interchangeably throughout the book. In ancient Inca, Pachamama was a fertility goddess. In Quechua (the indigenous language native to Peruvians and other South Americans), *pacha* means world or cosmos, and *mama* means mother. Pachamama translates as Mother Earth or Mother Cosmos.[2]

For those who may not have come across the use of dis-ease before, this is not a typo. I intentionally use dis-ease instead of disease in the book. Yes, your body can experience disease, but I prefer to separate it as a way to indicate that your body is experiencing a lack of ease. The prefix of *dis* in disease means apart, so, in essence, disease creates a separation from your true healthy state. Your body indicates when something is out of balance so you can place your attention on it.

What to Expect

This book has three sections. The first section discusses how we disconnect from our bodies and includes trauma, boundaries, thoughts, and emotions. The second section of the book discusses how to reconnect with your body and includes mindfulness, grounding, senses, energy and shamanism. The third section comprises one chapter to help you fully integrate and embody the principles of this book to live your life more authentically.

Each chapter will help you master and apply the concepts, connect and transform your relationship with your body, and become embodied. As you listen to, connect with, and accept and love your body, you will transform how you view yourself, and how you feel in your body, reflecting how you present yourself to the world.

Chapter 1 is about trauma, and explores the following:

- The ways people disconnect from their bodies.
- The roles of the parasympathetic and sympathetic nervous systems, how they affect your body, and what you can and cannot control.
- The fight-flight-freeze response, and three lesser-known responses—fright, faint, fawn.
- How you are affected by different types of trauma.
- The Window of Tolerance to understand how you have been affected by trauma.
- How guilt and shame can cripple how you see yourself.
- The benefits of reconnecting with your body.

Chapter 2 is about boundaries, and explores the following:

- What boundaries are, how to find them, and why they are essential as you start to reconnect with your body.
- The different types of boundaries: rigid, permeable, and diffuse.

- Boundaries apply in the following six areas: mental, emotional, physical, material, sexual, and spiritual.
- Boundary violations and indicators. What happens when you have damaged, unhealthy, or missing boundaries.
- The different ways to set healthy boundaries, such as speaking up and saying no.
- How to teach others your new limits, and to recognize other people's boundaries.
- The benefits of boundaries.

Chapter 3 is about thoughts, and explores the following:

- How your thoughts lie to you.
- How to check in with your thoughts and challenge them.
- Core negative beliefs and cognitive distortions that keep you from seeing yourself rationally and truthfully.
- How thoughts influence you, and how to listen to them so you can challenge and change them.
- How to change your thoughts, shift your mindset, and recognize that words have power.
- The benefits of changing your thoughts.

Chapter 4 is about emotions, and explores the following:

- The theories of emotions.
- The different types of emotions.
- How to name your emotions.
- The 10 most common emotions, along with their synonyms.
- Emotional dysregulation.
- The difference between repressed and suppressed emotions.
- Self-awareness and how to become self-aware.

- How emotions communicate with the body and are expressed in the body.
- Emotional mastery and what a healthy expression of emotion entails.
- The benefits of allowing yourself to have, express, and feel your emotions.

Chapter 5 is about mindfulness, and explores the following:

- Self-awareness and bodily awareness.
- Mindfulness—what it is and how to practice it.
- *What* and *how* skills to become more mindful in your everyday awareness.
- Meditation, its history, and the common misconceptions people have about meditation.
- Different types of meditation.
- The power of intention.
- The benefits of mindfulness.

Chapter 6 is about grounding, and explores the following:

- The difference between centering and grounding.
- How we have become disconnected from Mother Earth.
- The science behind grounding.
- The different ways you can ground yourself.
- The philosophy of Aikido, a Japanese self-defense and martial art form.
- The four elements (earth, air, fire, and water), and how to be more grounded like the earth element.
- What it means to connect with Mother Earth, and what she provides.
- The benefits of grounding.

Chapter 7 is about your senses, and explores the following:

- The sensations your body feels.
- The eight primary senses: sight, smell, taste, hearing, touch, vestibular, proprioception, and interoception.
- How you can connect with your senses for deeper awareness, and understand what's happening in your body.
- Intuition and how to repair your relationship with your intuition.
- Inner knowing—what it is, how to listen to it, how to connect with it, and how to use it to help you make sound decisions.
- The different ways of knowing through clairvoyance, clairaudience, clairsentience, and claircognizance.
- The benefits of connecting with your body through your senses.

Chapter 8 is about energy, and explores the following:

- What energy is and how to feel it in your body.
- Reiki—a hands-on healing technique, and how it can support you.
- The different energy bodies.
- The understanding of intention.
- How to give yourself healing energy.
- How energy influences your thoughts and feelings.
- Energetic cords—what they are, how to break unhealthy cords, and how to protect your energetic boundaries.
- How stuck energy can create dis-ease in the body.
- How to clear unwanted energy from your body and your surroundings.
- The benefits of mastering energy.

Chapter 9 is about shamanism, and explores the following:

- What shamanism is and what a shaman does.
- How to utilize shamanic practices to support the healing and release of emotional wounds.
- How to create a sacred space when you do healing work.
- The concept of a *mesa*, a medicine bundle, and how to create your own mesa for healing.
- How to find your healing power stones.
- How to create a mandala on the land to release stuck emotional wounds.
- How to create a *despacho*, a prayer bundle, to return to your natural healed state.
- Shamanic journeying as a means of going beyond your self-awareness.
- The benefits of working with shamanic tools and practices.

Chapter 10 is about your authentic self, and explores the following:

- The four S's: self-compassion, self-forgiveness, self-acceptance, and self-love, and how to implement these into your life.
- How to see yourself more clearly, in a nonjudgmental way, and support the best version of yourself.

Let your journey of self-discovery with your body begin!

PART I
DISCONNECTION

1

TRAUMA—
EVERYONE HAS EXPERIENCED IT

*"Trauma is a fact of life. It does not,
however, need to be a life sentence."*

Peter A. Levine

My first diet, at the age of 14, severely restricted my caloric intake. I'd always thought that had been the beginning of my rollercoaster relationship with food, eating, and weight issues. I only now realize that I was thin; I didn't gain any weight back for more than a year after I'd first lost it. My weight issues didn't start because of my first diet, but they did play a part in what ensued. My excess weight was due to sexual abuse. I had experienced a trauma that irrevocably changed how I viewed myself, my body, and men.

The summer of 1982 was the best and worst summer of my life. I was in Greece with my family, and almost 16 years old. We were going from city to city and village to village to visit our relatives. On this particular day, my parents, an uncle, and I were in Athens to visit my aunt.

I remember I was wearing a cute blue-and-white-patterned sundress with slim straps. Having lost around thirty pounds the year before, I was the thinnest I had ever been. I felt confident, happy, and beautiful for the first time in my life. Guys were paying attention to me, even flirting, which never happened back home. I felt attractive and desirable and was excited by all the attention. If only I could have captured those feelings and saved them for the future, as that was the last time I felt that way about myself.

My parents were up on the roof with my aunt and I was downstairs with my uncle. I'm not sure why I had lagged back with my uncle. We stood inside, at the bottom of the stairs that led to the roof. He teased and tickled me in what, I believed at the time, was innocent playfulness. How naive I was. Before I knew it, his hand was down the front of my sundress, and he'd grabbed my breast.

I pushed him away and shot up the stairs faster than a jackrabbit. When I reached the roof, I cowered like a small child behind my dad. My uncle came up to the roof and sauntered over with an innocent look on his face. I couldn't look at him; I was in complete shock. My heart raced; I couldn't think. I watched him out of the corner of my eye to ensure he stayed away from me.

My brain couldn't process what had happened. I didn't know concepts like sexual abuse or sexual molestation. After I calmed down, I did what many people do. I ignored it, and buried it. I went about the rest of my summer as if it hadn't happened, and chalked it up to an innocent mistake. But my body knew, and would never forget.

I never told anyone what happened that summer until later in life. I instantly disconnected from my body as it was shameful and no longer safe. Part of my brain equated thinness with vulnerability. Since I had no outlet to process the trauma, I began to eat. I used food to build a wall of protection around myself. This trauma initiated years of weight gain, and loss with every new diet.

How You Became Disconnected

There are several reasons why you disconnect from your body:

- Criticism from people that say your body isn't okay.
- Disgust or hatred toward your body.
- Illness or disease.
- Injury.
- Chronic pain.
- Limiting or negative beliefs. For example, "My body isn't safe."
- Physical abuse or neglect.
- Rejection.
- Sexual abuse.

Being Disconnected

Disconnection from the body will be different for each individual. Some people rely on their thoughts and ignore feelings or sensations that emanate from their body. I am analytical by nature, so I did this naturally. I thought, *Why should I listen to my body when my mind tells me everything I need to know?* This belief is flawed. Your mind lies to you. You have thousands of thoughts daily, but those thoughts aren't necessarily factual. (See more on thoughts in Chapter 3.)

Some people may dissociate from their body. Dissociation is when you feel like you are outside of yourself—like you aren't fully present. You may have lapses in time, even if it's seconds. Dissociation often results from a traumatic event. The trauma is too difficult to process, and the brain is brilliant: it disconnects you from your body so you don't have to fully experience the trauma. Many people who experience dissociation state they were above themselves looking down at what was happening. They didn't feel anything. People check out of their body in several ways:

- Food
- Sex
- Drugs
- Cigarettes
- Alcohol
- Shopping
- Gambling
- Plastic Surgery
- Thrill Seeking
- Porn
- Social Media
- Internet
- Video Games
- Work

Some people may recognize they are experiencing something in their body. However, it's too scary or uncomfortable, so they stuff it down, pretending it doesn't exist. Unpleasant sensations can manifest as pain, dis-ease, or intense emotions felt viscerally. For example, when someone is anxious or panicked, "The body responds by producing high levels of adrenaline resulting in symptoms such as confusion, light-headedness, excessive sweating, racing or irregular heart rate, heartburn, nausea, and difficulty swallowing."[1] Who would want to feel these uncomfortable sensations? (See more on sensations in Chapter 7.)

Nervous System

Trauma can have an impact on your physiology. When you experience trauma, your brain and body react unconsciously to ensure your survival. The nervous system communicates through electrical signals to and from your brain and organs. It is comprised of three systems. The central nervous system consists of the brain and spinal cord. The brain controls the body's functions. The peripheral nervous system involves a complex set of cranial and spinal nerves that extend throughout the body, relaying information to and from the brain and body through nerve impulses. Finally, there is the autonomic nervous system (ANS). It automatically controls essential bodily functions, such as breathing, heart rate, blood pressure, and body temperature. As such, you don't have to be consciously aware of those functions.[2] The ANS consists of the parasympathetic nervous system (PNS) and the sympathetic nervous system (SNS).

Parasympathetic Nervous System

The PNS regulates organ and gland systems when the body is at rest. These bodily functions occur automatically. The functions include salivation, lacrimation (crying), digestion, urination, defecation, and sexual arousal. This system initiates the rest-and-digest or feed-and-breed responses. This system is activated more slowly, and is considered a dampening system (less intense). It does not require an immediate reaction from the body.[3]

Sympathetic Nervous System

The SNS maintains homeostasis (balance) in your internal organs, and initiates your body's stress response. It requires a quick response, and is considered a mobilizing system. In response to stress, it activates the fight-flight-freeze response by secreting adrenaline. It produces the following effects in your body:

- Accelerates heart rate and lung action.
- Constricts blood vessels.
- Decreases sexual arousal.
- Dilates pupils.
- Creates hearing loss.
- Increases goosebumps.
- Increases sweating.
- Inhibits tear production and salivation.
- Loss of peripheral vision (causing tunnel vision).
- Raises blood pressure.
- Relaxes the bladder.
- Stops or slows digestion.
- Uses fat and glucose to support muscular action.

When someone experiences stress or a traumatic event, these two systems function opposite of each other. The SNS is excitatory and triggering, while the PNS serves to relax, decrease, or modulate a bodily function.[3] In a state of stress, the SNS's unconscious automatic processes can enhance the body's disconnection. Once the body returns to a rest-and-digest response, a person can reconnect with their body and process the stress or trauma.

Fight-Flight-Freeze Response

The limbic system, or midbrain, houses your emotion and learning centers. It "evaluates everything as either agreeable (pleasure) or disagreeable (pain/distress). Survival is predicated on the avoidance of pain and the repetition of pleasure."[4] The limbic system contains the amygdala and the hypothalamus. The amygdala, an almond-shaped mass inside your brain, is where emotions such as anger, fear, and sadness reside along with your survival instincts. It scans for any perceived threat. The amygdala is also where aggressive behavior originates. Fear and other emotions help to protect you from danger.

The base of your brain contains the cerebellum and your spinal cord, or brainstem, and is referred to as your reptilian brain. When your amygdala signals danger, it activates the thalamus in the limbic brain. The thalamus conducts motor signals and relays information, such as emotion, memory, or arousal, from the brainstem to the cortex. It incites your lower reptilian brain to drive the fight-flight-freeze response. This primitive part of your brain sustains your life through basic functions such as reflexive behaviors, balance, muscle control, heartbeat, breathing, digestion, and reproduction. Your reptilian brain kicks in automatically, much quicker than your rational brain, to ensure your survival. From years of evolution, your reptilian brain remembers when cavemen had to flee from dinosaurs and other predators. As such, your mind can misread situations as unsafe when they are harmless, and send out warning signals that trigger the fight-flight-freeze response.[4]

When the fight-flight-freeze response is activated, it opens up your past negative experiences to scan for danger and help you survive the current situation. Troubling memories can heighten your fight-flight-freeze response. Also, you can have difficulty assessing facial expressions, which results in you misreading neutral cues as dangerous or threatening. The fight-flight-freeze response can be activated by stress, a perceived threat, an argument, social withdrawal, depression, anxiety, substance abuse, watching television, the computer, social media, or playing video games.[5]

Males and females respond differently during the fight-flight-freeze response. Males tend to become aggressive, while women tend to flee or freeze. However, it is essential to note that both men and women can experience any one of the fight, flight, or freeze responses. You don't have a conscious choice; you are not in your rational brain. Your survival instinct kicks in, and your rational brain is offline. Many people find it difficult to process a traumatic event, where their body didn't respond the way they wanted, and to accept the situation. Again, I reiterate, you don't have a choice. It happens in a fraction of a second. Your brain is brilliant and will choose whatever response it needs to keep you alive.

Fight

The fight response is activated when you physically want to fight someone, hit someone, or verbally attack. If the fight response becomes the person's go-to in all situations, whether they feel unsafe or not, there may be a subconscious belief, "If I can control a situation, and have power over others, I will be safe."

Flight

The flight response is activated when you run away. For example, you may leave the room if the flight response becomes activated during an argument or disagreement. Sometimes, there is no visible or current experience for the body's need to flee, but there is a physiological response. Long-term, this can lead to anxiety and panic disorders. For some, the flight response is so strong they need to get in their car and drive, or want to leave their city and move away.

The fight and flight responses produce psychological and physiological symptoms of hyperarousal, which is an abnormal state of increased response to environmental stimuli. See Window of Tolerance later in the chapter for more information on hyperarousal.

Freeze

The freeze response produces psychological and physiological hypoarousal symptoms, which is a lack of response to environmental stimuli. See Window of Tolerance later in the chapter for more information on hypoarousal. The freeze response can render you unable to move your body. However, it can also present as numb or shut down, addictively tuned out (e.g., watching endless hours of Netflix, or constantly surfing social media), or depression. There is also a term known as a *functional freeze*. A person presents as calm or serene on the outside, appearing to function normally, but, in actuality, they are frequently in the freeze response, operating automatically. They ignore their feelings, shove down the signs and symptoms of stress, and disconnect from their body.[6]

According to ethologists, who study animal behavior, the freeze response occurs as a first response to a potential threat. Stopping allows one to assess the level of threat and determine the appropriate reaction: fight or flee. As such, a freeze response can also present as hyperarousal through hypervigilance, or a need to be alert or on guard to danger.[7]

Going about your daily life can trigger the fight-flight-freeze response. Stressful life experiences continue to add up—loss of a job, divorce, moving, sickness, a pandemic, or death of a pet or loved one, to name a few. This continual activation increases emotional overwhelm, and engages the body's SNS, which floods the body with adrenaline and creates the physiological symptoms discussed above.

Embodied Exercise

I'll speak more about supporting and reconnecting with your body in the Reconnection section, but I wanted to give you a quick exercise. Suppose you experience a fight-flight-freeze response due to stress, anxiety, or flashbacks. Flashbacks are when you re-experience a traumatic episode from your past in the current moment. They occur suddenly, and are intense. They often leave you feeling out of control, and can be re-traumatizing. The following exercise will help you get back in your body, feel calm and grounded, and return your body to the PNS state of rest-and-digest:

- While standing, place your back against a wall with your feet shoulder-width apart.
- Let your back slide down the wall to a comfortable squatting position, as if you were going to sit down on a chair.
- Ensure your bum is not lower than your knees, or you'll find it hard to stay in this position long, as you would place a great deal of pressure on your knees.
- Immediately, you will feel the weight of your body as it pushes your feet onto the floor.
- If your legs start to shake, slide yourself back up the wall for a few minutes. Then, when able, bring yourself back down.
- Place your hand on your belly and slow your breath.
- Inhale deeply through your nose, and down into your belly. Your hand should rise as your belly expands. Then, exhale slowly through your mouth.
- As you continue to breathe deeply, you can do a technique called five-four-three-two-one.

- Move your head slowly from left to right as you look around the room. Start to name five things you see, five things you hear, and five things you feel.
- Then, four different things you see, hear, and feel, and then three, two, and one.

It becomes more challenging as you try to find the different things you see, hear, and feel. This process helps you get out of the fight-flight-freeze response because it gets you back into your rational brain. Once back in your rational brain, remind yourself there is no current threat and that you are safe.

Other Survival Responses

Many of you have likely heard of the fight-flight-freeze response before reading this book, but there are three more survival responses you may not have heard of.

Fright

Fright, or tonic immobility, is a defense response used by slow-moving vulnerable organisms when confronted by large predators, such as when an opossum plays dead. If the predator presumes the prey is dead and loosens its grip, there is an increased chance of escape or survival. The fright response is often displayed by sexual assault victims during the assault.[7]

Faint

Fainting, or syncope, literally translates to "a thorough cutting off" from awareness of the physical body, as a result of blood, injection, or injury-type phobias. Blood-induced fainting increases survival because blood loss or cardiovascular shock is minimized by a radical drop in blood pressure. Female and child non-combatants likely could not outrun a young male adversary. As such, non-combatants who inherit the fainting response at the sight of blood or a sharp object possess a survival advantage. Fear-induced fainting non-verbally communicates that they are not a threat and can be ignored, which allows a chance to survive violent conflicts.[7,8]

The faint response can also take the form of a psychological syncope through dissociation, such as losing contact with your physical body to avoid uncomfortable, stressful experiences or a loss of consciousness via memory loss of a traumatic event. Psychological syncope is not only a defense mechanism, but also a psychic state of awareness. When some people dissociate, they experience autoscopy, which is *seeing yourself* from a position outside of your body. During autoscopy, you may observe the event from a distant perspective or you may float on the ceiling looking down on yourself. An out-of-body experience is a transcendent psychic state. Some refer to this as spirit walking, astral travel or projection, or lucid dreaming. Your soul or astral body separates from the physical body to travel to distant places. "It appears some of us have the ability to cognitively perceive ourselves as separate from our physical body's experience when we are threatened, by psychically separating from harm, while at the same time staying connected to the intuitive capacities of the new mammalian brain, which gives us a cognitive capacity for insight from an expanded, nonphysical transcendent perspective."[8] The faint response through dissociation, is the body's innate wisdom to know when to hang out and when to leave.[8]

Dissociating from the body during an incident can lead to Dissociative Identity Disorder (DID). DID is a "severe form of dissociation, a mental process which produces a lack of connection in a person's thoughts, memories, feelings, actions, or sense of identity."[9] DID is not *spiritual* in nature—even though it may have been practical at the time it can lead to mental illness if not processed properly.

Fawn

The final response is called the fawn response. The term was coined by Pete Walker, a psychotherapist who specializes in working with adults who have experienced complex childhood trauma due to repeated abuse and neglect.

If you cannot fight or flee, you initiate the freeze response, appease, or dissociate. "The appease response, which is also known as 'please' or 'fawn,' is another survival response which occurs [when] survivors read danger signals and aim to comply and minimize the confrontation in an attempt to protect themselves."[10]

As with the fight-flight-freeze response, the fawn response becomes activated by a need for safety. A person forgoes their needs and wishes, and merges them with others. "They act as if they unconsciously believe that the price of admission to any relationship is the forfeiture of all their needs, rights, preferences, and boundaries."[11] In a nutshell, fawning is people-pleasing. When a person engages in the fawn response, it helps them feel safe and secure, diminish conflict, and feel accepted by others. Below is a list of frequent behaviors associated with fawning:

- People-pleaser.
- Being nice.
- Difficulty sharing thoughts and emotions.
- Feel unseen and misunderstood by others.
- Put others' needs before your own.
- Compromise your beliefs and values.
- Inability to say no when you want or need to.
- Unable to advocate for your needs.
- Need to compliment others and make them feel good.
- Low self-esteem.

- Unwanted release of excessive emotions or unload emotions onto strangers.
- Conflict avoidance.
- Feel guilty when angry at others.
- Feel responsible for other people's reactions.
- Feel taken advantage of.
- Worry about fitting in.
- Difficulty taking up space and setting boundaries.[10,12]

People who fawn miss out on being fully authentic. They have to be whatever the other person needs them to be, or what they perceive the other person wants. Because the patterns were ingrained early, they have a hard time noticing or understanding what the other person *really* wants and can't help themselves.

People with a history of complex childhood trauma and abandonment are more likely to experience codependency in their relationships. In a codependent relationship, a person relies on their partner for all their emotional and self-esteem needs. They cannot express their needs, recognize their rights, and don't know how to set and maintain healthy boundaries. Abuse or neglect and exploitation can often result in codependent relationships for people who have a fawn response.

—⁓—

Humans are "biologically wired to respond to change with an adrenal stress response—an instinctive fear reaction."[13] All of the above survival responses are expressions of a reaction to fear, including:

- Fear of death.
- Fear of isolation.
- Fear of change.

- Fear of loss: meaning, purpose, freedom, and safety and security.
- Fear of rejection or abandonment.
- Fear of engulfment or enmeshment.

Any of these can ultimately lead to the biggest fear: loss of self.[13]

The chapters and exercises in this book can help you increase your self-awareness and connection with your body, so you notice when your body has triggered the fight-flight-freeze-fright-faint-fawn response, and diminish the mental, emotional, and physical symptoms once activated. When you connect with your body and become embodied, you increase your self-identity. Connecting with your body will result in improved clarity of thought, the ability to feel your emotions and release them, and help you engage in healthy and supportive behaviors.

Trauma

Many of my clients believe they haven't experienced trauma because it wasn't something big like abuse or a major accident. However, we all experience wounding from stressful or disturbing events, and each person's response to their experience will be different. Some people are more resilient than others. For example, a physically abused child may grow up without the abuse having any effect on their life. They worked through it and did not let it define them. For others, maybe they are more sensitive and still can't get over the time a teacher yelled at them in class. The memory of the experience continues to affect how they see themselves, and how they act in the world. A trauma can be anything that has troubled or disturbed you.

Eye Movement Desensitization and Reprocessing (EMDR) is a therapy modality recognized as an effective treatment for people who experience Post-Traumatic Stress Disorder (PTSD), trauma, and other mental health disorders. EMDR uses eye movements, looking to the left and right, by following the therapist's hand movements or a light source. I provide small hand-held tappers that sit in the palms of your hands. One buzzes, then the other one buzzes, and they buzz back and forth for a minute or two. When I stop the machine, we discuss what you noticed. This continues throughout the session(s) until the disturbing event or issue is no longer troubling. Both the eye movements and tappers create bi-lateral stimulation, which connects the left and right sides of the brain. The left brain is the rational, analytical brain; the right brain is the creative side, holding memory, emotion and the subconscious. The right brain is also how you connect to Spirit. Connecting the two sides with EMDR allows you to fully process, desensitize, and reframe disturbing images, thoughts, emotions, and body sensations.

I use EMDR with patients who have experienced trauma or are struggling with mental health issues. When you experience a trauma or stressful event, and it is not fully processed and integrated, memories become dysfunctional—stuck in a raw, maladaptive form. When you store maladaptive memories in their state-specific form, it means you store that memory with feelings of fear, danger, and the other overwhelming emotions you experienced at that time. As a result, you are more likely to become triggered, experience flashbacks, and re-live these unprocessed memories. Trying to access memories where adaptive information resides becomes problematic. Raw, unprocessed memories are like many rooms in your brain that you cannot access. There are no doors or windows to other rooms where you coped with stressful events and processed them fully. Imagine the unprocessed memory room is full of cobwebs and you ask your neighbor for a broom to help sweep them up. Through EMDR, you reprocess these maladaptive memories to integrate them into adaptive memory networks, which helps resolve symptoms and create new insight and learning.[14]

Single Trauma

A small "t" trauma is a single traumatic event, such as being scolded by a parent when you were young, or laughed at in class for something you said. Don't discount this type of trauma. These experiences can leave you with lasting negative beliefs about yourself that inform how you interact with others and how you view the world. A big "T" Trauma is a single traumatic event, such as a motor vehicle accident, sexual or physical assault or abuse, the death of a loved one, or a natural disaster.

Complex Trauma

Complex trauma is an accumulation of traumatic events experienced repetitively over time. Complex trauma can arise from wartime or natural disasters. It can also arise from recurrent physical, mental, emotional, financial, or spiritual neglect and abuse within a family system or intimate relationship. It can also result from harmful experiences within organizational systems like government, culture, society, media, school, hospital, church, or foster facility. As discussed above, when one trauma occurs and is not processed and integrated, it affects your mental, emotional, and physical body, and you become easily triggered. When more than one trauma occurs, no adaptive memory networks exist, or can't be accessed. Each new trauma compounds the existing trauma(s).

Ancestral Trauma

Your ancestors include everyone who has come before you, starting with your parents and going back in time. Your genes and DNA link you to your ancestors. If you can get your eye color, hair color, and other features from your ancestors, then it's possible for them to pass on trauma memories. Plus, you were an egg in your mom when she was a fetus in your grandma.

Epigenetics is a term coined in the early 1940s by Conrad Waddington. He defined epigenetics as the branch of biology that studies the "causal interactions between genes and their products, which bring the phenotype into being."[15] A phenotype refers to a person's observable characteristics or traits. More specifically, ancestral trauma relates to how your inherited genes affect your behavior. If traumatic experiences impacted your ancestors, they might be epigenetically inherited—passed to you via molecular memory.

Everything you experience has energy, and that energy is not only felt in your body, but it has a resonance that permeates the cellular structure. If one of your ancestors experienced a traumatic event, or several events, it affected them mentally, emotionally, physically, and behaviorally. The cell becomes infused with traumatic memories. Ultimately, that cellular resonance is passed on to future generations. Because, when a cell dies, the blueprint for that cell creates the new cell.

—◦◦◦—

My mom, Aspasia, grew up in the small village of Kastri, Greece. German and Italian soldiers occupied Greece during World War II. My mom's village was occupied for several years when she was a young child. Due to the occupation, all the men and boys left the village for fear of being shot. They hid in the mountains or went to fight in the resistance. When my mom was six years old, her mother asked her to go to a neighbor's house to get some matches so they could start a fire to cook. On the way, an Italian soldier spotted movement and involuntarily shot at her because he thought she was a threat. Luckily, another soldier called out, "*piccolo, piccolo*," which means small in Italian, and he stopped shooting.

I can only imagine how frightening and traumatic that experience was for her. And then to not have her brothers and father there for comfort and support. She wouldn't have had the ability to process this trauma. She may have feared leaving her home, or created a belief that the world wasn't safe. My mom tends to be a bit on the anxious side, fearful of potential danger and unknown threats. Did this result from this experience? Did her cellular memory get passed on to my brother and me?

I don't believe I was anxious or fearful as a child. I was fortunate. I did not live in a war-torn country. I became distrustful and cautious of men when I experienced inappropriate sexual touching by strangers and my uncle. If my parents had traumatic experiences with suspicious people, they could have passed on that cellular memory. I could have been predisposed to being distrustful of people. I don't know if I was that way from birth. As discussed at the beginning of this chapter, since my first traumatic experience was at age four, it's hard to know which came first—being inherently distrustful or becoming that way from an experience.

There may be no direct correlation between my parents' experiences and my own. But that doesn't mean I didn't inherit their traumas. I certainly absorbed their energy around it growing up. As a psychologist, I have clients who present with behavioral, physical, and mood disturbances that are direct results of their parents' traumas.

I want to emphasize that you may be affected by your parents' traumas. I do not mean to scare you into thinking you have no control over your body, or your body's reaction to events. Also, you cannot blame your behaviors and mental and emotional states on your parents. I share this because I want you to understand that you can be affected by more than just your own experiences; there may be a pre-determination to how you view the world and act in it.

Your body is astounding. It continually seeks balance and healing. If you recognize you have been affected by ancestral trauma, it's normal to feel worried. The knowledge, skills, and tools provided in this book can help you gain greater awareness and connection to what happens in your body. Also, the following can help to alleviate any compounding effect from ancestral trauma, and your own trauma:

- Live in an enriched and stable environment.
- Recognize resiliency from past challenges you've overcome.
- Set up sound support systems.
- Utilize tools and coping strategies.

Ancestral Belief Patterns

It is not just your ancestors' traumas that are passed down to your DNA. You can also inherit your ancestors' feelings and beliefs, and express them as your own. You believe these are your unique struggles, but they are rooted in the experiences and beliefs of your ancestors. As these are very subtle, it can be hard to distinguish between your struggles and what resulted from your ancestors. Here are some indicators that you may carry ancestral belief patterns:

- Repeat familial habits or coping strategies.
- Experience anxieties and fears that don't match your past or current reality.
- Beliefs and patterns you feel you were born with and cannot change.
- Success or failure stories passed on through family lore.
- Thoughts of family history (known or unknown) feel heavy.
- Feel stuck and don't know why.[16]

Here are some examples of ancestral belief patterns:

- Want to change careers, but fear holds you back.

- A chronic health issue prevents you from thriving.
- There isn't enough food to eat even though there has always been abundance.
- Difficulty trusting or fearing men, even though you have never been harmed by one.
- Can't hold onto money, and you always lack financial stability.
- Something bad always happens when things are going well.
- Difficulty keeping relationships or making friendships.
- Meet everyone else's needs except your own.
- Need to rescue or fix others.
- Angry at an extended-family member for no apparent reason.
- Chronic irrational anxiety, panic, or fears.

Embodied Exercise

Everyone carries ancestral belief patterns, but that doesn't mean you have to struggle with them for the rest of your life. Here are some steps to help clear ancestral belief patterns.

- Identify the patterns or areas where you feel stuck and struggle the most—mental, emotional, and physical health, relationships, money, low self-esteem, etc.
- What belief do you think is at the heart of this pattern? For example, "I don't deserve to be happy." (Check out Chapter 3 for common limiting or negative beliefs.)

- Trace the belief back to the first time you experienced it. Then continue going back in time to a time before you were born—a time when an ancestor may have believed this. Trust whatever comes up—an image, something you hear, or an internal knowing. (The chapters in the Reconnection section will provide information and exercises to embody this practice.)

- Explore the belief's function. Why was it needed? What was going on at the time?

- Light a candle, and set up sacred space. (See Chapter 9.) Write a letter to yourself about all the ways this ancestral belief pattern shows up in your life. Feel all the emotions and body sensations as you write the letter. If you are sad, cry. If angry, yell. Using your breath, blow your feelings out of your body into the letter using a *ha* sound. Write all that needs to be said, and release all the emotions from your body. Burn the letter once complete.

- Write a letter to your ancestors to acknowledge and validate their sacrifices. Thank them for all they did to survive and protect themselves. Ask for support from your ancestors to release this belief pattern. Tell them that your life is very different from theirs, and you no longer need to carry this pattern. Burn the letter once complete. Visualize speaking with your ancestors, and state what you wrote in the letter. You may see a contract appear, or have an internal knowing that an ancestor created a contract around this belief. If yes, imagine the contract being lit on fire, exploding, or disintegrating into dust, and being absorbed by Mother Earth. Afterward, state, "I release the contract from all past, current, and future lifetimes for the highest good of everyone involved."

- Write down a new belief to replace the old ancestral belief pattern. For example, "My body is healed and whole." Repeat this new belief several times aloud as you visualize bringing it in through your crown chakra (the top of your head), permeating throughout your whole body, into every cell, to the core of your DNA.[16]

Generational Trauma

Another type of trauma, but on a much bigger scale, is generational trauma. Generational trauma is also known as intergenerational, multigenerational, or transgenerational trauma. First-generation trauma survivors experience complex trauma that results in PTSD. As such, they pass down their trauma to subsequent generations. Generational trauma is passed down through the DNA like in ancestral trauma, but it is not only from your ancestors' experiences. It is from a whole culture's or group's experiences, which inherently influences future generations. Some examples of generational trauma include:

- 911 terrorist attacks affected survivors, families of survivors, and a whole nation.
- Effects of World War I, World War II, and the Vietnam war on veterans, their families, and the countries.
- Mass genocide and slavery of Native Americans when the Spaniards reached our shores, and the continued racism and mistreatment of Native Americans through land confiscation, residential schools, and extreme poverty.
- Mass genocide of Jews during World War II, and the atrocities they experienced in concentration camps.
- Slavery and dehumanization of African Americans, and the continual racism, prejudice and violence perpetrated on this culture.

These are, sadly, a few of the well-known groups of individuals who have experienced generational trauma. For those who have experienced these atrocities, ingrained feelings and experiences become a part of their cellular memory. Healing from generational trauma may take several generations.

Trauma to the Body

Trauma can be something you have personally experienced, or received by witnessing someone else's traumatic experience. When you experience trauma, your body goes into survival mode. As discussed previously, the SNS engages and your fundamental instinct for survival rules. You automatically go into a fight-flight-freeze response. The amygdala can't distinguish between a perceived threat and a real threat. A perceived threat to your survival results in your prefrontal cortex, or rational brain, going offline, and you can't reason. Primal instincts kick in to protect you. Say you were in a closed room and a grizzly bear burst through the door. In a split second, your brain would assess whether you could fight the bear, run from the bear, or play dead. You don't have a conscious choice.

Some symptoms people experience due to trauma:

- Avoid certain people or places that may bring on disturbing feelings or traumatic memories.
- Disconnect from themselves and their body.
- Experience anger, irritability, mood swings, sadness, hopelessness, anxiety, fear, guilt, shame, or self-blame.
- Experience confusion, loss of memory, or difficulty concentrating.
- Experience flashbacks or nightmares.
- Feel dread and worry for the future.
- Feel numb, experience being out of their body (dissociate), or lose time.

- Feel unsafe and need to stick to a routine.
- Find it challenging to engage in daily living activities.
- Inability to trust others.
- Startle easily and need to check their surroundings constantly.
- Withdraw or isolate themselves from others.

Below are five basic needs that can become disrupted by trauma:

1. **Safety for Yourself and Others**—the need for you and others to be free from harm caused by yourself, others, or the environment.
2. **Trust in Yourself and Others**—the need to trust your own judgment and others.
3. **Control of Yourself and Others**—the need to be in charge of your actions and influence others.
4. **Esteem for Yourself and Others**—the need to value your thoughts, emotions, and beliefs, and value others.
5. **Intimacy with Yourself and Others**—the need to know and accept your thoughts and feelings, and be known and accepted by others.[17,18]

People often disconnect from their body after trauma because they believe they should have done something different. They think they had a choice when they didn't. They may perceive their body betrayed them, and they no longer trust their body.

Trauma Stored in the Body

Trauma is the result of a disturbing or troubling external experience. Every external experience has consciousness—it has energy. It is this energetic consciousness that causes the trauma. The external experience is processed as a thought, emotion, and behavior energetically. Uncomfortable thoughts, emotions, and body sensations are not processed fully because you unconsciously cannot wholly feel them. Your brain and body need to protect you, so you mentally and physically check out. Your body creates resistance and constricts the energetic consciousness, and you cannot move the energy out of your body. Your body then stores the trauma. Thoughts, emotions, beliefs, and behaviors are supposed to be felt, then moved through the body. Your body is never meant to store the energetic consciousness of trauma.

As you are unconsciously aware of this stored trauma, your body tries to protect you from future traumas by creating a trauma response. You cannot stop yourself from feeling and experiencing future traumas. Still, because you have no conscious awareness of your stored trauma, you respond with thoughts, emotions, beliefs, and behaviors to situations the brain perceives as new trauma. People are constantly mirroring their traumas to each other. A trauma response may manifest as blaming, ridiculing, judging, belittling, name-calling, controlling, manipulating, jealousy, greed, anger, rage, or fear. Trauma responses will happen with individual people, but also with the collective. When you become more conscious and self-aware of individual and collective trauma responses, you will see how to free yourself from the cycle.

Someone who projects their thoughts, feelings, and beliefs onto you is unconsciously trying to protect themselves from their own trauma response. If you are unconscious of this trauma response playing out, you will perpetuate it by believing the person's words or deeds, and may think there is something wrong with you. You take it on as your stuff. It is not yours, it is theirs. Or, it belongs to the collective. You are only responsible for your own trauma responses.

You can support yourself by consciously becoming aware of your trauma responses. How do you typically respond when verbally attacked? When you experience a trauma response, recognize you are triggered and feel whatever thoughts, emotions, beliefs, or body sensations you are having without judgment. Your brain is trying to protect you.

Recognize the trauma response in other people, or the collective, so you don't take it on as yours and trigger your trauma response. You can do this by observing and witnessing what is happening without reacting. When you can recognize people's or the collective's trauma responses, it frees you not to react, speak your truth, and set boundaries For example, the current COVID pandemic. Collective trauma is being perpetuated by governments, the media, and the polarization of people's views.

Utilize the tools and techniques in the Reconnection section of this book to process, clear and heal your traumas. Alternatively, seek out a trauma-informed counselor. When you clear the energetic consciousness of your traumas from your body, you will no longer respond to situations with a trauma response, and will be able to express your Divine nature. You will naturally respond from a compassionate, aligned, heart-centered state.[19]

—∿∿—

The exercises in this book can support reconnection with one's body even after trauma. However, for others, it will require working through the trauma with an experienced trauma-informed counselor. Working with a counselor can reduce disturbing emotions or triggers, unwanted physical symptoms, and unhealthy negative thoughts and beliefs. This book will help you reconnect with your body in a healthy way, become embodied, regain your confidence, feel present and at peace, and allow your authentic self to shine.

Embodied Exercise

Get out a pen and paper and write out a timeline of all the stressful events, wounds and traumas (little "t" and big "T") you have experienced. Don't compare your experiences to those of others and shrug them off as "no big deal." Your wounds and trauma are yours. If they still affect you, address them. It matters, you matter.

Next to each event, assess it on a scale from zero to ten, where zero is neutral, or not disturbing, and ten is the highest disturbance you can imagine.

Anything higher than an eight may need a therapist's help to process, especially if it results in a state of hyper- or hypoarousal (see Window of Tolerance below) that can't be self-regulated.

You will learn tools in this book to help you self-regulate and release emotions and energy blockages in your body from unprocessed trauma. You can journal about these events to see what is still troubling. If you notice being out of your Window of Tolerance, and become hyper- or hypoaroused, stop journaling and engage in a self-soothing strategy. (The Introduction lists some examples.) Journaling is a valuable tool to help process feelings and emotions, and to recognize limiting or negative beliefs so you can challenge them, and reframe them into more accurate, positive beliefs. Below are some questions you can ask yourself as you journal:

- What is still troubling or disturbing about this incident?
- Am I experiencing any guilt or shame?

- What limiting or negative beliefs do I have about myself?
- What emotions am I experiencing?
- What body sensations am I experiencing?

Window of Tolerance

Dr. Dan Siegel coined the term Window of Tolerance. This concept describes what happens in the body due to intense stress or trauma. If your caregivers nurtured you, and gave you room to explore, you experienced healthy attachments. Your brain then created neural pathways to support the self-regulation of intense emotions, which helped you be resilient during stressful events. Children can end up with unhealthy attachments as a result of abusive and neglectful caregivers. If caregivers cannot provide comfort to a distressed child, the child's resiliency to stressful situations weakens. The child isn't able to self-regulate because they didn't establish those neural pathways. As such, everyone's level of resiliency is different.

The diagram below shows how a healthy nervous system deals with the ups and downs of emotions. If you experience a stress response, the SNS kicks in and you start to experience more excitatory physiological reactions in your body. After a while, your body self-regulates, and begins to settle down, which initiates the PNS so you can rest-and-digest again. You don't go out of your Window of Tolerance unless you experience an unusually stressful event.

The two horizontal lines indicate your Window of Tolerance. Your emotions and physiological response go up and down depending on your experience to stressors. On the lower end of the curved line, you may, for example, feel sad because you got a low grade on your exam. On the higher end of the curved line, you may feel nervous, for instance, because you're going for an interview tomorrow. In each of these scenarios, you don't go outside of your Window of Tolerance. You quickly find ways to manage the stress. When you maintain optimal arousal, you engage in the following ways:

- Adaptable
- Empathetic
- Feel Calm and Relaxed
- Feel Emotions
- Feel Open and Curious
- Feel Safe
- Flexible
- Grounded
- Maintain Boundaries (yourself and others)
- Present
- Self-Regulate
- Think Rationally
- Tolerate Feelings

Window of Tolerance

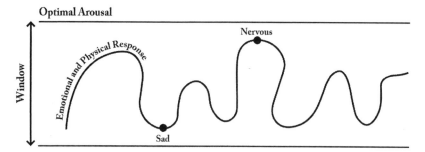

When you experience intense stress or trauma, your window gets smaller. What you could handle before, you can no longer manage, and it takes longer to self-regulate. You are now out of your Window of Tolerance. On the upper part of the scale, you experience hyperarousal. The SNS has kicked in, and you undergo the fight-or-flight response. Symptoms can include:

- Addictions
- Anger or Rage
- Anxiety
- Chronic Pain
- Digestive Issues
- Emotional Reactivity
- Racing Thoughts
- Feeling out of Control
- Heightened Startle Response
- Hypervigilance
- Impulsivity
- Chaotic
- Overwhelmed
- Panic
- Restlessness
- Sleeplessness

On the lower part of the scale, you experience hypoarousal. Hypoarousal creates blunting (reduced emotional reactivity) in the PNS, which results in a freeze response. Symptoms can include:

- Depression
- Disconnection
- Dissociation (out-of-body)
- Lack of Emotion
- Exhaustion
- Lack of Energy
- Memory Loss

- Not Present
- Numb or Zoned Out
- Passive
- Poor Digestion
- Separate from Self, Emotions, and Feelings
- Shut Down
- Withdrawn[20]

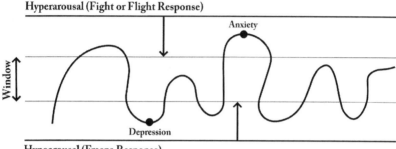

Window of Tolerance

If this is the first time you've heard about the Window of Tolerance, and the effects of stress and trauma, you may feel overwhelmed. Depending on your level of stress or trauma, you may need a counselor's support to explore and process your experience in a way that is not re-traumatizing.

Over time, you can increase your Window of Tolerance to its normal range, or an expanded range, and help your body to self-regulate again by slowly titrating uncomfortable experiences a little at a time. You can activate your PNS to return to rest-and-digest when you experience hyper- or hypoarousal by engaging in self-soothing and coping strategies several times a day. When your body is supported, it starts to settle more quickly, symptoms lessen, and your window expands. In the Reconnection section of this book, you will learn several techniques, and engage in exercises to self-soothe and calm your body, regulate your emotions, and process stress and trauma through the chapters on:

- Mindfulness
- Grounding
- Senses
- Energy
- Shamanism

Guilt and Shame

There is a whole chapter on emotions, but I thought it relevant to talk about guilt and shame concerning trauma. Guilt is about action. *It is something you have done or not done.* People experience guilt from trauma either as a result of their actions or unforeseen circumstances. For example, a driver of a vehicle gets into an accident. They may feel guilty if someone gets hurt, whether the accident was their fault or not.

Some people experience survivor's guilt because they survived a traumatic experience when others didn't. Maybe they were supposed to be where the event happened but weren't—like missing a flight that crashes or when a whole family dies in a fire except for one person. Survivor guilt is not constructive. It can become crippling. Guilt results when you:

- Cause harm to another person or yourself.
- Do something illegal.
- Do something immoral or unethical.
- Do something you believe is wrong.
- Go against your values or beliefs.
- Don't do something you said you would do.

When you've harmed someone, there is an opportunity to make amends:

- Apologize or ask forgiveness.
- Make amends or fix damages.
- Make changes in your behavior.[21]

Shame occurs when you internalize the situation and place blame or create limiting or negative beliefs about yourself. *It is something you say about yourself.* For example, "I am bad," or "I am responsible." You carry shame. Shame gets stronger when you hold onto it and don't talk about it. It becomes a secret you bear, and it grows and festers like an open wound. Unless you talk about it, it becomes an entity that lives inside and rots from the inside out.

There can also be outside pressure to perpetuate the secret by a perpetrator, friends, or family members who have a vested interest in ensuring the secret is not revealed. For example, a sexually-assaulted child never talks about the abuse because their perpetrator manipulates them with statements such as:

- It's a secret.
- No one will believe you.
- I'll harm you if you tell anyone.
- I'll harm a family member or the person you tell.

It is not the child's or victim's fault. The perpetrator is solely responsible. Sometimes, a sexually-assaulted child internalizes their abuse as something shameful about themselves.

Shame can show up in the following ways:

- Avoidance or withdrawal from people.
- Concave body posture.

- Grovel or try to appease others.
- Hide characteristics from others.
- Lack an ability to speak.
- Look away from people.[21]

Shame increases when you don't talk about it and diminishes when you tell people your story. It can be vulnerable to discuss your experience for the first time. If you don't have someone you trust to share your story with, seek out support from a counselor. Alternatively, you can journal your thoughts and feelings, and look at the situation from a third-party perspective, as if it happened to someone you loved, to see it more realistically and compassionately. More specifically, find a counselor who will not judge, blame, or shame you further. When you share your story, it helps you heal the burden of carrying the secret. Healing shame is about forgiveness of self. I can't tell you how many times I've asked a client how they feel after sharing their story for the first time. Many clients report feeling relieved, as if a weight had been lifted.

Why You Need to Reconnect

Maybe you're thinking, "Who cares? I've gotten this far without a connection to my body. Why should I start now?" You picked up this book for a reason. There is something that doesn't feel right or it no longer works for you to be disconnected. It is a part of human nature to grow, transform, and seek ways to improve and live more fully.

As stated above, your thoughts often lie to you, but when you learn to connect to your body, become embodied, and listen to it, it will not lie to you. Tapping into the body is like tapping into a wealth of knowledge. It is where your Higher Self and inner knowing lie. (I discuss your inner knowing in Chapter 7.) You already have all the answers to your health, well-being, and life. When you create a deep connection with your body, it becomes your crystal ball. Your body tells you what it needs from you and what to do.

There is no doubt that you get something out of being disconnected from your body. Maybe it keeps you safe. It might keep you from experiencing troubling, disturbing, or unpleasant sensations and feelings. Perhaps it keeps you stuck in your story, and, in doing so, you get help, support, or sympathy from others. It could be the scared part of you that doesn't like change. You may wonder what you would be like if you connected to your body. Will people still like you?

How you view yourself, and how you connect and interact with others socially, is a big part of what it means to be human. In existential-humanistic psychotherapy, James Bugental talks about five existential givens of living. Each of these givens brings about an "inescapable circumstance called a 'confrontation.'"[22]

Basic Given	Confrontation
Embodiedness	Change
Finitude	Contingency
Ability to Act or Not Act	Responsibility
Choicefulness	Relinquishment
Separate-but-Related-ness	A-Partness

Being embodied forces you to either recognize or repress that you are continually changing—not only are you in flux, but also the world is in flux. As such, you try to make time stop, or decide not to change—as if you can control the inevitable.

Finitude means you are finite, that you will ultimately die. You cannot do everything and you cannot know everything. Contingency helps you to determine the outcome of your efforts.

Your efforts allow you to take action. You are not an idle observer in your life. Your actions make a difference, and it is your responsibility to take action.

Responsibility connects to your choices. You get to select from several possibilities, while at the same time, there is a continual need to relinquish those infinite possibilities.

Finally, the paradox of being related to, but at the same time separate from, others. You have to confront your aloneness, and accept the need to bond with others.[22]

Embodied Exercise

Get out a pen and paper and journal on the following two questions:

- How does it serve me to stay disconnected from my body?
- What will I lose if I become connected to my body?

Benefits of Reconnecting With Your Body

There are many benefits to reconnecting with your body:

- Accept and love yourself for who you are and not what others want you to be.
- Access feelings, sensations, and intuitive perceptions.
- Acknowledge and relieve bodily disturbances.
- Become more fully available and present in the moment.
- Become more fully centered and grounded.
- Become more mindful of stress in the body.
- Decrease mental, emotional, and physical overwhelm.
- Connect to your inner self.

- Connect with Creator, Divine, God, Goddess, Higher Self, Mother Earth, Spirit, Source, or Universe for guidance and support.
- Connect with resources such as meditation, breath work, or energy work to heal the past, and balance mind, body, and spirit.
- Explore and trust your Higher Self and inner knowing.
- Feel more at ease in your mind, body, and spirit, and feel a greater heart-opening and emergence of joy in your life.
- Find balance in the emotional, physical, mental, spiritual, and creative areas of your life to support your well-being, and ability to function in the world.
- Gain clarity and tap into your intuition and inner wisdom.
- Reveal insights into your current behavior for growth and self-discovery.
- Gain self-acceptance and self-love.
- Gain clarity on possible triggers.
- Grieve losses by acknowledging and experiencing feelings and sensations as they occur.
- Have greater compassion for yourself and others.
- Improve worldview of self.
- Increase confidence and self-esteem, and other positive beliefs.
- Increase self-awareness and make any necessary adjustments as needed.
- Open yourself to receive love, and give love, fully and unconditionally.
- Set appropriate boundaries to create healthy relationships with your partner, family, friends, peers, and coworkers.

- Recognize and release negative beliefs about your body and yourself.
- Know unhealthy or nonexistent boundaries, and strengthen healthy boundaries.
- Acknowledge your body's needs.
- Reduce unhealthy attachments, self-limiting beliefs, or disturbing behaviors.
- Reduce unhealthy behaviors that falsely try to meet your needs.
- Speak your truth freely, and present your authentic self at all times.
- Unblock resistances you hold in your body to help you bring greater focus toward your purpose, goals, and aspirations in all areas of your life: relationships, family, health, spirituality, education, and career.

I hope you found this chapter about the ways wounds and traumas have disconnected you from your body informative and enlightening. This chapter may have been intense; it may have opened up your memory bank of wounds, things you hadn't thought of in years, or didn't even realize were traumatic. Be kind and gentle with yourself. Support your emotional and physical needs and, if necessary, seek out support from a counselor.

Join me in the next chapter as I explore boundaries. You will learn what happens when you have damaged, unhealthy, or missing boundaries, and how to set healthy boundaries.

2

BOUNDARIES—
DON'T CROSS MY LINE

*"Boundaries are, in simple terms,
the recognition of personal space."*

Asa Don Brown

I experienced a handful of unwanted sexual touches before the age of 12. I was a vulnerable child with no voice. The people who perpetrated those violations knew what they were doing was wrong. They elicited their power over me because they could, without pause for the ramifications to my life.

However, there was an instance where I willfully participated in what I would, many years later, recognize as a sexual-boundary violation. In grade six, my teacher placed all the desks together in fours, making squares where the students would face each other. My friend, Sarah, and I got paired with the two most popular guys in the class—Steve and David.

Most of the girls in my class were skinny, and hadn't developed yet, but Sarah and I were already filling our bras. Steve and David made comments about our breasts. While sitting in the square, Steve grabbed Sarah's breast several times. Following his lead, David did the same thing to me. We giggled and feigned being upset by this behavior.

I told Sarah to switch desks. It was like a game. I was hoping Steve would grab my breast too, which he did, to my delight. It made me feel noticed and wanted by the two hottest guys in class. I didn't recognize this as harmful to my self-identity. To be liked, I permitted guys to touch me sexually for their pleasure.

You may relate to this experience. Maybe there were times in your life when you engaged in behavior you thought was consensual at the time. This experience isn't a trauma for me. It isn't upsetting or disturbing. Many may believe this was all playful fun, but, unfortunately, it wasn't. As a result of the sexual boundary violations I experienced, my healthy boundary became distorted.

As I will discuss later in the chapter, these experiences led to a diffuse and damaged boundary. I believed this is what people were allowed to do to me. As such, I willfully engaged in my breast being grabbed. When you add in the social pressure of wanting to be liked, I wasn't able to set healthy boundaries, and this damaged my self-esteem. Even when you provide consent, and have a healthy boundary, some situations may not be as black and white as you perceive. You need to factor in past trauma, age, and whether there is an understanding of healthy and unhealthy boundaries.

What is a Boundary?

Have you ever seen a political map of Canada and the United States? The border is shown as a line dividing our two countries. There isn't an actual physical line, but it is a real boundary nonetheless. The boundary you have around your physical self is similar. You can't see it, but it exists.

At a border crossing, an official stops your car and asks you several questions before deciding whether you can enter the country. Similarly, you continually take in verbal and non-verbal information to determine how you feel in an environment and with different people. Safety and trust are crucial for your ability to let others enter your space. There are multiple layers of boundaries. Some people get permission to touch you, while others need to maintain a distance. It is whatever you determine. It depends on the person you interact with, your relationship with them, and how comfortable you feel about allowing people to enter your space.

Factors Influencing Boundaries

Several factors shape boundaries:

- The region or country you live in or come from.
- Your culture or heritage.
- Your family dynamics.
- Your life experiences—including your wounds and traumas.
- Your personality—whether you are introverted, extroverted, or ambiverted (a balance of both).[1]

For example, many North Americans value and prefer independence, individualism, and the need for personal space, or physical distance, when interacting. Many cultural groups have immigrated to North America, and some of those parents include the cultural values of their country of origin when raising their children in a new country. Some of these cultures value collectivism. As such, all of the family's best interests are kept in mind when making decisions. These cultures prefer physical closeness within their extended family unit, and several generations may live under the same roof. As such, these children's boundaries may be quite different from other people's boundaries, even if they were born and raised in the same country.

Why Setting and Maintaining Boundaries is Important

It is vital to connect to, and get to know, your physical boundary. It allows you to experience where it begins, and where it ends. A boundary is continuously changing, so how you interact will be different for each person. Your boundary is also affected by your emotional state, and how you feel at any given moment. For example, if you feel fearful, your boundary will likely be close to your skin, but it will probably be several feet beyond your physical body if you feel comfortable and relaxed.

Setting and maintaining boundaries with people is vital for three reasons:

1. To stop people from coming into your space.
2. To prevent you from entering someone else's space.
3. To help you discover who you are in the world.

For some people, their boundary is their physical skin. For others, it may be a foot or two beyond their physical body, while for others, it may be across the street.

Your Skin as Your Boundary

Those who have their skin as their boundary may believe they aren't allowed, or don't deserve, to take up space in the world. The loss of a personal boundary can result from years of physical, emotional, or sexual abuse. It can leave a person fearful of anyone coming in close contact with them. A caregiver may have told them, "A child should not be seen or heard." Sometimes, parents don't permit their children to have control over their own body by saying no when something doesn't feel right for them. As such, they may believe they don't matter, or aren't good enough.

A Foot-or-Two Boundary

Those with a boundary a foot or two beyond their physical body typically feel good in their skin. They have good self-esteem, self-worth, and self-confidence. They can interact and connect with others, and ensure they meet their own needs when they interact with others.

Across-the-Street Boundary

Individuals with a boundary that stretches across the street were born highly sensitive. They quickly take on other people's energy and emotions as their own. They may not know where they end and other people begin. For example, a highly sensitive individual can step into a room and immediatcly sense tension or anger. They often experience heightened emotions and believe they have no control over them. They don't like being around many people, and are affected by intense stimuli such as noises or smells. They may feel lost and unsure of themselves as they move through the world.

Types of Boundaries

There are three different types of boundaries: rigid, permeable, and diffuse.

Rigid Boundary

A rigid boundary is represented by a complete circle.

The circle is closed, and nothing can get in or out. People who have rigid boundaries have experienced emotional, physical, or sexual abuse as a child, potentially by caregivers who were substance abusers. Children and adults with some form or degree of Autism, may also present with a more rigid boundary, as they experience heightened sensations to sounds and touch. People with rigid boundaries feel they need to protect themselves, resulting in increased distrust and isolation.

Permeable Boundary

A permeable boundary is represented by a circle with small gaps in the line.

Have you ever made homemade nut milk? You need a nut milk bag to strain the milk from the nuts. This type of fine-meshed bag is what I mean by permeable, both good and bad things can escape through it. A person who speaks up about what is okay and not okay during interactions is able to maintain a healthy boundary.

Diffuse Boundary

A diffuse boundary is represented by a circle with much bigger breaks in the line.

Others are often able to influence people with diffuse boundaries. People with diffuse boundaries go to extremes—either taking everything from others, or giving everything of themselves. People with diffuse boundaries have typically grown up in a rigid household where their parents or caregivers were abusive, neglectful, had mental health disorders, or engaged in substance abuse. As adults, those children end up going to the opposite extreme to not be like their parents. They need to regain control, but in doing so, they create more hurt and confusion. People with diffuse boundaries don't know what an appropriate limit is for them.[2]

Embodied Exercise

Journal the following questions and notice any emotions, thoughts, body sensations, or memories that come up regarding your boundary. Boundaries can change throughout your life depending on your age, the experience, and who is involved.

- What kind of boundary do you have? Is it rigid, permeable, or diffuse? How did it come to be this way?
- What was your boundary as a child, adolescent, and adult? Did certain people influence your ability to set and maintain boundaries?
- Did your boundary change? If yes, why? If not, does it need to? If yes, how?

Areas Where Boundaries Apply

Boundaries are not only energetic fields around your body. There are six specific areas where boundaries apply to your life and well-being: mental, emotional, physical, material, sexual, and spiritual.

Mental Boundaries

When you have mental boundaries, you know, understand, and are responsible for your thoughts, ideas, values, and beliefs. Healthy mental boundaries include:

- Ability to stand firm on your opinions.
- Have an open mind about other people's opinions.
- Don't let others sway you from your thoughts, decisions, values, and beliefs.

Emotional Boundaries

When you have emotional boundaries, it means you can distinguish your emotions from others and not take on other people's emotions as your own or feel responsible for them. Healthy emotional boundaries include:

- Not being overly emotional, rigid, defensive, or argumentative.
- Not blaming others.
- Not feeling guilty for other people's problems or negative feelings.
- Not giving out unsolicited advice.
- Not taking people's comments personally.
- Not taking the blame for things you did not do.

Physical Boundaries

When you have physical boundaries, you know, and can maintain, your privacy, personal space, and body. Healthy physical boundaries include:

- Allow other people to touch you when you have given your permission to do so.

- Reveal only parts of your history, thoughts, ideas, or experiences with those you wish to disclose to.
- Touch others when they have permitted you to do so.

Material Boundaries

When you have material boundaries, you can assess and decide what you want to give or lend to someone else. Healthy material boundaries include choosing if, and when, to give or lend your time, money, car, food, clothes, or possessions.[3]

Sexual Boundaries

When you have sexual boundaries, you can make decisions about engaging in any form of sexual intimacy. Healthy sexual boundaries include:

- Ability to determine when, how, where, and with whom you want to engage in sexual intimacy with.
- Engage in sexual intimacy when you have given your consent.
- Engage in sexual intimacy with others when they have given you their consent.

Spiritual Boundaries

When you set spiritual boundaries, you engage in religion, spirituality, beliefs, rituals, and ceremonies that are right for you. Healthy spiritual boundaries include:

- Ability to hold firm to your spiritual practices when ridiculed by others.
- Don't let others dissuade you from your beliefs.
- Don't try to persuade others to believe or engage in your spiritual practices.

Spiritual practices can include a belief in Creator, Divine, God, Goddess, Higher Self, Mother Earth, Spirit, Source, Universe, or a specific type of religion.

Embodied Exercise

Write out the six different types of boundaries in your journal (mental, emotional, physical, material, sexual, and spiritual) and answer the following questions for each area:

- Are you able to hold this boundary?

  - If no, why? What is holding you back? Do you need a specific skill? Is there something missing that you need? Is someone blocking you? Are you experiencing any fear around this boundary?
  - If yes, how is this boundary supporting you? What has allowed you to hold this boundary? Experience? Skillset? Confidence?

- Are there specific instances where you struggle with this boundary? For example, under material boundaries, are you constantly giving money to your friends? Write out all the different scenarios where you struggle to maintain the boundary.
- How would you like to hold this boundary better? For example, "I would like not to be fearful of speaking openly about my spiritual beliefs."

This exercise is about information gathering. Later on in the chapter, I'll discuss how to set healthy boundaries.

Boundary Violations

Parents, caregivers, friends, teachers, mentors, bosses, coaches, acquaintances, or strangers can perpetrate boundary violations. Any form of violation is ultimately an abuse of power. There is a myth that when someone sexually assaults another individual, it is about sex. This is false. It is about power. It is the abuser's need to exert their dominance and control over another individual.

A child's boundary is intruded upon and breaks down when someone in authority, or someone much older, uses their power to get what they want. The child or teenager then loses their ability to feel safe and secure in their body and the world.

In the family unit, impairment to a child's boundary can occur when the child is either protected too much or not enough. This inconsistency leads children to turn into adults who have no boundaries, unhealthy boundaries, or close themselves off completely.

No Boundaries

People who have no boundaries are unduly influenced and can suffer in several different ways:

- Difficulty protecting themselves.
- Difficulty saying no.
- Low self-esteem, low self-confidence, and low self-worth.
- Further abuse and being taken advantage of emotionally, mentally, physically, materially, sexually, or spiritually.
- Take responsibility for other people's emotions, thoughts, and behaviors.

Damaged Boundaries

Other people end up with damaged boundaries. Sometimes they can set healthy limits, put themselves first, and take care of their needs and wants. Other times, they have difficulty establishing and maintaining boundaries. This inconsistency results in protecting themselves only some of the time.

Sometimes people end up putting up energetic walls around themselves to keep people away. This mode of protection may result from feelings of anger and fear. When people put up walls, they often become isolated, shut down, and no longer participate in life.

These individuals have difficulty seeing beyond themselves. They often only speak about their needs and wants, and how other people, systems, the world, or God create havoc in their life. They don't know how to take responsibility for their choices and actions. This inability to take responsibility is known as an external locus of control. Everything happens to the person as a result of other people, things, or situations. They aren't able to recognize they have the power to choose how they feel and the ability to take action. People can oscillate between putting up walls and responding from their damaged boundaries.[4]

Unhealthy Boundaries

There are several ways an individual may experience unhealthy boundaries:

- Difficulty trusting people—feel suspicious or paranoid about people's motives.
- Have you ever met a new person and, within minutes, they've told you their whole life story? This is oversharing—telling people everything without them wanting you to. This behavior includes:

- One-sided conversations.
- Personal attacks or rants on social media.
- Unfiltered accounts of ongoing dramas.
- Expect emotional support from friends and family at all times.
- Share intimate details to gain new friendships.[1]

- Can't say no—give their money, time, personal possessions, or engage in unwanted sexual intimacy.
- Easily persuaded—engage in behaviors or thoughts that go against their values and beliefs.
- Easily become intimate, or fall in love quickly with an individual they recently met.
- Engage in sex because their partner wants to, even if they don't.
- Take on other people's problems and become overwhelmed and burdened.
- Have you ever met someone who never goes against anything you say? You could say the sky is green and they would agree. These people-pleasers struggle to have any of their own ideas, judgments, or beliefs. If they do have them, they are unable to voice them because they want to be liked, or are fearful. They experience fawning.
- Unable to recognize when someone has crossed their boundary because their boundary is either nonexistent or damaged.
- Take unwanted advice, gifts, food, clothing, housing, money, or sex.
- Due to a belief of lack, they take from others for the sake of taking.
- Due to a lack of self-worth, they give for the sake of giving—which provides them with a false sense of worth.

- Let others define who they are in the world, how they should live their life, and decide their values and beliefs for them.
- Have you ever experienced an argument with your partner because he or she didn't do something you wanted them to do, but you hadn't told them? People with unhealthy boundaries believe others know their needs, even though they have never voiced them. No one can read your mind.
- Expect their needs will be immediately fulfilled by another person.
- Rely on others to take care of them—often falling apart so they can feel loved and wanted.
- Engage in self-harming behaviors—cutting, suicide attempts, drugs, alcohol abuse, food addiction, or sex addiction.
- Engage in the world as a victim and have a self-pitying, poor me, attitude.[5]

Healthy Boundaries

Setting healthy boundaries will allow you to feel in control, safe, confident, and empowered. Individuals with healthy boundaries show up in the following ways:

- Ability to determine a person's character by what they say and how they treat others, provides a healthy, appropriate level of trust.
- Reveal small pieces of themselves to others over time, and assess how that information is accepted.
- When they reveal information to others, they notice that person's body language and attention. Are they listening? Do they look like they care about what I am saying to them? Are they making eye contact?

- Take their time when being intimate with others—getting to know them first and participating in increasing levels of intimacy like holding hands, hugging, and kissing.

- Look at the whole person—their likes and dislikes, values or beliefs, and other areas of importance to assess whether they are compatible with them. For example, if you hate guns and don't want to have anything to do with them, and a prospective partner is a gun owner and hunter, he is not compatible.

- Make decisions about when relationships are right for them.

- Stay in their power by choosing themselves first to support their needs, personal growth, and healing.

- Take the time to assess how their brain, heart, and body feel before engaging in sexual intimacy. Close your eyes, and take a couple of deep breaths. Ask your brain, "Do I want to engage sexually with this person?" Then ask your heart, "Do I want to engage sexually with this person?" Finally, check in with your body, "Do I want to engage sexually with this person?" You will get a yes or no answer to each of these questions. If the answer is no for one of these, then do not engage in any type of sexual intimacy at that time.

- Hold firm to their values and beliefs, and are not persuaded by what others want them to do.

- Recognize when someone is not able to hold their boundaries, or crosses other people's boundaries.

- Speak up and be aware when someone crosses their boundary.

- Say no to things they don't want. For example, sex, food, alcohol, drugs, or advice.

- Check in with the person to see if it's okay to touch them before doing so.

- Don't take advantage of other people's kindness.
- Treat everyone with respect no matter their age, education, sexual orientation, color, culture, religion, or socioeconomic status.
- Treat oneself with respect, and don't give any part of them away to be liked or accepted.
- Don't let people take advantage of their kind nature.
- Able to make appropriate decisions by taking in all the relevant information, and trusting their choices are accurate.
- Ability to be authentic—know their truth and reveal those parts to others who treat them with care and respect.
- Clearly and concisely present their thoughts, needs and wants to others, and recognize that people can't read their mind.
- Take time in their day-to-day life for self-care, self-reflection, and alone time.
- Talk about themselves to others and themselves with compassion, care, kindness, and respect.
- Acknowledge their body's needs, and treat their body with respect and love.
- Empower themselves to take appropriate action on their needs and wants.[5]

Indicators of Unhealthy and Healthy Boundaries

Your body may display certain physical characteristics, and you may experience certain emotions or states of being when you have unhealthy and healthy boundaries.

Unhealthy Physical Indicators	Healthy Physical Indicators
• Head and eyes focused downward. • Difficulty looking someone in the eye. • Shoulders are rolled forward and turned inward in a concave body posture. • Cower, shrug away from people. • Difficulty speaking up or finding your words. • Speak quietly, stutter.	• Head and eyes focused forward. • Ability to look people in the eye. • Shoulders naturally rest back, able to stand tall, and have a strong body posture. • Ability to maintain boundary. • Able to speak your truth and find your words. • Assertive, speak clearly.
Unhealthy Emotional Indicators	Healthy Emotional Indicators
• Anxious • Nervous • Fear • Doubt • Anger • Resentment	• Calm • Confident • Secure • Content • Safe • Empowered

Embodied Exercise

A lack of boundaries can occur due to neglect, a lack of attachment to caregivers, or trauma. A person may not believe they can take up space in the world or they feel small and insignificant. There is a loss of identity and a feeling of not belonging. If you struggle with setting and maintaining boundaries, the exercise below will help you connect with and expand your boundaries.

Materials

- Red wool or string.
- Different colored rectangular pieces of felt.
- Scissors.
- Journal and pen.

Part I

- Find a place to sit on the floor comfortably. If you are unable to sit on the floor, you can sit in a chair. Ensure there are no obstacles around you for approximately three feet or more.
- Have the wool and scissors close.
- Take a couple of deep breaths and feel into your body. Let yourself get comfortable.
- Breathe in through your nose. Feel the air enter down into your chest and deep into your belly.
- With every breath, imagine bringing light, or vital life-force energy, into your body. Breathe out any tension.
- As you continue to breathe with your natural rhythm, take a moment to scan your entire body mentally.

- Start from the top of your head and scan down to your toes. Notice anything that draws your attention, then let it go.
- Sense into your inner body and feel a deep relaxation.
- Notice how your body radiates heat.
- Imagine that heat, which is your life force, radiating out into the world.
- Notice how far your life force goes. Is it close to your body, a few feet away, or even farther?
- Unravel the wool, and create a circle around yourself according to how far your life force went out from your body.
- Look at the boundary you created; notice what it's like to see this boundary around you. Are there any specific thoughts or emotions that come up? Are you surprised by what you see?
- Notice how it feels in your body as you look at this boundary. Is there tightness or tension?
- If there is tightness, meet the pressure by pushing your arms out from your shoulders. Bend your elbows with your hands up by your shoulders. Face the palms of your hands outward, and slowly push your arms out until parallel with the ground.
- As you push your hands outward, repeat the following statements:

  - I get to be here.
  - I am enough.
  - I am going to take up all the space I need in my life.
  - All of you stay right over there. Don't go away; stay right over there.

- Keep repeating the above statements a few times, and keep pushing outward.
- Notice anything that comes up—thoughts, emotions, body sensations, or memories.
- Take a look at the red string and see if it needs to move.
- What do you notice now in your body? Where do you notice any sensations? Does it feel like there is a little more space? If yes, take it in by breathing deeply into your body and saying to yourself, "There is more space."
- Notice the breath coming into your body.
- Notice if there is a word, or words, to describe how you feel now.
- With the next several breaths, speak the word(s) out loud.
- Journal anything that came up for you in the session—thoughts, emotions, body sensations, or memories.

Practice five to seven minutes a day spreading out the yarn, sitting in the circle, repeating the above statements, pushing out your arms, and saying the word(s) to yourself.

Part II

- Use men's and women's different types of shoes to represent the people in your life—Mom, Dad, siblings, friends, partner, colleagues, or boss.
- Use the different shoes to trace outlines on the felt material, and cut them out.
- Keep the pieces of shoe cut-outs near you.
- Lay out the red string, and sit inside the circle.

- Take a few moments to settle into the circle, and adjust the string to where it feels comfortable.
- Take a few moments to breathe deeply into your belly; notice your stomach expand as you inhale and deflate as you exhale out any tension.
- Take one of the shoe cut-outs depicting a person you know and place it outside the circle.
- Notice how that feels in your body. If there is any tension, repeat the statements in Part I above and push out your arms.
- Place the shoe cut-out on top of the red string and notice how that feels in your body. This person has now entered your space, but is not fully inside. Do you feel comfortable, uncomfortable, or fearful? Keep breathing and notice any thoughts, emotions, body sensations, or memories. Repeat the statements, and push your arms outward if necessary.
- Finally, place the shoe cut-out completely inside your circle. Notice what comes up, repeat the statements, and push your arms outward if necessary.
- Repeat this process with other shoe cut-outs to represent the different people in your life.
- Journal any new insights, thoughts, feelings, emotions, body sensations, or memories.

Were you able to stay present during the second part of the exercise? Did your circle want to shrink or expand with specific shoe cut-outs? Did you want them in your circle? Did you dissociate or check out of your body? Whatever comes up is valuable information for when you start to engage with these people in real life. Are you able to have self-awareness when you lose or shrink your boundary with these people? Are you now able to firmly hold your boundary?

You may be amazed by this exercise. Some people get to be in your inner boundary, while others need to stay outside it or be quite far from it. Take this process slowly. It's not so much that the boundary is the string. The boundary is the sensation you feel in your body!

Values

Write out five to ten significant values for how you want to live your life. (There is an Embodied Exercise on values in Chapter 3.) Take note when someone challenges or treads over these values, and you feel uncomfortable.[1] For example, let's say you value honesty for yourself and the people in your life. If you witness your friend lie to another friend, this will bump up against what you value. If this person is willing to lie to another friend, she may easily lie to you. If being honest is your value, this person is crossing a boundary, and is not the type of friend you can trust or want in your life.

Speaking Up

When you start to notice what is right for you, what you need and want, and where your boundaries lie, you will have to start speaking up for yourself. People can't read your mind, so you will have to tell them what you need from them. Be assertive in a clear and nonthreatening way. Being assertive can be a terrifying prospect, and you may experience fear around speaking up. That's normal.

Use "I" statements when setting boundaries, and when expressing your emotions, thoughts and opinions. When you speak up and put yourself first, you display confidence and assertiveness. An assertive statement has four main parts:

I feel   _____

(use exact feeling word)

When (you)   _____

(explain the situation)

Because   _____

(describe precise consequence for you)

What I need is   _____

(describe what would happen when the problem is solved)

For example, "I feel disrespected when you don't inform me that you're going to be late for our date. I feel like my time isn't valued. What I need from you is a text or call when you're going to be late to let me how long you're going to be."

Ask yourself, "What's the worst thing that could happen if I speak up?" Maybe there is a fear your partner will leave you. If it's a healthy relationship, where there is equality, respect, and give and take, then the likelihood they would leave you for stating your needs is highly unlikely. They may even be happy to see you stand up for yourself instead of giving away your power.

Look at that worst thing realistically. Is it even possible or is it a false perception? (See more in Chapter 3 about how our thoughts lie to us.) Whatever the outcome, tell yourself you will be okay and able to work through it—either by yourself, or with the help of a friend, family member, or counselor.

Start to speak your needs and wants with small things and with safe people. If your food order is wrong, tell the waitress. Ask a co-worker to turn down the radio because it's too loud and distracting. Find ways to speak up and set micro-boundaries throughout your day.

For those who have had trauma from neglect and abuse, you may not know what you need and want. You may not have been allowed to have a voice, and you learned to be something for everyone else in your life. It may be hard to know what you like. Sometimes it's easier to start with what you don't like or don't want to be. Create a list of the things you don't like. Then write the opposite of that thing or behavior. Speak up about what you don't want. As you slowly discover what you like, need, and want in your life, hold your boundaries.

Saying No

One aspect of setting healthy boundaries is saying no. People struggle with saying no because they have never, or rarely, done so in the past. A person's boundary may not have been accepted or allowed in their family. Whatever their parents or caregivers wanted was what they expected them to do.

To support yourself in creating healthy boundaries, start by saying no to things that don't feel right or that you don't want. People in your life are used to you doing what *they* want. As you begin to assert yourself, be prepared for those people to escalate their behavior to get what they want.

If your friends are used to getting their way with you, you will see who your real friends are when you begin to hold your boundaries. A true friend will be okay with you asserting yourself and expressing your needs and wants. It won't be a big deal to them if you say no. They should be proud of you!

A not-so-true friend would manipulate you to appease them. Understand, this person will try to get their way. Be prepared. If they can no longer control you, they may stop being your friend. If that happens, they weren't your friend in the first place. Let's say a not-so-true friend is used to getting your help because you always drop whatever you are doing to help them. When you start saying no, they aren't going to understand.

They will take it as a personal affront—you are selfish for not helping them. They may get angry and escalate their anger to get their way without any thought to your wishes.

You may hear a lot of hurtful comments attacking your character. People's aggression may be cutting. For example, "What do you mean you aren't going to help me? I'm always there for you." A person may act in a passive-aggressive manner. When someone is behaving passive-aggressively, they become aggressive in an indirect way. They put up an impenetrable barrier. They can sulk or become stubborn. They shut down, making it hard to connect with them emotionally. They may display a victim mentality, "Nobody wants to help me. Nobody loves me." A victim wants you to feel sorry for them so you'll do what they want. If you cave even once, the person will know they've won because they escalated their behavior. Now, they have a new level of escalation they can use in the future to get their way.

As you work on setting healthy boundaries, take the time to assess your friendships and other relationships. You should be able to speak your truth, or say no to something without a person attacking you or your opinions. The response from a true friend would be "no problem," or "I understand." If someone doesn't respect your boundary, then it's time to reassess your relationship with that person. As you start to weed out unhealthy relationships, you need to start building new ones with like-minded people. Find your tribe. It will help you feel accepted for who you are. Attend courses, workshops, retreats, and events that interest you, to find other like-minded people. Check out Eventbrite, Facebook events, Meetup, or check out the notice boards at your library and local stores for events.

Setting healthy boundaries with people is listening to yourself about what is appropriate for you, and telling others your limits. For people to recognize your new boundary, you need to be consistent. When you say no, you mean it, and you don't give in to another person's pressure.

How Do I Say No?

You need to give yourself time and space to say no to things. The first thing is to know what you want and don't want in the situation. For some people, it's not only about setting a boundary. It is about understanding themselves and what they want. When someone asks something of you, you have a choice to say yes or no.

When you have difficulty saying no, do not respond immediately to someone's request. Take a moment to consider your response. Someone says, "Can you help me move out of my house this weekend?" and the first thing out of your mouth is, "Sure, no problem," even though you had plans to go away for the weekend. Whether you have plans or don't, say, "I'm not sure. I'll get back to you in..."

It's essential to set a time to get back to them because, otherwise, you may get pestered with calls or texts for an answer. If they persist, and say they need to know now, keep repeating the above statement. You could add, "I need to check my schedule," or "I need to speak with my husband to see if we have plans." If someone asks something of you, take the time to check in with yourself about whether or not you want to do this thing. If you already have plans, then definitely say no. Otherwise, you can be flexible to decide your priorities.

Here's another example. "I'm hosting a party Saturday night. Can you come?" Instead of responding yes immediately, which is likely your go-to response, tell them, "Thank you for the invitation. I'm not sure. I'll have to check my schedule and talk to my mother. I'll get back to you on..." Do not say, "Can I get back to you?" because they may say, "No, I need to know now," and you would likely respond with the usual, "Yes, sure, I'll be there."

Now that you have given yourself time before you respond, take time to think about what you want. If you have a partner, include them in the decision-making process. Don't assume that just because *you* feel obligated to go or participate, they should too. When you decide without consulting your partner, it can be a bone of contention. Roping your partner into doing things they don't want to do can lead to arguments, as they feel a loss of control by being left out of decisions.

If you decide you can and want to go because you have no other commitments, then call or text and say, "Yes, I'll be there." If, however, you don't want to go, or already have other plans, then respond on or before the deadline you gave them. Keep the response simple. Do not back peddle. You do not need an explanation. Remember, "No" is a complete sentence.

If the person doesn't back down, you can change the subject, leave the room, get off the phone with them, or stop responding to their texts. If you have been ghosted by someone, it's not a great feeling. However, in this situation, the person isn't respecting you and is pestering you. To maintain your boundary, don't feel guilty for not texting back.

If you said you would go to an event, or participate in a request, but do not feel well that day, or don't want to go, you can cancel right up to the last minute. If that person is a true friend, they will understand. They may feel disappointed, but that is their emotion to deal with. You are not responsible for their emotions, and you are not the cause of their emotional state. They choose their emotions. (See more on emotions in Chapter 4.)

When you start saying no to people, it's helpful to practice out loud. Write out a script, and repeat it several times. See how the words come out. You can look at yourself in the mirror as long as there is no judgment. When you start to speak up for yourself, it may feel difficult or uncomfortable. If you respond to their request over the phone, you can have the script in front of you. If you are with them in person, and have practiced, your words will come effortlessly. Short and simple is best. You do not need to defend yourself for saying no—stick to your script.

Emotions and Negative Beliefs

Setting new boundaries is scary. Fears, emotions or negative beliefs may show up to keep you from speaking up or asserting your boundaries.

Don't be surprised if you feel guilty. You are used to saying yes, or going along with other people's choices. There may be several reasons why you feel guilty:

- You don't like to hurt people.
- You don't want to disappoint people.
- You have a need to be liked.
- You are afraid they won't be your friend anymore. (See Chapter 3 on limiting or negative beliefs, and Chapter 4 on when it's appropriate to feel guilty.)

We all want to feel we belong, but staying with someone who is toxic or unsupportive, for fear of being alone, is not a reason to rupture your boundary. Stick to your guns. Don't back down from doing what you want to do. Maintaining your boundary will be hard at first, but the more you say no, the better you will feel about your choices, and the easier it will become.

Ask yourself, "What is my biggest fear if I say no to someone or if I speak my mind?" Then ask, "What is the likelihood of that happening?" There may be a slight chance of it happening, or not at all. It may be only a perception or assumption, and not factual. Alternatively, ask yourself, "What if my biggest fear comes true?" Tell yourself you will be okay, and you can deal with whatever happens.

A possible negative belief is, "I have no choice but to go along or agree with this person." That is a false belief. You always have a choice. For example, if your boss is a tyrant, and you go home and cry every day, your boundaries are being crossed. It isn't a healthy work environment. I'm not going to say you need to quit immediately, as you likely wouldn't be able to financially. But you do have choices. For example:

- Stay in the job—which may mean you will continue to struggle mentally, emotionally, and physically.
- If it's safe to do so, speak to your boss about how his or her behavior affects you.
- If it's not safe to do so, talk to someone in Human Resources about your options.
- See if you can get transferred within the organization.
- Look for a new job.

It's entirely normal for fears, emotions, and negative beliefs to show up. Work through them and continue to hold your boundaries. In the long run, holding firm to your boundaries will be beneficial in all areas of your life.

Always Saying Sorry

If you are the type of person who says sorry for everything, even when it's not your fault, this may be a challenge. Saying sorry all the time is a good indicator of someone who has diffuse boundaries. "My needs don't matter. I don't matter. It's my fault for experiencing needs and wants." You get to have a voice. You get to have needs and wants. It may also stem from limiting beliefs about being wrong, bad, or not good enough. You take on self-blame and a heightened sense of responsibility when it's not warranted.

If you have good friends, or a life partner, ask them to point out every time you say sorry. Increase your awareness around it. Think of a situation, and determine if it warrants you saying sorry. Notice your words in your head before you speak. When you hear yourself wanting to say sorry, catch yourself, and don't say it unless you really mean it.

Sorry is not only used to apologize, but a way to express sadness, empathy, or sympathy for something that someone is going through. Here are some examples of when it's appropriate to say sorry:

- "I'm sorry that I bumped into you."
- "I'm sorry you lost your job."
- "I'm sorry to hear about your mom's passing."
- "I'm sorry that I yelled at you."

When you make a sincere apology, you repair the relationship. Do not apologize for saying no to somebody, or for stating your needs or wants. They don't go hand in hand. It's not "I'm sorry I can't make it," say "I can't make it," or "I won't be able to help you with that."

Embedded in our Canadian culture is a tendency to apologize for everything. It doesn't matter what culture you come from or which culture you currently live in. If your needs and wants never counted, you lost the ability to speak for what is okay for you. People whose voice and boundary went unacknowledged tend to apologize for everything. It may be challenging to meet your needs when you have little experience with feeling heard. As a result of trauma and loss of boundaries, you may feel like you don't have a right to take up space in the world—that you have to apologize for being alive.

Notice Your Body and Listen to It

I want you to notice your body posture when you are around certain people, and when they request something from you.

Do you tend to look down? Does your body turn inward and your shoulders roll forward? Are you in a cowering position? Notice if this is a familiar stance for your body. It may be your go-to. An upright body posture is essential to support healthy boundaries.

If you are speaking to someone in person, or even over the phone, lift your head. Allow your shoulders to rest naturally toward the back. Keep your feet facing forward, and have them shoulder-width apart to keep you balanced.

You will learn more about grounding in Chapter 6, but for now, ground yourself before you speak to someone. Even if you text this person, ground yourself. Imagine your feet are encased in big cement bricks, anchoring you to the ground. Feel solid in your body. Take several deep breaths.

Listen to your instincts and intuition when dealing with others, or in specific situations. What does your gut say about this person or situation? Do you feel safe? Are you able to have a voice and share your emotions, thoughts, or opinions?

Notice how it feels in your body when there is something you don't like to do. Your body will respond physically—increased heart rate, sweating, nervousness, upset stomach, pressure in your throat, tightness in your chest or shoulders, or balled fists.[1] You may also experience pain or discomfort in other parts of your body, or uncomfortable sensations. These are all indicators something isn't right.

As you learn more about listening and connecting with your body in upcoming chapters, you will recognize how your body continually informs you, and doesn't lie. Take a moment to close your eyes, and bring up something you don't like—notice how your body feels. Maybe there is pain, tension, nervousness, or discomfort. Shake those sensations off. Now close your eyes again, and bring up something you like, and notice the sensations in your body. Your body may feel light, relaxed, calm, or at peace. Your body always informs you when your boundary is maintained, or if someone or something violates it. Use your body as a gauge to help communicate what is okay and not okay.

When you are in conversation, or interacting with another person or persons, notice their body language, their tone of voice, the words they speak, and where they stand within your boundary. Are they too close or too far? What is your body experiencing during this interaction? Do you feel safe or uncomfortable? You are energetically affected by their presence within your boundary, and will receive sensations in your own body about whether or not this situation is acceptable. If it feels good, utilize all your senses to create an open channel to receive. Be present in the interaction, and allow yourself to create a true connection with this person. If it doesn't feel good, remove yourself from the situation as quickly as possible. Support any physical or emotional dysregulation through self-care and self-soothing techniques. (For example, deep breathing, journaling, going for a walk, taking a bath, or speaking to a friend.)

Embodied Exercise

This exercise will help you feel more confident, grounded, secure, unwavering, and connected to your body when dealing with people, saying no, or confronting anyone about anything troubling.

- Shake your arms and legs to let go of any nervousness or tension.
- Take a couple of deep breaths.
- Feel the air come in through your nose, down your chest, and deep into your belly.

- Colors have psychological properties. As you inhale, imagine breathing in one or more of the following colors for whatever support you require:

  - For physical courage and strength, breathe in the color red.
  - To speak clearly and feel calm, breathe in the color blue.
  - To feel confident, friendly, and emotionally strong, breathe in the color yellow.
  - To feel balance and harmony, breathe in the color green.[6]

- When you exhale, imagine releasing any tension in your body.
- Keep your body balanced with feet shoulder-width apart, and knees slightly bent.
- Allow your shoulders to rest naturally toward the back with your arms at your sides.
- Have the palms of your hands open and facing forward to allow you to be open and to receive, if the situation is supportive.
- Alternatively, keep your hands neutral at your sides to allow your body to be more relaxed and feel safe.
- Keep your head up and make eye contact.
- Have a smile on your face. If you don't like the person you are interacting with, or don't feel particularly happy, turn up the corners of your mouth ever so slightly. Your brain will respond as if you are happy, and your body will release *happiness* hormones, including dopamine, endorphins, and serotonin.

- Speak loud enough so the other person can hear you, and speak your words clearly and concisely.

Practice this body stance as often as you like, or until it becomes second nature.

Safeguard Your Space

Setting boundaries is not always about speaking your needs or saying no. Technology continually invades our privacy and boundaries to monitor, control, or manipulate us. A loss of boundaries can occur in your personal and work relationships. You can put practices into place that support setting healthy boundaries without ever interacting with a person. Set boundaries to create a physical or emotional space, protect your belongings, and protect your time and energy. Here are some examples:

- Lock personal items in a drawer or cabinet.
- Use passwords, or other security features, on your phone, computer, and other devices.
- Block or remove people from your phone, email, and social media accounts.
- Remove apps from your phone, or remove yourself from social media accounts.
- Turn off your phone in the evening, or at a specific time during the day, to not be interrupted.
- Set up an automatic response for emails when you are out of the office for vacations, or state you are only available during work hours.
- Set a cut-off time to stop answering texts or emails.
- Do not answer work texts or phone messages if they are on your personal phone.

- Take your breaks at work, don't work through them. Don't stay at your desk to eat.
- Schedule time for yourself to work out, take a nap, read, watch TV, garden, sew, meditate, or journal.[1]

Work on Setting Healthy Boundaries

If you don't have the healthiest of boundaries, don't beat yourself up. It can take time to master skills, and perseverance to re-assert your boundaries. Make small changes daily. Along with doing the exercises in this chapter, choose one specific boundary, or one in each area you would like to improve. Practice it for several weeks or months until it becomes second nature, and then move onto another area of struggle.

Take a look at the Healthy Boundaries section at the beginning of this chapter. Choose one or several areas you would like to focus on. In the second exercise in this chapter, you started to gather information about the areas where you are thriving and the scenarios where you may be struggling. Use the information you gathered to choose what you would like to work on first. Maybe it's the most challenging area you struggle in, or perhaps you do well in one area, but want to focus on improving. For example, maybe you are excellent with not lending money to friends, but continue to lend money to family members. If that's the case, focus on stopping this aspect of the boundary violation.

If you are struggling with a specific problem, search online. For example, "How do I set healthy boundaries with family?" There are over 89 million results as I'm writing this, so your next question is likely, "How do I choose which article is best?"

Having so much information and too many choices can cause confusion. My suggestion is to go to psychologytoday.com. Type in the search field whatever you are struggling with, and it will list all the related articles. *Psychology Today* has hundreds of articles on many issues experienced by people. They are written by psychologists and other mental healthcare workers with abundant knowledge and years of experience. The articles are generally not too long, and give practical tools to support new ways of being.

Setting new healthy boundaries and maintaining them is not easy, especially if you are dealing with friends or family members experiencing mental health or personality disorders, depression, anxiety, suicidal ideation, or trauma-related symptoms. Seek out the support of a counselor to help you create and maintain your boundaries.

Teach Others Your Boundaries

When you start to teach others your new boundaries, you need to be consistent. Decide what the boundary is you want or need to keep, and stick with it. Don't say no to someone's request for money one day, then give it to them the next. Don't change your mind. I don't expect you to be 100 percent perfect, but that's what you are working toward.

Tell people what your boundary is, and tell them often. "Please stop asking me for money, as I will no longer give you any." "Please don't touch me without my permission." "Please don't speak up for me unless I ask you to."

Tell people that if they don't respect your wishes, you will leave the room, end the phone call, or block them on texts or social media. You may have to tell them that you will no longer be their friend.

Be prepared to walk away from people. If they keep trying to change your mind, you can say, "It doesn't appear you are hearing me. I am not going to change my mind. If you can't accept my decision, then I'm going to have to leave / hang up the phone / block your number." Follow through—do what you say you are going to do.

State your needs and wants in your relationships. For example, maybe you've always done laundry for your partner, but that is no longer okay for you. You could say, "I know in the past, I've always done the laundry, but I need it to be a shared responsibility now." If a couple never discusses who will be responsible for what in the home, women end up taking on traditional women's roles like cooking, cleaning, and taking care of the kids. You may have taken on a role you hadn't consciously thought about or chosen. Discuss your new boundaries even if you haven't done so in the past. Communicating what is right for you will need to be an ongoing process. Address your needs and wants as they arise.

Of course, compromise in a relationship is also essential.

If your belief in setting boundaries builds a wall around you and keeps people out, this belief is false. Change your mindset to realize that when you set healthy boundaries with people, you strengthen relationships. (Mindset will be discussed more in Chapter 3.) Boundaries allow you to recognize when something or someone is harmful. If your boundaries are continually being crossed or violated, listen to your instincts, and know this isn't okay. You get to choose and have a right to your thoughts, opinions, decisions, beliefs, values, emotions, spirituality, sexuality, privacy, and material possessions.

Honor and Recognize Other People's Boundaries

Although you get to be the star with your boundaries, you also have to learn to recognize and honor other people's boundaries. If you can't identify your own boundaries, it may be difficult to recognize those of others. That's okay. Below are some helpful hints for recognizing other people's boundaries.

You can become aware of how people assert their boundaries and create space for themselves by the cues they give off. Social cues can be present through physical distancing. An exception to this is the result of mandated social distancing and fear during the COVID pandemic. If you tune into your body, you may feel this energetically (more on this in Chapter 8) from their body language, and verbal and nonverbal communication. Here are some things you may notice in others if you cross or violate their boundaries:

- Limited responses to your conversation, uninterested.
- Excessive nodding.
- Excessive *uh-huh*-ing.
- Talk fast or laugh nervously.
- Sudden higher-pitched voice or other changes to the tone of voice.
- Lack of eye contact or a blank stare.
- Inconsistent facial expressions to words spoken.
- Turn away from you or to the side.
- Back away from you.
- Nervous or defensive hand gestures.
- Stiff posture or folded arms.
- Flinch or wince.

Cues will be slightly different for everyone. Some people's cues may be hard to read. Some will be affected by their culture. For example, in North America, we value—and see it as respectful—to make eye contact when speaking and listening to people. However, in Japanese culture, this is seen as a sign of disrespect. Some people may not be able to provide eye contact because they are shy, have low self-esteem or low self-confidence, experience Autism, or are on the spectrum, or have other developmental disabilities. It is crucial to be inclusive and discerning of those you meet, and the cues you receive.

Ultimately, the easiest way is to ask someone. For example, "Is it okay if I ask you a question?" or "Am I bothering you?" Checking in with someone is the best way to ensure you are not crossing or violating their boundaries.[1]

Benefits of Setting and Maintaining Healthy Boundaries

The benefits of setting and maintaining healthy boundaries include:

- Feel safe and secure mentally, emotionally, physically, materially, and spiritually.
- Treat yourself with respect by listening to and meeting your needs.
- Increase self-esteem and self-confidence.
- Increase independence and personal agency.
- Ability to have and feel your emotions.
- Ability to be vulnerable.
- Ability to own your thoughts.
- Ability to speak up for yourself and make decisions.
- Ability to say no.
- Feel more content and happy with choices.
- Improve relationships.
- Increase comfort when socializing.
- Feel more authentic—true to yourself.
- Feel empowered and in control.
- Trust yourself.

―⁓―

I hope you found this chapter helpful in recognizing whether or not you have rigid, permeable, or diffuse boundaries, the six areas requiring boundaries, the differences between unhealthy and healthy boundaries, and the ways you can begin to change and create new healthy boundaries.

—✺—

Join me in the next chapter as I explore thoughts. You will learn how to notice your thoughts, decipher if they are factual or not, and learn how to change your thoughts to create a healthier and supportive mindset.

3

THOUGHTS—
DON'T BUY INTO THEM

*"A sick thought can devour the body's flesh
more than fever or consumption."*

Guy de Maupassant

Growing up, I didn't have much enthusiasm for elementary school. I was more interested in visiting and talking with my fellow students. I rarely did homework, or applied myself to assignments, unless they were of interest to me. I never read books. In grade three, the teacher gave us points for each book we read. She displayed the student's name and the number of books they'd read in the classroom. The student with the most books would be the winner. To receive a point for the book you read, you had to explain it to the teacher. I, in my brilliant wisdom, read the back cover of the book, and a bit in the beginning, middle, and end, so I could say enough to get me a point.

In junior high, my marks averaged in the mid-70s. I struggled with tests, and was told I needed better test preparation. I can laugh at this now because they never taught us how to write tests or study for them. How do you prepare when you don't know how? As my parents emigrated from Greece, and English wasn't their first language, they couldn't help by teaching me study habits.

My grade 10 and 11 high school marks dropped to the mid-60s. At this point, I had no study skills and no motivation to do homework. By grade 12, I was averaging marks in the mid-50s. The year I graduated, they brought in departmental diploma exams, which counted for 50 percent of our grade. In three of the five exams, my marks were in the low 40s. I barely passed with averages in the low 50s.

I remember taking a career aptitude test in high school; the top choice was a nurse. I didn't even think about whether I wanted to be a nurse or not, it just became my career choice. So, off I went to college. I still had no idea how to study. I remember highlighting the majority of my nursing books. I thought it was all relevant information. No surprise, I failed, and was thrown out of the program after the first semester. I was distraught. I believed my world had ended. I adopted the thoughts *I'm stupid* and *I'm not smart enough for university or college.*

Not knowing what I wanted to do with my life, I took a course to become an administrative assistant. I worked several clerical jobs, and finally ended up working as an administrative assistant at the University of Calgary in the Faculty of Medicine in 1992. I was good at my job, but unhappy and unfulfilled. Ten years later, a work colleague said she wanted to take a university course. I thought, if she does it, I'll do one too. Surprisingly, I got an A-. I was shocked. If I was able to get this grade, it meant I wasn't stupid.

No one taught me study skills growing up, so I didn't have the tools to succeed in the school system. I recognize now that I was, and am, extremely bright, with a high IQ; as such, I wasn't challenged and, therefore, bored in school. I didn't study, and took short cuts because I learned how to do enough to get by. My abilities and intelligence were not nurtured. I bought into the system and believed I wasn't smart enough. All this wasted time thinking I was incompetent kept me stuck and small. I had bought into my negative thoughts and beliefs, and it became my story.

Thoughts

Have you heard the adage, "You are what you think?" Those words are accurate in terms of how we think about ourselves and our story—the specific memorable experiences, our wounds, or our traumas. We tend to get stuck in that story—not only as a victim, but because of the way our brain functions, and how we view ourselves.

Our thoughts are all-encompassing. We have 50 thousand to 80 thousand thoughts per day, with approximately two thousand to three thousand thoughts per hour, and most of them are recycled.[1] That's a lot of thoughts!

Our thoughts tend to be negative, it's part of our survival mechanism. Have you ever wanted to change something about yourself or your life but fear comes up? Then you start saying things like *you can't do that, you're not smart enough,* or *you're not good enough.* The survival part of our brain wants us to keep the status quo. It fears change, thinking it would put our survival at risk.

"I don't need to get a new job. I'm good where I am. I have a nice place to live. I can buy food and clothes. So what if my boss doesn't treat me great? If I get a new job, what if I'm not good at it? I could lose that job. If I lose my job, I won't be able to pay my rent. If I can't pay my rent, I'll get evicted. Then I'll be living on the street with no food, clothing, shelter, or safety."

This scenario may sound extreme, or even ridiculous, but this is what runs subconsciously with many of our decisions. Our brains are hardwired to survive.

Limiting or Negative Beliefs

We create a limiting belief when we conclude something about a life experience that is ultimately false.[2] Our perception is due to a lack of information. Something happens, and we don't have all the information we need, so we fill in the missing information from our previous experiences and that creates a new belief. We also conceive limiting beliefs by the need to protect our ego or self-worth.[3] For example, "I didn't pass my exam because I am not smart enough." Limiting beliefs allow people to feel good. It protects them from seeking out information to address their issues, and from seeing the situation more realistically.

We create limiting beliefs as early as three to five years old. We continue to develop limiting beliefs throughout our formative years. However, within the first seven years, we have ingrained all the beliefs about others, ourselves, and how we fit in with people and the world. Limiting beliefs occur due to what we see, hear, feel, sense, and experience. We witness the people around us, and mirror what we experience, and believe to be true. These thoughts are ingrained in our subconscious mind. As a result, we walk around in the world with this programming running below the surface. For example, if I don't feel worthy of love, I may seek out unhealthy or abusive partnerships repeatedly. When we have limiting beliefs, they stay with us until we recognize them and start to challenge them.

―⁓⁓―

My parents had a home in Regina where they rented out rooms. When I was approximately four years old, we had renters living in the basement. They gave me a big brown paper bag filled with plastic dishes. The bag was as big as me. I was so excited and happy. For a four-year-old, this was like winning the lottery. I remember carrying the bag upstairs and going outside into the backyard to play with my new dishes. After a while, my mom called me to have lunch, and I left the bag outside. When I came back out after lunch, the bag was gone. I began crying hysterically, and my mom came outside to see what was wrong. She realized the garbage truck down the street must have taken it along with the other garbage, because I had set it down on the ground next to the garbage cans. Even at four years old, my brain wanted to fix the situation. I remember thinking, why can't we go stop them and get my stuff back? It was rightfully mine, and they took it without my permission. My mom said there was nothing we could do now. I sat on the step and cried and cried and cried.

In this defining moment, I created the negative belief, *I am powerless*. This belief often reared its ugly head throughout the first 30 or so years of my life. I had hardwired it into my brain and my brain continued to search for instances where I would feel powerless. Instead of believing I had power and could create my destiny, the world mirrored back to me what I thought about myself—I am powerless. I was magnetically attracted to situations where I felt powerless. It's like having blinders on. I was unable to see anything but what was directly in front of me, missing opportunities for positive situations that I could control, just outside my line of vision.

—⁓—

Do you keep repeating the same scenarios over and over again? Maybe you wonder, "Why do I keep attracting this into my life?" It's the *same shit, different pile* mentality. One or more limiting beliefs is running subconsciously. Negative beliefs are like money in the bank—the more you have, the more interest you make. As a result of multiple experiences, you can have several negative beliefs floating around in your subconscious.

For me, *I am powerless* was also influenced by the negative beliefs: *I am not good enough*; *I am a bad person*; *I am not lovable*; and *It's not okay to show my emotions.*

When you trigger one negative belief, it can trigger several others, like a domino effect. Negative beliefs can be insidious. The only way to counter the subconscious patterns running in the background is to challenge them. When a situation occurs, start to listen to the rattling in your head. What are you saying about yourself?

Core Negative Beliefs

In EMDR therapy, one of the questions I ask in the assessment phase is, "What is your negative belief about yourself concerning the current issue or experience?" This question helps access the client's core negative beliefs. For example, in trauma, a core negative belief may be, *I am not safe*. In families where there has been abuse or neglect, or when parents are hypercritical, it may manifest as *I am not good enough* or *I am not deserving*. Whatever the situation, you have several core beliefs running in your subconscious. Below are some of the more common negative beliefs and their corresponding positive beliefs. They comprise four overarching themes: Self-Defectiveness, Responsibility, Safety/Vulnerability, and Control/Choice.

Negative Cognitions	Positive Cognitions
Self-Defectiveness	
I am a bad person	I am a good person
I don't deserve love	I deserve love
I am worthless	I am fine as I am, I have value
I am shameful	I am honorable
I am not lovable	I am lovable

I am not good enough	I am good enough
I am not deserving	I deserve good things
I am stupid	I am intelligent, I am able to learn
I am insignificant	I am significant/important
I am a disappointment	I am okay just the way I am
I am weak	I am strong
I am permanently damaged	I am (can be) healthy
I am different (don't belong)	I am okay as I am
I am ugly (my body is hateful)	I am fine (attractive)
Responsibility	
I should have done something	I did the best I could
I should have known better	I do the best I can
I did something wrong	I learned (can learn) from it
I should have done more	I did my best
It's my fault	I did my best
Safety/Vulnerability	
I am not safe	I am safe now
I am in danger	It's over, I am safe now
I can't trust anyone	I can choose whom to trust
I can't trust myself	I can (learn to) trust myself
I can't protect myself	I can take care of myself
It's not okay to feel (show) my emotions	I can safely feel (show) my emotions
I can't stand up for myself	I can make my needs known

Control/Choice	
I am not in control	I am in control now
I am weak	I am strong
I am powerless	I have choices now
I can't get what I want	I can get what I want
I am helpless	I control my destiny
I am a failure (can't succeed)	I can succeed
I have to be perfect (please everyone)	I can be myself (make mistakes)
I can't be trusted	I can be trusted
I can't trust myself	I can trust (learn to trust) myself[4]

Which limiting beliefs resonate with you? Do they trigger other negative beliefs that aren't on the list? Maybe you are unsure which limiting beliefs relate to you. If that is the case, ask yourself the following questions: What role did I play in my family while I was growing up? For example, maybe you were often sick, had an ailment or disease that diminished your ability to thrive. Your limiting belief may be, *I am a burden.* What were my pain points growing up? What difficulties did I experience? For example, maybe you were bullied in school, or had no friends. Your limiting belief may be, *I am not likable.*

Embodied Exercise

- Write out all the negative beliefs that resonate with you.
- Rank them from the most troubling to the least troubling.

- Choose one negative belief to work on. Maybe it's the most troubling, or perhaps the least.

- Write out all the ways and situations this negative belief shows up in your life. For example, *I have to be perfect.* Is that with everyone or only specific people? How often? Occasionally or daily? When does it typically show up? What types of situations?

- The more information you can get, the more you can challenge this negative belief.

- Challenge the negative belief. (I'll discuss challenging your thoughts later in this chapter.) If your negative belief is *I have to be perfect*, is someone telling you you need to be perfect? Likely no. *You* create the need to be perfect.

- Write out all the scenarios and situations that disprove this negative belief. Find the exceptions, and focus on them. Re-read the list often to remind yourself you are not this negative belief.

- When you speak the negative belief out loud, or when you hear it in that voice in your head, stop yourself, cancel it out, and replace it with a positive belief.

- Write out the positive belief and say it to yourself daily. Repetition is key. Place it on post-it notes around your house. Put it as a screensaver on your phone and computer.

- Your negative belief has been around for most of your life. It will take a while for the truth to sink in.

- Work on it for several weeks or months until you believe it in the core of your being.

- Then, choose another negative belief from the list to work on.

Cognitive Distortions

Limiting or negative beliefs are not the only way we misread our thoughts and experiences. Cognitive distortions are when our mind exaggerates or creates irrational and false thoughts about ourselves, others, or situations. Cognitive distortions arise because we want to reinforce our limiting or negative beliefs. We buy into these cognitive distortions, believing they are rational and truthful, but they are false, and keep us feeling inadequate. Below are 15 of the most common cognitive distortions, and how to counteract them.

Filtering

Have you ever heard of the expression "wearing rose-colored glasses"? When someone wears rose-colored glasses, they look at things optimistically and positively. Filtering is like wearing black-colored glasses. If your focus is pessimistic, it distorts the situation. When you use filtering, you magnify and focus on negative details while filtering out the positive aspects of a situation. For example, in your annual review with your boss, she tells you that you need to work on time management. You get stuck on this one critique, and go home and tell your partner or friends how your boss thinks you don't have adequate time-management skills. Then you discuss all the times you've mismanaged your time, which makes you feel even worse. If you stopped to look at the review in its entirety, you would recognize your boss commended you on your ability to think on your feet, being supportive and helpful to your colleagues, being a team player, speaking up in meetings with great ideas, being punctual, or being a hard worker. By focusing only on one negative detail, you distort the whole perspective of the situation. If you recognize you use filtering, stop magnifying the negative and expand your view of the situation. Look at it realistically from all sides. What else was said? What else happened that was positive in the situation?

Polarized Thinking

Polarized thinking is seeing things from the extreme—either black-or-white thinking or all-or-nothing thinking. If you tend toward polarized thinking, you can never win. Let's look at the belief *I have to be perfect*. If you are not completely perfect, you are a complete failure. There are no shades of gray. For example, "If I don't work out seven days a week for two hours each day, I'm a failure." This type of thinking can result in you never achieving your goals. If you believe you aren't perfect, your mind stops you from ever starting, or stops at the first sign of not meeting your expected ideal. Living life perfectly doesn't exist. Stop comparing yourself to others and look realistically at what is preferable for you. If you want to be more fit, will that happen if you work out several days a week? Yes. But, you won't be fit if you do nothing.

Overgeneralization

When a person overgeneralizes, they take a single adverse event, or piece of evidence, and conclude that it will happen every time. This results in feelings of defeat and hopelessness. For example, "My boyfriend cheated on me in the past, so *all* my boyfriends will cheat on me." Negative beliefs show up as well. "All my boyfriends cheat on me because I am not..."—*attractive enough*, *sexy enough*, or *lovable*. Look for instances to disprove your overgeneralization. As in this example, which boyfriends did *not* cheat on you?

Jumping to Conclusions

When a person jumps to conclusions, they believe they know what another person is thinking, or feeling (mind-reading). They predict something terrible will happen, or know precisely why the other behaves the way they do (fortune-telling). This cognitive distortion negatively interprets a situation where there is no factual evidence to back it up. For example, "I know my friend is angry at me because she hasn't returned my text for several days, so she won't want to go out with me this weekend." There are no assumptions or perceptions allowed. Ask the person directly how they feel or think about you or a situation. You have to have factual evidence to prove your claim. If it hasn't happened yet, then it's not true.

Catastrophizing

When someone catastrophizes, they believe the worst-case scenario is going to happen. It's future thinking at its worst. There are two types of catastrophizing. One way is to magnify a situation to extremes. For example, "My coach told me I need to work on my volleyball serves." You then interpret this as, "I'm going to get kicked off the team." The other type of catastrophizing is minimizing. A person downplays significant events as being not that big of a deal. For example, "My husband drinks a lot and then yells at me, but it doesn't happen that often." To stop catastrophizing when magnifying a situation, ask yourself, "What is the truth?" If it's not happening currently, then it's not happening. Stay out of future thinking and only look at the present situation. If you are minimizing, take yourself out of the situation and imagine it happening to your sister or best friend. How would you feel if it was happening to them?

Personalization

Personalization is when a person believes everything someone says, or does, is directly about them. They take everything personally, even when not intended. A person who thinks this way tends to compare themselves to others. For example, while sitting in the passenger seat of their car, a friend says they hate when people drive so fast, and the driver interprets this as a direct attack on their driving. In personalization, a person can also blame themselves, and take responsibility for an adverse event that has nothing to do with them. For example, "My mom and I got into a car accident today because I was late leaving the house with her." To help not take everything personally, recognize we all have egos. This makes us believe the world revolves around us and that we are self-important. Get out of your ego. When a person states something, unless they directly implicate you, it is not about you. When you blame yourself for something that has nothing to do with you, look at the situation in terms of correlation or connection between two things: cause and effect. Would leaving the house late result in an accident? No. However, driver error, or poor weather conditions, could.

Control Fallacies

Control fallacies, or mistaken beliefs, are about a need to control situations in our lives. This cognitive distortion includes both externally-controlled and internally-controlled fallacies. In externally-controlled fallacies, we believe we are helpless victims of fate. For example, "I did poorly on my test because the teacher made it too hard." In internally-controlled fallacies, we take responsibility for other people's unhappiness and pain. For example, "I'm not a good mother because my child is always anxious." For externally-controlled fallacies, notice what you have control over in a situation, and where it is beyond your control. For internally-controlled fallacies, take responsibility only for what is yours, not other people's stuff. You can only control yourself—your thoughts, emotions, and behaviors. You can't control others, and you can't control situations beyond yourself.

Fallacy of Fairness

In the fallacy of fairness, a person becomes resentful when others don't agree with what they believe should be fair. They become angry, bitter, and hopeless about situations they think should be fair when they're not. Because they believe life isn't fair, things don't work out in that person's favor. For example, a woman is outraged when she finds out her male co-worker receives a higher wage than her even though she started before him and is more qualified. Life is full of injustices and times where you have no control over what is fair. Instead of creating more suffering by trying to change an unchangeable situation, recognize you have control over your response. Accept it, let it go, and focus on the positive in the situation. You can also advocate for change in your circle of peers, workplace, community, or city.

Blaming

In blaming, a person puts the responsibility for their emotional pain onto others, or blames themselves for every problem outside their control. For example, "My boyfriend flirted with the waitress and he made me feel bad about myself." No one can make you feel anything. You are responsible for your beliefs, thoughts, emotions, and reactions. You have a choice about how you feel in any situation. See the situation clearly and truthfully. Speak up when you think something is not okay.

Shoulds

When people use *should, must, ought,* or *have to* statements, they judge and criticize themselves or others based on some rigid rules about how people should behave. They feel guilty if they break their own rules, or get angry when others break the rules. People believe *shoulds* motivate them into action. When, in actuality, they punish themselves by doing something they don't want to do, or label themselves as something they aren't. For example, "I should volunteer at the hospital," even though they faint at the sight of blood. Remove *should, must, ought,* and *have to* from your vocabulary. Do something because you want to do it. Accept who you are.

Emotional Reasoning

In emotional reasoning, a person believes whatever they *feel* to be automatically correct. The person's emotions take over their rational thoughts, and they have difficulty thinking logically. If they experience an uncomfortable emotion, then it must reflect how they feel. For example, "I feel nervous; therefore, I must be an anxious person." Get out of your emotional mind and connect to your rational mind. You are not your feelings. You experience emotions, but they do not define you. (I'll discuss emotions in detail in Chapter 4.)

Fallacy of Change

In the fallacy of change, a person believes if they pester a person to change, they will. Their happiness and success depends on the other person changing. This cognitive distortion often shows up in relationships. For example, "If my husband would only work harder, we would be able to afford a new house." You can't make people change. They will only choose to change if it benefits them. Focus only on what you can change in yourself.

Global Labeling

Global labeling is also known as mislabeling. A person creates a negative global judgment of themselves or others, from one or two defining qualities, into unhealthy universal labels. This cognitive distortion is overgeneralization to the extreme. The person evaluates themselves only by their mistakes or negative experiences. For example, *I'm stupid* after getting one lousy grade. People may use colorful and emotionally-laden language to describe a person or event. For instance, if a stranger sees a mother scolding her child, she may say she's a horrible mother who is emotionally abusing her child. By mislabeling, you add assumptions and perceptions about yourself, someone, or an event. You infer it falsely because you don't have all the information. Look at a situation from all sides and speak kindly about yourself and others.

Always Being Right

With this cognitive distortion, the person needs to prove their opinions and actions are correct. They go to great lengths to prove they are right because it is unthinkable to be wrong. You may feel you are on trial with people who engage in this cognitive distortion. They always have to be right, and they always have to win an argument. They don't care if they hurt your feelings. Their need to be right is more important. Maybe you know someone like this. If you do, don't engage in an argument with them. Acknowledge their side even if you don't agree with it, and know your opinion is valid. If this is you, then see other people's views as also being valid. There is no one hard-and-fast truth for any area under discussion.

Heaven's Reward Fallacy

The final cognitive distortion is a false belief that you will receive a big payoff by some unseen Divine force if a person denies or sacrifices themselves. People can become bitter when they don't receive a reward for all their hard work and sacrifice. For example, a woman in an abusive relationship believes sacrificing her life for her children by staying in the marriage will eventually be worth it. Do not deny or sacrifice any part of you. God has given us choice and agency. Create the life you want.[5]

After reading through this list, you may recognize several cognitive distortions of your own. Maybe even all of them. That's okay. Increasing your self-awareness is what's important here. Once you have an awareness of something, you can start to change it. Check in with your thoughts and self-talk daily. Notice if you use cognitive distortions. If you do, name it, then change your thoughts to accurate, factual statements. Negative thinking will lessen and truthful, balanced, and rational thoughts will be restored.

Embodied Exercise

Below are some steps to help you change your cognitive distortions.

- Start paying attention to your negative self-talk to bring it into your conscious awareness, and stop reacting out of habit.
- Get out of your head, and write out your distorted thoughts on paper. Writing it out can help you see things more rationally.
- Write down the event along with your negative thoughts and emotions.
- Challenge your negative thoughts by asking the following questions:

  - What evidence do I have to prove these negative thoughts? Facts, not opinions, assumptions, or perceptions.
  - Am I overly critical of myself?
  - What successes have I had in the past?
  - What is a more positive way to view these thoughts?
  - What would I say to a friend in this situation? Apply it to yourself.
  - What are the advantages of believing this negative thought?
  - What are the disadvantages of believing this negative thought?

- Test the validity of your cognitive distortion. For example, "My friend thinks I'm a burden because I have anxiety." Ask her directly instead of staying stuck in your false beliefs.

- Talk to yourself more compassionately, as you would to a friend.
- See things in shades of gray. Scale yourself from zero to 100 percent on the accuracy of this negative thought.
- Survey other people to gauge their experiences in similar situations. Ask for their opinion as to whether your negative thoughts are realistic or distorted.
- Look at the world more positively and change, "I should..." to "It would be nice if..." For example, "I should stop smoking" to "It would be nice if I no longer wanted or needed to smoke." This curiosity opens up new thoughts about wanting to change, or not wanting to change.
- Look at the responsibility of all those involved. Don't put the blame solely on yourself.
- Think of positive outcomes for the situation when stuck in a worst-case scenario.
- Use a mantra, a simple word or phrase, to help calm your mind. For example, *everything is fine,* or *my life is good.*
- You can't change the past, and your future is unknown, so stay in the present moment.[6,7,8]

Preceding Event

When you check in with your thoughts, you'll find there was an event that preceded them. For example, you may have received some disturbing news, maybe you had a fight with your boyfriend, or perhaps you won the lottery. (Now *that* would be something!) The event will affect your thoughts, emotions, sensations in your body, and your behaviors.

River of Life

The event influences your mental, emotional, and physical response. According to the Lazarus Theory of Emotion, thoughts are necessary before emotion can be present. There will be a stimulus (i.e., an event), then there will be a thought, then you will simultaneously experience a physiological response in your body along with emotions.[9] The thought-emotion happens so quickly that you don't even notice it, and appears as if you go directly to an emotion without prior thought.

Let me give you an analogy—the River of Life. There is an event, and as you proceed down the river, you get to some rapids. These are your emotions. Then, as a result of the emotions, you proceed down the river and come upon more rapids, and you react to those emotions with unwanted behaviors. Lastly, as you head down the river even farther, a new event occurs, and the process starts over again.

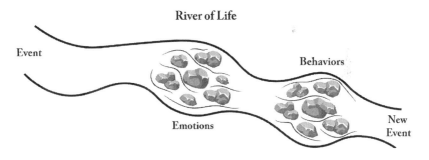

River of Life

Event

Behaviors

Emotions

New Event

"Wait a second, Vicky, what about your thoughts? Shouldn't those be in the River of Life?" Absolutely!

Influencing Thoughts

Your thoughts continually influence you, and you need to discern which thoughts are lies, and which are truths. I'm going to give you a scenario, and then I'll plug it into the River of Life.

Event—You are at work and your boss calls you into his office. He proceeds to yell at you because you haven't completed the report he needs for his meeting tomorrow.

Emotions—You believe you didn't deserve to be treated that way and feel hurt, upset, or maybe even angry.

Behavior—You go home, and yell at your spouse or your kids. It's not about your family. They've done nothing wrong. It's about the work situation, and the thoughts you had about that event influence your emotions and behavior.

You perceive emotions as a direct result of the event. Yes, an event and emotions are valid and correlate, but your thoughts also influence them. These thoughts are called automatic thoughts. You have a running dialogue in your mind about what you are experiencing—what you feel emotionally, what you sense physically, and what you believe about the situation. These automatic thoughts dictate how you feel about the situation, which influences your behavior. Because automatic thoughts happen automatically, you are often unaware they are occurring. They happen instantaneously, and appear rational and believable. You forget to check in with the chatter in your brain, and question if those thoughts are factual.[10] If you stop to listen to the chatter, you may hear negative thoughts or limiting beliefs. Your thoughts precede your emotions. As a result, they influence how you feel and how you respond. In this particular scenario, the automatic thoughts preceding the emotions may sound something like this:

Thoughts—*My boss hates me. I am so stupid. I am lousy at my job. I never do anything right. I am going to get fired.*

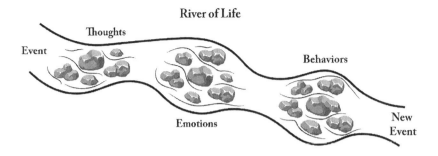

These automatic thoughts influence how you feel about your-self, and how you react in response to those thoughts. In this example, she's not angry at her spouse or kids, she's mad at herself. If she were to look more in-depth, she might be sad about not doing a good job, disappointed in herself, or fearful of losing her job. Her thoughts influence her emotions and behaviors after the event.

The key here is to know your thoughts. Thoughts are just that—thoughts. We have thousands of thoughts a day, but that doesn't mean they are factual. You need to look at each thought, and decipher if it's true or not. Let's look at each thought above:

My boss hates me—How does she know her boss hates her? Did he tell her directly?

I am so stupid—Stupid is a relative term. It is a generic word that holds different meanings for different things. She got this job. She probably went to school and passed. She probably had other jobs where she completed her work effectively.

I am lousy at my job—What indicates she is terrible at her job? Was she told in a review that she doesn't know what she's doing?

I never do anything right—Really, never? Never is an all-encompassing word. That means there is not one instance where she has done something right, which is highly unlikely.

I am going to get fired—Did her boss say she was going to be fired? Has she been reprimanded before? If yes, did her boss state he would fire her if she doesn't get it together? He probably would have fired her at that moment if this were true.

It's helpful to know your thoughts. Challenge them, and recognize how they influence you. Are your thoughts factual or false? Thoughts can only be factual if the evidence supports them as if you were in a court of law.

The River of Life scenario above reveals that how you *think* about a situation will influence how you feel and behave. However, it is essential to recognize that thoughts, emotions, and behaviors are all interrelated. How you *feel* about a situation will also affect how you think and behave. Finally, how you *act* in a situation will affect how you think and feel.

The purpose of this book is to get you out of your head and into your body, and not to get tripped up by your thoughts or let them rule how you live your life. I recognize unpacking your thoughts can be challenging, especially if they result from childhood wounds or trauma. As such, you may require support from a counselor to explore these issues more extensively.

As Above, So Below; As Within, So Without

The ancient Greeks deemed the Greek God Hermes and the Egyptian God Toth as Gods of Wisdom, and combined them into Trismegistus or Thrice-Greatest. Hermes Trismegistus gave rise to several teachings, and sacred religious and philosophical texts known as the *Corpus Hermeticum*. Hermeticism is a Gnostic tradition that focuses its pursuit on the knowledge of spiritual mysteries. One of the sacred texts of Hermes Trismegistus refers to the seven hermetic principles. These principles, or laws, help people understand how the Universe works and how we can master the three planes of existence—mental, physical, and spiritual. In 1908, the Three Initiates compiled the teachings into *The Kybalion*.

According to *The Kybalion*, the second principle is the Principle of Correspondence. It declares the law, "As above, so below; as below, so above. As within, so without; as without, so within."[11] The Principle of Correspondence sees the macrocosm (greater cosmos) as a reflection of the microcosm (smaller parts) and vice versa.

Since the chapter is about your thoughts, let's see how this principle affects the mental plane. With *as above, so below*, what you experience in your mind is what you present in your body and environment. With *as within, so without*, you express and reflect what you think within yourself out into the world. Also, what takes place in the world is a reflection of your inner thoughts. Your thoughts create what you see and experience and, as such, are reflected in your life circumstances.[11,12,13] For example, if you believe you are a terrible person, then the world presents you with experiences that validate your belief about yourself.

The more conscious you become about your thoughts, negative beliefs, and cognitive distortions, and start to challenge and shift your thoughts, the quicker your world will reflect a more positive perspective. Keep this principle in mind as you begin to listen, challenge, and change your thoughts.

Listen to Your Thoughts

Start to listen to your thoughts, and notice the type of comments you say about yourself. You might be shocked by the number of negative and hurtful comments. When your brain says, for example, *I am a failure*, try to catch yourself, then counteract the negative belief with a truthful statement. Tell your brain, "Thank you for the comment, but that is not true." Then state what is truthful about the situation. Maybe, "I did the best I could," or "I may not have won the race, but I'm an accomplished runner."

To stop the subconscious programming from running amok, become aware of what you say, challenge it, then replace it with the truth. Challenge your thoughts continuously as you have years of programming to reprogram. I find it helpful to speak this out loud. When you notice a negative thought, you can say "STOP," or "ENOUGH," "That is not true, I am..."—fill in the blank.

Thoughts Attract Similar Thoughts

Become aware of when you say something negative to yourself. Your thoughts affect what you bring into your world. You energetically attract what you believe and say about yourself. You carry that resonance in your body and it becomes manifested into your life. So, when you casually say, *I'm a disappointment*, the Universe will continue to bring you more instances to prove you are a disappointment. It's like you are on a loudspeaker shouting to the world, *I'm a disappointment*. The Universe will respond with, "I hear you loud and clear. I'm bringing you more ways to be a disappointment." When you recognize you aren't your negative thoughts and beliefs, and change your dialogue, you will have a more realistic mindset about the person you are. You will see yourself truthfully and not with distortion.

Cancel Out Negative Thoughts

When you notice negative self-talk in your head, or speak it out loud, say the words *cancel, clear, delete*, or *cancel, cancel, cancel* afterward. This will negate the negative belief. Then replace it with a more accurate statement, or what you want to be true in the future. For example, if I say, "I can never find my words when I speak to people," I would immediately say *cancel, clear, delete*, and then I would replace it with, "I easily find the words I wish to speak."

I Don't Believe It

Maybe it's something you don't yet believe, but want to be true. For example, perhaps your negative belief is *I am ugly*. If you replace it with *I am beautiful*, you're not going to buy it because you don't believe it to be accurate. Your body will reject the positive thought. Your body is a radar for your thoughts and can be used to assess whether or not something resonates as truthful or supportive. Your body's antenna is why affirmations don't work. Your body rejects it, and you aren't able to take in the positive statement. Instead, use the words, "I am *learning* to recognize my beauty," or "I am *working on* seeing my beauty." Can you feel the difference in those sentences, and how your body is able to accept it and take it in? Let's try an exercise to work on this more.

Embodied Exercise

This exercise will help you feel into your body, while experiencing a negative belief, to recognize and understand how your negative beliefs influence your physical body. You will then shift the negative belief into a positive belief to see how your body responds—whether it will accept it or reject it.

- Find a quiet place to sit, and check in with yourself for a few minutes undisturbed.
- Take a negative belief you have about yourself. It can be your most troubling one, or something not as burdensome.
- Close your eyes. Get comfortable. Take a couple of deep breaths and center yourself.
- Say the negative belief out loud.

- Scan your body from the top of your head to the tips of your toes. Notice how those negative words sit in your body. Maybe you feel sick to your stomach, or there is tension or tightness in your body. What type of sensation is it? Is it jabbing, stabbing, aching, tense, throbbing, or numb? (Check out Chapter 7 for more descriptive sensation words.)
- Change the negative belief into a positive belief, and say it out loud.
- Notice any new sensations, or maybe you feel the same uncomfortable feelings in your body. Notice if you can take this positive belief into your body or not.
- If yes, fantastic. What type of sensations are you experiencing now? Do you feel calm, alive, excited? How strong is this feeling? Is it a whisper, or does your body believe it and want to shout it from the rooftops?
- If not, is there an energetic wall it can't get through? Does it bounce off? Does it fade away? Does it feel so far away you can't even imagine it as truth? Feel into those sensations as uncomfortable as they are.
- If you were unable to take in the new positive belief, change the statement to include either, *I am learning to...* or *I am working on...* and say it out loud.
- Notice if re-framing the statement helps your body accept it.

Journal any insights, and write down the positive statement that goes with your negative belief. When the negative belief rears its ugly head, state *cancel, clear, delete,* and say the positive statement that your body accepts. Before you know it, you will be living it, and the Universe will bring you more instances that support your positive belief.

Change Your Mindset

Once you become aware of your negative beliefs, thoughts, and cognitive distortions, you can start to change your mindset. To cancel out the negative, look for accurate and factual information by gathering truthful information about yourself. The truth is you are not those negative beliefs or thoughts. You are so much more. Recognize and acknowledge all parts of yourself: the things you have accomplished; your values and beliefs about the type of human being you are; how you interact in your relationships.

> **Embodied Exercise**
>
> Grab your journal and pen, and write down as many things you can think of under the following categories:
>
> - List the positive qualities that describe the type of person you are. For example, kind, caring, efficient, or hard-working. To make it easier, check out my article, *What Kind of a Person Are You?*[14] There you will find a list of over 600 personality characteristics.
> - Write out a list of your accomplishments and successes. For example, graduating from grade 12 or university, participating in a piano recital, or volunteering in your community. It can be anything you deem as an accomplishment. Don't shortchange yourself. Write out everything, especially the things your brain says aren't that big of a deal.
> - Write out a list of your values. You can use the same list from my article. Choose a list of the top ten qualities you value about yourself, and what you expect from others. Start showing up as the person you want to be in the world.

Sometimes it's difficult to see these qualities in yourself. I encourage you to ask your friends. Tell them you are experimenting, and you want to know how others see you so as to compare that to how you see yourself. What makes you a good friend? What qualities do they admire about you? What do they see as your accomplishments? Ask friends who love you for who you are unconditionally, and who support and want the best for you. As discussed in Chapter 2, you may not have healthy relationships where you feel supported and uplifted. Your relationships may be abusive or manipulative. If that is the case, do not ask those people to give you feedback about your character. It could be harmful and, likely, not truthful.

—⟋⟍⟍—

When I created my website, I tried to find words to describe the type of person I am. I wanted to bring that through in my text so prospective clients would know what they would get when they worked with me. I asked my friends, and they were kind and helpful. It gave me new insight into how others viewed me.

—⟋⟍⟍—

It is easy to get caught up in your negative beliefs, or not to see yourself truthfully. When you do this exercise, you will start to recognize and acknowledge the significant impact on, and contribution to, those around you.

For some, this may be a difficult assignment because you believe you are being narcissistic or bragging. Parents sometimes teach children it's not okay to brag or be boastful, as it makes one appear conceited. There is a big difference between someone who simply and proudly acknowledges their accomplishments and contributions and someone who is full of themselves. This exercise is about recognizing and acknowledging your worth and achievements, so you can take stock and have a clear, truthful picture of who you are.

These are the facts and truth about you. It's helpful to write them out, so when you feel down due to negative self-talk, or when you experience hurtful comments from others, you can go to your list and read your truth.

I believe the world would be a better place if we told people how much we appreciate them, the beautiful qualities they possess, and why we are grateful they are in our life. We tend to only focus on the negative things people do, instead of telling them how great they are. This tendency applies to ourselves as well.

You can also look at previous work reviews. What were the positive comments about your skills? If you haven't had a review in a while, ask your boss for some feedback. Remind yourself that you will also receive constructive feedback about your work, and areas where you may need improvement. Do not equate, "I notice it takes you longer to complete work assignments, and I would like you to increase your productivity," as *I am incompetent*. Don't take feedback personally. It is about your work, not who you are as a person.

If, however, your boss attacks your character, and says something about you personally, for example, "You are a terrible person," you need to assess the situation truthfully. Is this an accurate reflection of the type of person I am? What kind of a person is my boss? Does he personally attack other people? This question is a great way to help your brain recognize it isn't about you. If you can put other colleagues in your place, and your boss says similar things to them, you know this is his issue. You will have relationships with people who have not healed their wounds and trauma. As such, they become triggered by personal and professional stress, and may lack healthy interpersonal skills.

When you get emotional about something someone has said to you, it's because you have a resonance to that comment. When you get emotional about a comment, it is the subconscious programming coming to the forefront. For example, I tell my friend, "I slipped and fell on my ass today at the grocery store in front of everyone," and she responds, "You are so clumsy." If this is a negative belief I have about myself, I would get upset, defensive, and wonder how my friend could say such a mean thing. It opened up my subconscious filing cabinet to all the other situations that prove I am clumsy. However, if I tell my friend the same story, and she responds the same, but I agree and we burst out laughing, this comment isn't a trigger. There is no negative belief attached to her comment.

Let's look again at the negative belief *I am stupid* to see how to change your mindset. What proof do you have that you are smart? Did you pass grade 12, get a higher education, get a job, or get several jobs? The likelihood is you're not stupid.

There is more than one way to measure intelligence, and there are different types of intelligence. You can have book smarts, emotional intelligence, and street smarts. Some people are great at mental intelligence, but have difficulty understanding social norms, understanding their emotions, and connecting with people. For others, if you put them out in the streets, they might place themselves in harm's way because they don't see signs of imminent danger. All of these intelligence types are valid, and you may excel in one or more. It doesn't matter. What matters is you know your genuine intelligence, and that there are many ways to measure how smart you are.

Embodied Exercise

Grab your journal and pen. Write down all the things you know to be true about your intelligence in the following three areas:

1. **Mental Intelligence**—Tests and grades aren't the only way to measure mental intelligence. Have you completed training for your job? Do you understand how to do your job? Are you able to complete assigned tasks? Do you have specialized skills?

2. **Emotional Intelligence**—is the emotional understanding of yourself and others. Can you read people's body language and sense how they feel? Can you see through people to their true character? Can you feel and name your emotions and those of others? Are you able to connect and interact with people? If this is an area you struggle in, stay tuned, I will discuss this in Chapter 4.

3. **Street or Survival Intelligence**—is about how you interact with the world around you. When placed into a new environment, are you able to tune into the people, places, sites, and get a sense of what is going on? Are you aware of your surroundings and able to determine if it's safe? Are you able to find your way around and get to where you need to go?

This exercise will help you recognize your intelligence in these three areas. Sometimes, due to stress, life circumstances, lack of sleep, or ill health, your abilities suffer. Take inventory of your life, and what may be hindering your ability to be at your best.

Words Have Power

Words have power. They can shape how you view yourself and what you believe to be true. When you stay stuck in negative thoughts, beliefs, and cognitions, you not only diminish your value, but you affect the well-being of your body.

Dr. Masaru Emoto, the author of *The Hidden Messages in Water*, studied the effects thoughts and words had on water molecules. He froze the water, and using high-speed photography, discovered the crystals created different patterns. Water from clear springs and regular water exposed to loving words formed crystals that were "brilliant, complex, and [had] colorful snowflake patterns."[15] Polluted water and regular water exposed to negative thoughts formed "incomplete, asymmetrical patterns with dull colors."[15]

Seventy percent of the average human body is water. As such, your negative beliefs, thoughts, and words alter and affect your body's cells negatively and create dis-ease. These experiments are proof your negative thoughts can affect your physical health. Dr. Emoto states, "The vibration of good words has a positive effect on our world, whereas the vibration from negative words has the power to destroy."[15]

Take the time to pay close attention to the words you use to describe yourself and others. Start to change those negative thoughts into positive and realistic truths. Do you want to be someone who uplifts themselves and others, or do you want to be someone who harms and destroys? I hope you choose to use words that can heal and transform yourself mentally, emotionally, physically, and spiritually.

Gratitude

We can get stuck in our negative beliefs. What we feel and believe is what we put out to the world. If you change your negative thoughts, perceptions, and beliefs, you acknowledge what is truthful. You then begin to be grateful, and see the positive things in your life.

Get a journal specifically as your gratitude journal. Keep it by your bed and, every night, write three to five things you are grateful for that day. It can be anything—friends, family, health, job, finances, sunny day, found a penny, or someone smiled at you. Then express gratitude for three to five things that facilitated the fulfillment of your future desires. For example, if you don't have healthy friendships, you could state, "I am grateful for the new loving and respectful friendships in my life." As you sleep, you program your subconscious mind to problem solve and find creative ways to create the outcomes you desire. The more you utilize your gratitude journal, the more you will notice instances to be grateful for, and the Universe will bring you more positive experiences. When you are struggling, go back and read what you wrote to remind yourself of the blessings in your life.

If you have a family or partner, and would like them to be involved, create a gratitude jar. Decorate it together. Place it somewhere where everyone can see it. Have multi-colored pieces of paper and pens so each person has their own color. Pick a time at the end of the day for everyone to write down and say out loud what they are grateful for that day. If someone is feeling down, they can pull one or several of their colored pieces of paper to remember that experience. It will help change their perspective, and to see how good life is. At the end of the year, create a ceremony of pulling out all the pieces of paper and reading them aloud to each other. There is nothing better than starting the New Year with a reminder of all the beautiful experiences of the previous year. Where you place your attention, is what you create in your world.

The brain doesn't know the difference between a current experience, a memory of a previous experience, or a visualization.

You feel all the same sensations and emotions assigned to that experience, or the sensations and emotions you would feel if that visualization came true. The brain is powerful. That is why so many athletes visualize winning a race, or going through their routine over and over again. It is a precursor to making it a reality.

Benefits of Changing Your Thoughts

- Change perceptions of yourself from falsehoods to the truth.
- Increase self-esteem and self-confidence.
- See the world and the people in it realistically and factually.
- Gain a clear understanding of your identity, and who you want to be in the world.
- Accept the truths others see in you.
- Think more clearly and rationally.
- Ability to make sound decisions.
- Maintain emotional regulation.
- Have a more positive outlook.
- Diminish unhealthy behaviors.
- Engage in authentic behaviors.
- Ability to stay out of your head and connect into your body.
- Increase vitality.
- Increase psychological and physical well-being.
- Improve the immune system.
- Decrease stress.
- Ability to cope during stressful situations and hardships.
- Greater acceptance of self, others, and your experience.
- Greater life satisfaction.
- Increase life span.

- Decrease depression and anxiety.

———〜〜〜———

I hope you gained some new insights into your limiting or negative beliefs, cognitive distortions, and negative thoughts so you can challenge them and shift your mindset. The more you do so, the easier it will be to quiet your inner chatter and get out of your head to connect with your body in a more fulfilling and meaningful way.

Yes! I want you to challenge your thoughts.
Yes! I want you to challenge your limiting beliefs.
Yes! I want you to challenge your cognitive distortions.
But, ultimately, I want you to **Get • Out • of • Your • Head**.

I want you to connect with your body, because your body doesn't lie.

———〜〜〜———

Join me in the next and final chapter in the Disconnection section. In the Emotions chapter, I discuss how to name your emotions and feel them in your body as you work toward becoming more connected with your body.

4

EMOTIONS—
FEEL THEM AND LET THEM GO

"Your emotions make you human. Even the unpleasant ones have a purpose. Don't lock them away. If you ignore them, they just get louder and angrier."

Sabaa Tahir

To me, there is nothing better than a summer vacation. I loved riding in the back seat of the car as a child, and getting the semi-trucks to honk their horns. I would keep a look out for any animals—bears, big mountain sheep, and moose. I would be in awe of the size of the mountains, and dense forest of fir trees. To this day, there is nothing like driving to the mountains and going for hikes. It brings me instant calm and joy. Even though I was born landlocked, I am a water baby. The best part of my summer vacation was swimming in the pool or lake for hours at a time. I was happier than a pig in mud on my summer vacations.

The summer I was 12 years old, we went to Penticton, British Columbia. There were several kids at the motel we were staying at. I met a girl, and we started hanging out. And, of course, there was a boy I found interesting hanging around. I told the girl I liked him, and thought he was cute. It isn't a good summer vacation without a sweet innocent summer crush. He asked us to go to the arcade, but I wasn't allowed. So, off the two of them went. Later that day, as I went up the stairs to my room, I saw them together at the edge of the railing, kissing. I froze in shock. I'm sure it was mere seconds, but I eventually slithered away back down the steps. I was devastated, feeling betrayed by my *new friend*.

Fast forward to high school, and the pattern repeated. My best friend and I were in the locker room at school, and I was changing out of my gym clothes. I told her I liked a boy we both knew. The next thing I knew, she's flirting with him, and they started going out. I felt betrayed by her, and our friendship—she'd known how I felt, and intentionally went after him. Yet, did I have a right to feel betrayed?

The first experience created a subconscious limiting belief that *people betray me*. That reinforced the second experience. This memory subconsciously triggered me, and I had no idea it was running behind the scenes. My subconscious thought became, "Vicky, people betray you. Why did you tell her you liked him?" However, in both situations, I wasn't in a relationship with the guy. I hadn't told them I liked them, nor had they told me they liked me. We weren't boyfriend and girlfriend. I remember my friend from the second example telling me that she liked the boy too. He was a popular guy, sweet, kind, and good looking. I'm sure half the school wanted to go out with him.

I felt hurt and sad in both situations. I was hurt because I disclosed a confidence to someone, who appeared to then use that information against me for their benefit. It felt like a betrayal, but it was not. To betray someone is to break their trust or confidence. As far as I know, neither girl told the respective guy I liked him. I was sad that I hadn't been the one he'd chosen. I focused on the betrayal, and didn't let myself feel the hurt and sadness.

Emotions

First, let's define the difference between feelings and emotions. When you feel something, it is your physical experience—how you feel sensations in your body. For example, an upset stomach when you are nervous. Emotions, on the other hand, are psychological states or moods influenced by thoughts, feelings, behaviors, and experiences. For example, frustrated or annoyed.

Growing up, I didn't have the tools to feel my emotions and understand them. I've said it time and time again—why aren't we teaching children about emotions in school? Here is what *everyone* needs to learn about emotions:

- What emotions are.
- Which emotions are theirs and which belong to others.
- How to name each emotion.
- How each emotion feels.
- Which sensations are present when they feel their emotions.
- How to cope with each emotion.

We are doing a disservice to children, and all of humanity, by not giving them the tools to name, feel, understand, and connect with their emotions. We discount and disconnect children from their birthright of emotional intelligence.

Some may wonder, "What is the point of emotions? Emotions make life complicated and confusing." Some emotions are uncomfortable to experience, but you can't live without them. God gave us emotions for a reason. Emotions help motivate your behavior and prepare you for action. They provide you with information about a situation you want to change or make better. They help you overcome obstacles. They tell you when something isn't okay or safe. They allow you to communicate effectively with others, and also to influence others. They help you to connect with people.

Emotions communicate what is going on in a situation. They can be a signal or alarm. You experience emotions viscerally. You get a *gut feeling* about something, and your body imparts information for you to pay attention to. The urge to act on specific emotions, along with facial expressions, body language, and tone of voice, are hard-wired into our biology.[1] This means you don't have complete control. Emotions are hard-wired to support your survival instinct. If a saber-toothed tiger was charging at you, and you didn't feel fear, guess what? He'd eat you.

There are two types of emotions: primary and secondary. A primary emotion is how you feel in response to your interpretation of an event. The situation could be an external event. For example, you lose your job, and your primary response might be shock. It could also be an internal event, such as an automatic thought, image, or memory, that triggers a primary emotional response. Your secondary emotions are your feelings in response to the automatic thoughts triggered by the primary emotional response. Let's go back to the earlier example. You lose your job and you feel shocked. If you received messages growing up that you are nothing if you are not contributing to society, then your limiting or negative belief may be, *I'm a failure.* This belief triggers other emotions, such as devastation, shame, or worry. These are your secondary feelings, or how you feel about your feelings.[2]

Can you imagine a world where people had no emotions? People would behave stoically, speaking only about facts and not feelings. We already have computers and robots, thinking machines devoid of life. Emotions give meaning to your life.

Theories of Emotion

Three components make up emotion:

1. Physiological arousal.
2. Expressive behaviors.
3. Conscious experience.[3]

There are three main theories on emotions. According to the James-Lange Theory of Emotion, emotion occurs due to physiological reactions to an event. You experience an external stimulus, which results in a physiological response, and as you interpret those reactions, you feel a corresponding emotion.[1] For example, let's say you are watching a scary movie. You notice your heart is beating out of your chest, and maybe you are even shaking. You then interpret those physical reactions in relation to your context, and conclude you are frightened. When you, in fact, are shaking because you are cold. For example, "I am shaking; therefore, I must be afraid." In other words, you are not shaking because you are frightened; you are frightened because you are shaking.

In the Cannon-Bard Theory of Emotion, you feel emotions and experience physiological symptoms simultaneously. One does not cause the other. When there is an event or stimulus, the thalamus sends signals to the amygdala, where emotions are processed. It also sends signals to the ANS, which results in a physiological reaction, such as upset stomach, sweating, shaking, or muscle tension.[4] For example, it's your wedding day, and you feel happy, nervous, excited, and you may be sweating, and have an increased heartbeat.

The Schachter-Singer Theory of Emotion suggests we first experience physiological arousal, and then we cognitively interpret and label the experience resulting in an emotion. They propose people infer emotions based on physiological arousal.[5]

For example, let's say you were out in the garden working all day. You are sweating, hot, thirsty, tired, and your heart is racing. Then your son comes home and tells you he dented the car. Your immediate response is anger. These theorists believe you are more likely to get angry because of your aroused state than if you were calm.

Remember, these are theories. Like thoughts, your emotions are not facts; they reflect your perception and experience of a situation. Just because you feel a certain way doesn't mean it's the truth. You are usually not responding emotionally to a situation that's occurring. Instead, you react to your interpretation of that event, as discussed in Chapter 2 on River of Life. An event occurs, your mind interprets the situation through thoughts, and responds to the interpretation by expressing emotions.

With the James-Lange theory, even though a person's body may experience physical sensations, it doesn't automatically mean they relate to a corresponding set of emotions. For example, people with anxiety receive constant messages from their body telling them something is not okay, but they need to look at what is happening. What are the facts? Are they in danger? Is something unsafe? Often, there is no threat, but the body responds as if there is. Hence, by connecting with your body and emotions, and engaging your logical thinking to assess a situation factually, you learn what is truly happening for you at the moment. You can decide what you need to do to support your body and emotional well-being.

Emotions are complicated, as is the body's response to emotions. Knowing as much as you can about how your body reacts, and how you experience emotions, will provide you with much-needed knowledge about yourself and how you engage in the world. No two people are alike, so even though you know about your emotions and body language, it doesn't mean you know what someone else is feeling. The only way you can know for sure is if you ask them directly. Have you ever had someone say you look angry, or *are* angry when you aren't? They keep insisting you are angry when you're not, so by the time this silly conversation is over, you've become angry. No one can read your mind, and you can't read someone else's mind about how they feel.

Your Emotions Come From You

Your emotions are yours alone. Emotions arise energetically from your internal state. They come from you, and it is your responsibility to acknowledge them, accept them, and find ways to deal with them if they are overwhelming. As a psychologist, I often hear clients blame their emotions on others. For example, "She did that on purpose to make me angry," or sad, or fill in the blank. No one, and I mean no one, can make you feel anything. They don't have that kind of power.

Sensorium

It sounds like a made-up word, but, I promise, I didn't make it up. In the medical dictionary, sensorium is defined as the entire sensory apparatus of the body. It is deemed the *seat of sensation*, where the brain receives, processes, and interprets sensory stimuli from the external world.[6] If it didn't exist, you wouldn't be able to feel emotions and sensations from your experiences. Life would be gray and meaningless without it. Sadly, people have become cut-off from their emotions. They don't know how to sense and feel their emotions, have become disconnected, and shut down their sensorium.

We *choose* to check out of our emotions and our life. We are easily distracted, hijacked, and can get sucked down the rabbit hole for hours by fear-based news, the Internet, social media, advertisements that purport we will be happier or healthier with particular products, video games, and Netflix binges. In his book *Spirit Hacking*, Shaman Durek calls this onslaught *aggravated stimulation*. He states:

[aggravated stimulation] disconnects people from their sensorium by flooding their systems with information that is wholly unnecessary for them to adapt and to thrive. The only thing aggravated stimulation serves is the darkness. Aggravated stimulation overwhelms us and creates disturbance frequencies in the body, mind, and spirit that further separate us from our intuitive capabilities and make it that much harder for people to feel imbalances that are threatening the well-being of this planet at this time.[7]

If you are easily hacked, and have become disconnected from your sensorium, or are now finding out for the first time that it exists, don't worry. The tools and techniques in this chapter, and the second part of this book, will help you reconnect with your sensorium and your body. Your sensorium will become a finely tuned instrument readily available at a moment's notice.

As Above, So Below; As Within, So Without

In Chapter 3, I discussed *The Kybalion*, more specifically, the second principle known as The Principle of Correspondence. "As above, so below; as below, so above. As within, so without; as without, so within."[8] As with thoughts, you reflect your emotions out into the world.

Let's look at how this affects the physical plane. With *as above, so below*, the thoughts and emotions you experience in your mind become sensations and energies in your body and environment. With *as within, so without*, you express and reflect what you feel out into the world energetically. What you sense inside of you is what you create and experience outside of you. You are interconnected energetically with everything in the Universe. What you feel is reflected out into the Universe and back to you.

Every cell in your body is comprised of energy and all emotions are energy. Emotions are impermanent. They take form, move through you, and change from one emotion to the next. Your emotions have a vibrational frequency and, when manifested, affect every cell in your body. Anger, resentment, and sadness are examples of low-frequency emotions. Love, joy, and happiness are high-frequency emotions. For example, if you are angry and stomp around the house, you energetically emit your body's anger into your environment, but it doesn't end there. You now affect other people's energetic frequency, which can create anger in them where there wasn't any. Remember, this is new awareness and understanding; this isn't about judging yourself and your emotions as good or bad. It is recognizing how you, and the world around you, are energetically affected. As you become more conscious of your emotions, and engage with more high-frequency emotions, you create a positive, energetic ripple effect internally throughout your body, and externally out into the world.

Different Types of Emotions

There are several different theories about how many primary emotions we possess. Emotions reflect culturally-universal facial expressions. Some say there are four, others say six or seven, and others say eight. It doesn't matter who is right. What matters is that you get an understanding of some of the basic emotions so you can:

- Name the primary emotion you are experiencing.
- Choose the best word that describes your emotion.
- Know the physical sensations you experience with the emotion.

Naming Emotions

It is essential to put a name to your emotion. You may recognize you are sad, but I want you to go even deeper. What kind of sadness is it? Hurt sad? Lonely sad? Maybe sad isn't quite the right word. Perhaps it's heartbreak, disappointment, or misery.

The more explicit you get with your emotions, the more in tune you will be with yourself and your body. Below are ten of the most common emotions we feel and their respective synonyms:

Anger: aggravation, agitation, annoyance, bitterness, devastation, dislike, displeasure, exasperation, ferocity, frustration, fury, grouchiness, grumpiness, hate, hostility, indignation, irritation, loathing, outrage, rage, resentment, scorn, spite, vengefulness, wrath.

Disgust: abhorrence, antipathy, aversion, condescension, contempt, dislike, derision, disappointment, disdain, distaste, displeasure, hate, loathing, horror, judgment, repugnance, repulsion, resentment, scorn, spite.

Envy: bitterness, craving, discontent, desire, displeasure, dissatisfaction, greed, jealousy, longing, malice, pettiness, prejudice, rivalry, resentment, spite.

Fear: agitation, alarm, angst, anxiety, apprehension, aversion, cowardice, despair, dismay, distress, distrust, dread, foreboding, fright, horror, hysteria, insecurity, nervousness, panic, shock, suspicion, terror, timidity, trepidation, uneasiness, worry.

Guilt: blame, culpability, dereliction, dishonor, disgrace, failure, fault, indiscretion, lapse, offense, regret, remorse, reprehension, responsibility, shame, sin, transgression, wickedness.

Happiness: amusement, bliss, cheerfulness, contentment, delight, eagerness, ecstasy, elation, enjoyment, enthusiasm, euphoria, excitement, exhilaration, glee, hope, joy, jubilation, merriment, optimism, pleasure, rapture, relief, satisfaction, thrill, zeal, zest.

Jealousy: carefulness, caution, cling, defense, desire, distrust, envy, grudge, heed, insecurity, mindfulness, mistrust, possession, protection, resentment, rivalry, solicitude, spite, suspicion, vigilance, wariness.

Love: admiration, adoration, adulation, affection, altruism, arousal, attachment, attraction, benevolence, care, compassion, desire, devotion, endearment, fondness, friendliness, goodwill, idolatry, infatuation, intimacy, kindness, liking, longing, lust, passion, rapture, regard, romance, sentimentality, sympathy, tenderness, warmth, worship.

Sadness: agony, alienation, anguish, blah, defeat, dejection, depression, despair, disappointment, discontent, dismay, displeasure, dissatisfaction, distress, gloom, grief, homesickness, hopelessness, hurt, insecurity, loneliness, melancholy, misery, neglect, pity, rejection, sorrow, suffering, sullen, unhappiness woe.

Shame: agony, chagrin, confusion, contempt, contrition, culpability, discomfort, discomposure, dishonor, disgrace, disgust, embarrassment, guilt, humiliation, insecurity, mortification, pain, regret, remorse, self-consciousness, shyness, sorrow, stupid, worthlessness.

Embodied Exercise

In this exercise, take time in your day to name your emotions.

- Choose how often you want to do this: once, twice, or three times per day.

- Set a unique ringtone on your phone so that when you hear it, you automatically check in to see which emotion(s) you are experiencing.
- If you are experiencing one or more of the ten primary emotions listed above, name it or them. For example, say to yourself out loud, "I feel happy."
- Use the list above, or search synonyms for emotions on your phone or computer, to see if there is an even better word than happy to describe how you feel. For example, pleased.
- If it's not one of the ten primary emotions, then name whichever emotion you feel. For example, bored or calm.

That's it. Right now, you don't have to do anything with your emotion. You are to name your emotion so you can acknowledge your experience in the moment. In 10–30 seconds, you become more deeply connected with yourself and your experience.

Happiness

Let's talk about happiness. When I ask clients what their goal is for therapy, and what would be different on the other side, invariably, their response is, "I want to be happy." The emotion of happiness, as with all emotions, is fleeting. Most emotions linger for about 90 seconds unless we stay focused on the story or the experience that created the emotion. Our emotions come and go throughout the day depending on the physiological arousal and expressive behavior arising from a conscious experience or thought.

Seeking happiness has become externally focused. We seek happiness through things. The Internet, social media, advertisements, influencers, and celebrities, are all selling happiness through artifice. We unconsciously seek out the next trending thing that will make us feel happy. "If I buy what Julia Roberts wears, I'll have a big smile on my face and laugh too." Happiness doesn't come from stuff. Happiness comes from within, from recognizing, speaking, and living your truth. Happiness comes from being your authentic self every day. (See more on this in Chapter 10.) If you don't listen, and aren't true to what is best for you, and, instead, let others tell you what you should feel, do, and be, you will struggle with feeling true happiness. When you work through your trauma and wounds, set healthy boundaries, shift negative mindsets, and use the tools in the Reconnection chapters, happiness comes naturally.

Emotional Dysregulation

Emotional dysregulation refers to a person's inability to regulate and control their emotions when triggered by an external stimulus. People aren't taught how to relate to their emotions, or how to manage them. As such, emotions feel overwhelming, and people are unable to get a handle on them. Emotions can come at times when they are not wanted. When emotions come quickly and intensely, there is a tendency for increased emotional reactivity. One second you're a bit frustrated, and the next second you are raging at everyone and everything.

The purpose of emotional regulation is to reduce suffering. This is not done by getting rid of emotions, but by feeling them, dealing with what triggers them, and supporting your body to reduce their intensity.

Being connected to your emotions, naming them, and understanding why they are there, will allow you to process them and release them more quickly. It will help reduce your suffering, make you feel less vulnerable when you experience intense emotions, and help you manage them better. When you can recognize and accept that you are emotionally vulnerable, you honor your experience and give yourself permission for better self-care. When you name and feel your emotions, you will automatically reconnect with your body, and become embodied. You will experience emotional regulation, allowing you to cope with life's challenges and bring your body back into balance.

Unwanted emotions are not only about feelings of anger, fear, or anxiety. They can also be positive emotions. One of the modalities I use in my practice is known as spiritually-directed therapy. This technique from my Embodied Awareness training allows the client to become mindful and turn inward to explore a thought or belief. During spiritually-directed therapy, after the client re-processes a wound or trauma by visualizing what they needed to happen, the client explores a source of support. This source can take the shape of anything: God, a field of grass, the ocean, space, a gemstone, a geometric shape, a stuffed bear. During a spiritually-directed therapy session, one of my clients visualized themselves at a waterfall; they felt such intense love that it overwhelmed them, and they had to come out of the visualization. You are not abnormal if intense emotions of love, pleasure, or happiness are too difficult to feel. You are not alone. You may have deeply ingrained limiting beliefs that make it difficult to feel positive emotions or you may be a highly sensitive individual. (I discuss highly sensitive people throughout the book in the Boundaries, Grounding, Senses, and Energy chapters.)

Anger

When people think about emotional dysregulation or overwhelm, the emotion that comes up most is anger. Maybe as a result of unhealthy boundaries, emotional repression, or difficulty expressing emotions, anger builds up, and can explode as rage at the most inappropriate of times. Anger can be a primary emotion or a secondary emotion. There are times when it is appropriate to feel angry. When anger is a primary emotion, it means the situation warrants the emotion of anger—righteous anger. Here are some relevant times to feel angry:

- Something didn't turn out as you expected it to.
- Someone crossed your boundary.
- You or someone you care about was threatened or attacked.
- Someone hurt you.
- Someone you loved died.
- Someone or something blocked an important goal.
- You are in physical or emotional pain.
- Loss of respect, status, or power.[9]

Anger is also a secondary emotion. When anger is a secondary emotion, you feel another primary emotion before the anger. Think about it like an iceberg. The top of the iceberg that sits on the surface of the water is anger. You can see it clearly, but underneath the surface is a deeper colossal iceberg where your primary emotion lies.

Anger Iceberg

Anger on the surface can be misleading.

Angry

There may be other emotions below the surface. Go deeper!

Hurt Regret **Trapped** Shame **Depressed**
Disappointed Rejected Embarrassed
Threatened **Annoyed** Stressed
Overwhelmed Anxious **Guilt**
Unsure **Insecure** Frustrated
Uncomfortable Helpless
Scared **Distrustful**
Shocked Envious
Sad **Attacked**
Fearful Tricked
Lonely
Jealous

Let me give you an example. I was standing in line at a fast-food place waiting to order, and there was a man who was visibly angry at his child. She was crying uncontrollably, and he kept telling her to stop crying loudly over and over again. His angered response heightened her dysregulation because she felt unsafe. The man was unable to console the child because her behavior had triggered an underlying emotion in him—embarrassment, panic, or a slew of other emotions.

Have you ever heard of the expression, *he flipped his lid?* When you are angry, or emotionally overwhelmed, as the child in the example above, you are not in your prefrontal cortex or rational brain. Your body reacts to the perceived danger and produces a fear response in your amygdala, which initiates your fight-flight-freeze response. Your body generates physiological reactions to let you know something is not okay. When this occurs, you need to soothe the emotional overwhelm first to bring down the physiological response screaming in your head, *danger, danger.* What the child needed was to feel safe to express her emotions. The parent needed to be present with his child to let her know it was okay to feel "X" emotion. Let a child experience their emotions, and only when they seek out support, help soothe and comfort them so they can learn to regulate difficult emotions.

Can you relate to this story? Perhaps it was not okay for you to express big emotions growing up. Your parents or caregivers couldn't handle them, or didn't know what to do with them. If this was your experience, you likely learned to turn off your emotions because it was unsafe to express them. You get to express your emotions, especially if you weren't allowed to do so growing up. Give yourself permission to feel all of your emotions, especially the more challenging ones. If you feel angry, or emotionally overwhelmed, feel the emotion, and then soothe yourself as you would a child. Even better, connect with your inner child and comfort her. What did your child-self not get that she needed in the past? What does she need now? If she needed to be talked to gently or hugged, visualize yourself embracing your child self and speaking the words she needed to hear. Then, do the same for your adult self. What do you need in order to soothe yourself and feel okay?

When you're angry, figure out your primary emotion. If anger is your primary emotion, then let yourself feel angry. You might scream or yell at the top of your lungs, punch a pillow, or journal your anger. Do not direct your anger onto someone else. Feel the anger, release the energy of it from your body, and let it go. If anger is a secondary emotion, do some self-reflection, or journal to reveal the primary emotion or emotions. You then validate your true emotions, but you also get insight into what you were really angry about. By taking the time to figure out and feel into your primary emotion, you will:

- Calm your anger as you start to feel into your body.
- Feel into your primary emotion, and where it sits in your body.
- Acknowledge the primary emotion, accept it, and let it go.
- Learn to course-correct your behavior when angry.

Embodied Exercise

This exercise will help you look beneath your anger to find out what your primary emotion is.

- Take some time to sit with yourself where it's quiet and you won't be disturbed.
- Have a journal, or a piece of paper, and pen handy to write what comes up.

- Let yourself get comfortable. Take four or five slow deep breaths. Feel the air come in through your nose and down into your belly. As you exhale, let go of any tension.

- Bring up the anger you feel toward the person or situation.

- As you feel into the anger, notice where the anger sits in your body.

- Mentally scan from the top of your head down to your toes, and notice any sensations where the anger resides.

- Explore this further. How big is the sensation? Is it on the surface of your body, outside your body, or inside your body? Does it have a specific shape? Does it have a particular color? Does it have a temperature? What type of sensation is it? Is it sharp, painful, stabbing, or throbbing? (See Chapter 7 for a list of sensations.)

- As you explore further, notice if it shifts or changes. You may get memories or images. If you do, take a mental note, and put that memory or image to the side.

- Ask the anger what it wants from you and how it is supporting you. Ask the anger what it needs to be resolved, or for you to let it go.

- Trust whatever your intuition or Higher Self says.

- Then see if you can go beneath the anger. Ask, "What is below my anger?"

- Reflect on any new emotions or sensations and explore those as above. Then ask again, "What is below this new emotion?" Keep going deeper until no other emotion is revealed.

- Like an onion, there will be many layers of emotions.
- Explore as many as you like. You may reveal a limiting or negative belief about yourself in relationship to the situation.
- Then, thank the anger for supporting you and providing information for you.
- You may tell yourself you don't need to be angry anymore, and that you will take care of your underlying emotions.
- Then notice how your emotions and body sensations have shifted.
- Allow yourself to gently come back to the room feeling calm and relaxed.
- Write out any insights that arose.

Repeat as often as you like with anger, or other disturbing or uncomfortable emotions.

Repressed Versus Suppressed Emotions

Repression is also known as dissociative amnesia, and it happens when you unconsciously forget or block troubling thoughts, feelings, or experiences. Repressed emotions are a defense mechanism. When you experience something difficult, that you cannot handle in your conscious, wakeful existence, you repress memories or emotions, push them back into your unconscious mind to forget them. Not only are they in your unconscious mind, but your physical body stores them as emotional energy. Trauma and wounds can result in difficulty naming or experiencing emotions because they become locked in the unconscious mind.

When you repress a memory or emotion, it is beyond your control. The memory or emotion was so intense that, for you to be okay, your brilliant brain locked it away in your unconscious mind as a survival tactic. But that doesn't mean that memory or emotion disappeared. Unprocessed memories and emotions can come up years later when you least expect them and turn your world upside down. When repressed memories result from trauma, you re-live that trauma repeatedly, and the emotions and body sensations can be overwhelming. If you experience this, it is best to see a counselor who has experience working with trauma.

Suppressed emotions are emotions you can't deal with, or don't know how to deal with, so you consciously avoid them. You choose not to feel that emotion. If you've ever experienced an intense emotion that you couldn't handle, or felt overwhelmed by it—fear, anxiety, or panic—and you pushed it away so as not to feel it, you suppressed your emotion.

People do this as a way to regulate their emotions, but it's not effective. It becomes your go-to. "Sad? Who has time to be sad? I've got to clean the house, take care of the kids, take them to their sports games or dance recitals, volunteer, bake cookies for the school meeting, go to work, and take care of my aging parents." Life can be overwhelming, but this is the reason you need to feel your emotions.

Suppressing emotions is ineffective as it often leads to increased symptoms later on. In a famous study about thought suppression, subjects were asked not to think about a white bear. As much as they tried to suppress the thought, it rebounded, and they became more obsessed and preoccupied with the thought of a white bear.[10] This is true for emotions as well. For example, the more you try to suppress your anxiety, that's all you'll think about, and all you'll feel.

Suppressed emotions become compounded. Imagine you have a garbage can in your torso, and every time you feel an uncomfortable emotion, you stuff it down into that garbage can.

Eventually, that garbage gets full, and it starts to shake and burst through the lid. When that happens, you feel anxious, panicked, or intense uncontrollable anger emerges. Have you ever raged at someone for no good reason, with the other person standing there stunned, not knowing what's happening? That's what can happen when you ignore and suppress your emotions. They don't go away. They come back to haunt you in the most inopportune situations.

Your Shadow Self

Carl Jung popularized the term *the shadow*, and referred to it as the *dark side* of our personality. It "consists chiefly of primitive, negative human emotions and impulses like rage, envy, greed, selfishness, desire, and the striving for power."[11] Although the shadow is largely negative, you can also hide and reject the positive parts of yourself. Your *bright shadow* can include your beauty, intelligence, emotional sensitivity, kindness, gifts, talents, or abilities. Your shadow encompasses the parts of your personality that you deny and disown. Your shadow parts become repressed and unconscious, and, therefore, your shadow operates without your full awareness. You say things you wouldn't usually say, and you express emotions and behaviors you later regret.

When you deny and bury the shadow parts of yourself, you see them in other people—you project these unwanted parts onto them. Projection is when you unconsciously take your unwanted, undesirable thoughts, emotions, and traits and attribute them to other people. Your ego wants to defend how it sees itself; so, to identify as *good*, it blocks your awareness of your projections. Your inner critic and idealized self-image are both a part of your shadow side. You can't eliminate your shadow parts; you can only bring them to the light through self-awareness. Below are some common examples of shadow behaviors:

- Impulsively judge others harshly because you don't want to be exposed in this way. For example, "Candace has gained a lot of weight."

- Point out your insecurities as flaws in others. For example, "Tanya is a horrible interviewer."

- Get angry with people in lesser positions of power to compensate for your feelings of helplessness. For example, getting angry at the waitress for taking too long to bring you your food.

- Play the victim no matter the situation, so you don't have to accept responsibility or take action. For example, "I can't find a job. Can you search online for me?"

- Manipulate and step on other people to achieve your goals and desires so you can boost your ego. For example, taking credit for your subordinate's idea at work.

- Don't acknowledge your biases or prejudices so you can continue to pretend you aren't racist, sexist, or homophobic, and you don't have to do the work to understand and override these disparaging stereotypes. For example, "Arthur refuses to recognize his white privilege. He's so entitled."

- Have a messiah complex where you believe you are the only enlightened one, and here to save others, so you don't have to deal with your emotional issues, wounds, and trauma. This is also known as spiritual bypassing. For example, "If you take *my* meditation course, you will heal your self-esteem issues."[12]

There is also the collective shadow. This can include groups of people, cultures, regions, countries, or the entire world. The collective shadow consists of the combined shadow of every human being on the planet. For example, racism, privilege, disease, trauma, or war. We carry an energetic resonance of our shadow parts, and that combined energy, although invisible, manifests into our world. Imagine the amount of energy everyone emits from their shadow parts, then multiply that force by eight billion humans on the planet. The energy is hidden, buried, like pressure building under Earth's surface, until it finally explodes like a volcano—spewing forth fire, steam, smoke, and lava.

When you bring your shadow parts to the light, you can shift your negative thoughts and beliefs, accept and feel all your emotions, set and maintain healthy boundaries, diminish unwanted behaviors, and improve your relationships. When you recognize, acknowledge, accept, and face your shadow parts, you become balanced, whole, authentic, awakened, and integrated as a fully self-actualized person. Self-actualization helps you realize your full potential by developing your abilities and your appreciation for life. (I discuss self-actualization more in Chapter 10.)

Why It's Important to Understand Your Emotions

Emotions are important because they help you know what is happening for you at any given moment. It's feedback about your state of being.

All Emotions are Valuable

When a situation occurs, you receive information and can understand how this event affects you emotionally and physically. When you become self-aware, and can name, acknowledge, and feel your emotions, you gain in-depth insight into yourself. When you unconsciously repeat the same emotions and scenarios in your life, and don't stop to understand why, you miss out on the lessons they have to teach you and the opportunity to change. When you connect and understand your emotions, you grow and evolve into a more conscious human being.

You can receive valuable insight when you question your emotions. "Why am I feeling this way?" For example, you feel an emotion, so you check in and recognize you feel hurt. You may wonder why you feel hurt, and a memory pops up from yesterday of your friend telling you your clothes aren't fashionable. Maybe she is projecting her shadow self around envy or desire. Maybe she has low self-esteem and is insecure about her looks. Perhaps she equates being fashionable with being valued, so when she sees that you dress however you want, this triggers her inability to not care what others think of her and how she dresses. The fact you feel hurt means there is some resonance of truth, and your shadow side is showing up. If you didn't care that your clothes weren't fashionable, you wouldn't feel hurt. You get to feel hurt, but you also need to look at why this affected you. If someone throws a barb at you, check out what it says about them, and what you believe about yourself. Figure out where the negative belief originated and process the wound with the help of a counselor, or use the tools in the Reconnection section of this book so you're no longer triggered by a similar event.

All Emotions Matter

Emotions matter because they let you know when something is okay and when it isn't. They allow you to feel your experiences and connect with your truth. They are not meant to be ignored, rejected, or stuffed down. Emotions help you be safe, respected, move forward, strive for your goals, learn about yourself, grieve losses, and connect with others. Emotions deeply enrich your life.

All Emotions Are Valid

Give yourself permission to experience all your emotions without judgment. If unchecked, your thoughts are brilliant at hijacking your emotions. We have a tendency to judge certain emotions as bad or wrong, which then equates to us being horrible people. Emotions are never wrong, and never bad. There are three levels to validating your emotions: acknowledge, allow, and understand.

1. Acknowledge the presence of the emotion you are experiencing.
2. Allow it, or give yourself permission to feel the emotion.
3. Understand the emotion—why it is showing up? This step can be the most difficult.[2]

When you can observe and describe the emotion you feel, it will support a deeper understanding of your experience. For example, maybe your boyfriend is frequently late to pick you up, but you haven't communicated to him that this is not okay. When you don't let him know, you haven't established a healthy boundary, and you end up giving away your self-worth and self-respect. When you finally get to your breaking point, it shows up as intense anger. Both he and you may be confused about where this anger originates. You allowed something that doesn't feel okay to continue because you weren't aware of how much it bothered you. Your body may have been giving you small indications that something wasn't right, but you weren't able to recognize them, or you chose to ignore them. Emotions are like a compass. They let you know when you are on the right path, or when you are off course.

Self-Awareness

I'll speak more about self-awareness in Chapter 5, but I want to give you an understanding of what it means to be self-aware in relation to emotions. Self-awareness is the state of being aware of oneself in any given moment through your thoughts, emotions, or body sensations. It is also what is driving you. What are your motives or desires at that moment? You want to be able to check in with yourself and discern what is going on. Being self-aware may feel foreign to you, but that's okay. With practice, you will be able to connect with yourself, understand how you feel, and course-correct as necessary.

How Do You Become Self-Aware?

To become more self-aware, tune into your body. Take a moment to reflect on what is happening to you, and make a concerted effort to check in as it won't be instinctive. When you check in, physically stop what you are doing, close your eyes, and notice what you are experiencing in your thoughts, emotions, and body sensations.

Your Body's Language

You might be wondering what emotions have to do with connecting with your body. It is a part of the body's language. Language allows humans to communicate through words that are either spoken or written. Communication also occurs through body sensations, and is influenced by thoughts, emotions, experiences, and energy. (Check out Chapter 8 for more on energy.)

Have you ever seen a cartoon where the character was so angry that steam came out of their ears? Well, you may not see physical steam coming out of your ears, but you will notice other sensations—like your ears feeling hot. You may tighten your fists into balls, raise your shoulders to your ears, experience tightness throughout your whole body, or build pressure behind your eyes as you stare intently. You may notice a need to stand taller, or lean forward, when you are in an argument, to feel larger or more threatening.

You will also experience changes in your physiology. You may have an increased heart rate, and feel like your heart is beating outside your chest. You may have increased blood pressure, resulting in pressure headaches or light-headedness. Your body will release adrenaline and cortisol due to increased stress. You may feel nauseated, perspire, or your body may shake. Your body may perceive imminent danger and engage in the fight-flight-freeze response.

Body Expressions of the Ten Common Emotions

If you are disconnected from your body, it may be hard to recognize that your emotions sit in your body, and your body expresses your emotions in physical ways. Below are the ten most common emotions, and how those emotions are expressed physiologically in your body. This list of sensations will help you increase your awareness of emotions and connect your emotions to your physical body.

Anger

- Tight muscles.
- Clenched teeth.
- Clenched hands.
- Flushed face.
- Hot throughout your body.
- Feel like you are going to explode.
- Expression of tears.

Disgust

- Feel sick or nauseated.
- Gagging, choking, urge to vomit, or vomiting.
- Lump in your throat.
- Loss of appetite.
- Faint.

Envy

- Tight muscles.
- Clenched teeth or mouth.
- Flushed face.
- Hot throughout your body.
- Rigid body.
- Stomach pain.

Fear

- Breathless.
- Increased heartbeat.
- Choking, a lump in your throat.
- Tense muscles, cramping.
- Clenched teeth.
- Nauseated.
- Anxious, butterflies in your stomach.
- Cold, clammy.

Guilt

- Hot, red face.
- Jittery.
- Nervous.
- Anxious.

Happiness

- Excited.
- Energetic.
- Flushed face.
- Calm, peaceful.

- Giggling, laughing.
- Open, expansive.

Jealousy

- Breathless.
- Increased heartbeat.
- Choking, a lump in your throat.
- Tense muscles.
- Clenched teeth.

Love

- Excited, energized.
- Increased heartbeat.
- Warm.
- Relaxed, calm.
- Open, expansive.

Sadness

- Tired, run-down, low energy.
- Lethargic, listless.
- Pain, hollow, empty.
- Difficulty swallowing, a lump in your throat.
- Breathless.
- Dizzy.
- Expression of tears.

Shame

- Stomach pain.
- Cowering.

- Head turned down.
- Covering your face or body.[9]

These are some of the ways your body typically expresses these emotions. However, emotions in the body can also become stuck energy, and show up in several body parts through physically uncomfortable sensations. When you cannot feel emotions because you don't know how, or they are too intense, you repress your emotions, but they are not gone. They are stored in your body until you allow yourself to feel, name, and release them. Below is an exercise to help you explore and connect with your body's emotions.

Embodied Exercise

This exercise will help you feel emotions in your body.

- Take some time to sit with yourself where it's quiet and you won't be disturbed.
- Have a journal, or a piece of paper, and pen handy to write what comes up.
- Let yourself get comfortable.
- Take four or five slow deep breaths. Feel the air come in through your nose, and down into your belly. As you exhale, let go of any tension.
- Allow your body to tell you where stored emotions reside.
- Do a mental scan from the top of your head down to your toes, and notice any uncomfortable sensations.
- Choose a sensation and body part to explore further.
- How big is the sensation? Is it on the surface of your body or inside your body?
- Does it have a specific shape?

- Does it have a specific color?
- Does it have a temperature?
- What type of sensation is it? Is it sharp, painful, stabbing, or throbbing? (See Chapter 7 for a list of sensations.)
- Explore every detail of the emotion and the sensations.
- Let yourself feel the emotion. If it's sadness, feel sad. Cry and sit with the feeling.
- Memories or images may come up. Make a mental note, and put that memory or image on the shelf for now.
- Ask the body part what it wants from you, and how it is supporting you. Ask the body part what it needs from you.
- As you reflect on the emotion and body sensations, notice any shifts or changes.
- Is the emotion or sensation ebbing, or has it completely gone?
- Thank the emotion and body parts for supporting you and providing information.
- Feel your fingers and toes. Wiggle them and stretch.
- Take your time to slowly and gently come back to the room feeling calm and relaxed.
- Write down your experience and any insights that arose.

Atypical Communication

What's marvelous about how the body communicates is that it's not always as typical as above. You may feel anger in your leg or your toe. You may feel happiness in your eyes. This concept may sound a little *out there*, but your body expresses emotions through physical sensations anywhere in your body. Follow the energetic feeling to wherever it resides in your body and be present with it. Connecting with your body is not only informative, but enlightening.

Your body holds all of your experiences. If you were to bring up a memory, your body would re-live that memory, and you would feel sensations in your body. Suppose you brought up two memories that you would categorize as similar in their experience. When you check out how each experience feels in your body, you might be surprised to find that your body sensations are different for each memory.

For example, let's say you brought up two different memories of you celebrating your birthday. There was cake, there were presents, and all your friends and family were there. In the first memory, your heart may be radiating love and joy and there may be a smile on your lips. Yet, when you bring up the second memory, there is a sense of unease in your stomach. As you take the time to sit with that sensation, you realize that experience was when you started to feel disconnected from your boyfriend, and several months later, the relationship ended.

Every situation and experience is unique. There will be other influencing thoughts, emotions, experiences, and extenuating circumstances that affect the sensations you experience in your body in connection with the event. It is vital to recognize and validate the information your body is telling you. Don't get sidetracked by your thoughts telling you to ignore your body's experience. Once you can recognize your body's sensations, feel them, acknowledge their truth, and learn from them. It will be easier for your body to feel heard, and let those sensations recede and, ultimately, let them go.

Emotional Mastery

It's not easy to feel uncomfortable emotions, but doing so will help you let go of emotional suffering. Do you remember the times you denied your emotions instead of feeling them? Here are some reasons why you may fear experiencing uncomfortable emotions:

- If they start, they'll never stop.
- They are too intense.
- I may lose control.

Below are the necessary steps to emotional freedom:

- Observe your emotion. (More on the *observe* skill in Chapter 5.)
- Experience and feel your emotion.
- Experience and feel into your body's sensations concerning the emotion.
- Remember—you are *not* your emotion.
- Practice loving all of your emotions.[9]

Similarly, Dr. Joan Rosenberg created a formula to help you achieve emotional mastery. Stop talking about your emotions as bad or negative. Instead, state them as either unpleasant or uncomfortable. "What we feel emotionally is felt in the body first as a bodily or physical sensation."[13] The sensation is what people try to distract from, not the emotion itself. Below is her formula:

- Choose to be fully present and aware of your experience moment to moment.
- Experience and move through the eight unpleasant or uncomfortable emotions of sadness, shame, helplessness,

anger, vulnerability, embarrassment, disappointment, and frustration to gain emotional strength and confidence.

- Moving through is about riding the wave, which typically lasts 60–90 seconds.

Emotions are temporary, and you can manage your feelings and uncomfortable sensations as they arise in your body. That is, of course, as long as you don't stay stuck in the story, negative thoughts, and limiting or negative beliefs that arise from the situation. Emotions will come, whether mildly or intensely, but they will always subside.[14] Let yourself feel your emotions, and the sensations in your body to experience emotional freedom in your life.

Healthy Expression of Emotions

A healthy expression of emotions means you can:

- Recognize and acknowledge emotions.
- State emotions to yourself and others.
- Feel emotions and not suppress them.
- Recognize, acknowledge, explore, and feel emotions as physical sensations in your body.

Benefits of Emotions

There are several benefits to naming, feeling, and expressing your emotions.

- Increase meaningful emotional states.
- Increase self-awareness and self-identity.
- Ability to be your authentic self.
- Promote self-growth and self-expression.
- Connect more deeply with your body.

- Feel comfortable in your skin.
- Create appropriate behaviors.
- Ability to cope with life's challenges.
- Increase concentration skills.
- Increase cognition and decision-making skills.
- Increase the organization of emotional memories.
- Improve working memory.
- Effective communication with others.
- Motivate others to respond to your needs.
- Increase vulnerability, intimacy, and connection with others.
- Express empathy, care, and compassion for yourself and others.
- Support healthy relationships.
- Increase comfort, calmness, and centeredness.
- Increase positive outlook.
- Lower blood pressure.
- Aid digestion.
- Strengthen the immune system.[14]

I hope this chapter brought you some insight into the different types of emotions, naming your emotions, and the importance of feeling your emotions in your body to understand how you currently deal with your emotions, and how to achieve a healthy expression of emotions.

You did it! You learned several ways people disconnect from their body. Join me in the next section on Reconnection as I discuss how to reconnect with your body, and become embodied.

In the first chapter, I explore mindfulness. Learn self-awareness and bodily awareness, the skills to become mindful, and the different types of meditation to support a deeper connection to your body.

PART II
RECONNECTION

5

MINDFULNESS—
BRING YOUR ATTENTION
TO THE PRESENT MOMENT

*"Mindfulness is a way of befriending ourselves
and our experience."*
*"Mindfulness means being awake.
It means knowing what you are doing."*

Jon Kabat-Zinn

"Live the actual moment. Only this actual moment is life."

Thích Nhất Hạnh

I started my Peruvian shamanic training in February 2010 in Bragg Creek, Alberta, and had the good fortune to travel to Peru the following July. Even though I had barely immersed myself in the training, I felt called to go on what I knew would be a healing and awakening journey. This trip wasn't your typical tourist vacation. Yes, I got to see and experience some wondrous places in Peru. However, it was the rigorous daily teachings, and conscious connection with myself and the land through ritual and ceremony, that provided a meaningful and transformational experience.

It was the intention of the organizers that we focus on the feminine during this trip to Peru. Connecting with the feminine within was appealing, as I felt I had become disconnected and disengaged from my feminine nature. My wounds and trauma had hardened me, and created walls of protection around me. I spoke aggressively and bluntly with little concern for others' feelings to ensure people feared me, and so I wouldn't get hurt. I didn't do this consciously, but unconsciously. I mirrored the behaviors I'd learned within my family system, and was influenced by the negative thoughts and beliefs that led me to be ruled by my brain's distorted thinking.

I'll speak more about the power of intention later in this chapter, but for now, intention is speaking or writing out what you wish to achieve. At the beginning of the trip, I wrote the following three intentions in my journal:

1. "Find my life's purpose, or at least know which direction to go in next."
2. "Get some much-needed healing for my health, my heart, and the releasing of negative emotions."
3. "Open up the feminine spirit within me to be able to express love. Be caring, kind, and nurturing to everyone I encounter."

To say this trip was a catalyst to a total life transformation is an understatement. Within months of returning from my trip, I found a Reiki Master, who helped me restore my immune system after contracting H1N1 and bilateral pneumonia eight months prior. Reiki is an energetic spiritual practice (not religious) that allows one's body to get to a state where it can naturally heal itself. (I will discuss more on Reiki in Chapter 8.) The Reiki Master had an extrasensory gift, not common to all practitioners, that provided me with angelic guidance. This influenced me to take my Master's in Counseling Psychology, and set me on the path to becoming a psychologist. I also started and completed my Reiki training with her and became a Reiki Master. I became softer, more loving, and caring to myself and others. I released many of my wounds, and rarely think negatively about myself anymore.

In the evenings in Peru, each individual worked through their wounds by feeling into the essence of their woundedness for every year of their life. We had to re-live each wound, and witness everything we saw, heard, smelled, tasted, and felt. We were instructed to start with our conception, and do increments of seven years of our life every evening. I spoke aloud each wound that came to my mind for each year. Memories of wounds came effortlessly. Words spilled forth of the loss that occurred due to these wounds—loss of innocence, safety, security, happiness, trust, connection to my body, power, acceptance, self-esteem, and self-worth, to name a few. I felt the emotions and sensations as they arose in my body. I released the wounds by blowing into *kintus*—three perfect coca leaves stacked one on top of each other. We slept with the kintus under our pillow every night and, when we completed the exercise, we burned them in a fire ceremony.

One evening on this trip still resonates as one of the most profound spiritual experiences of my life. We were all packed into a small room. Everyone was spread out on the floor to complete their *despachos*—a prayer bundle—leaving little space for my friend and me. (I discuss despachos more in Chapter 9.) We ended up in the back corner, where there was a tiny opening against the wall. There was no room for us to sit down, so we had to complete our despacho standing up. I became so mindful and present in the moment with the act of praying into my kintus, and prostrating myself to place my prayers into my despacho, that I became transported into another reality. The room fell away. I could feel the thickness in the air from the heat and energy we emitted. I felt every sensation in my body, and the intensity of my prayers as I blew them into the kintus. I was attuned and embodied with myself, my prayers, and the ceremony; nothing else existed. Through mindfulness, I tapped into direct communication with God.

—⁓—

There is no denying that mindfulness, meditation, and prayer are powerful tools to help you connect with your body, and become embodied. I chose Mindfulness as the first chapter in the Reconnection section of this book to help you become present in the moment with all of your experiences—your thoughts, emotions, and body sensations. Doing so will support you to deeply engage in the practices and ideas presented in the Reconnection section.

Let's begin your journey of self-discovery with your body, and help you to connect and become embodied.

Self-Awareness

To understand self-awareness, you first have to understand consciousness. Consciousness refers to being aware of your body, how you engage in your life, and the environment around you. It recognizes your existence from internal and external stimuli. Internal stimuli can include hunger, pain, thirst, sleepiness, and an awareness of your thoughts and emotions. External stimuli are what you receive from the environment, such as feeling the wind on your face, smelling the sea air, or hearing music. Our consciousness is continually moving through various states and different levels of awareness. Our consciousness can range from full awareness to deep sleep. Apart from these two extremes, we can experience different levels of consciousness such as meditative states, hypnotic states, daydreaming, drug-induced or alcohol-induced states, and sleep-deprived altered states.[1]

Self-awareness is about knowing and understanding who you are as an individual—your mind and body. Your individuality includes your personality or character traits, thoughts, emotions, actions, beliefs, values, desires, goals, needs, wants, and interactions with others. Through self-awareness, you become more consciously aware of who you are. As you engage with your world, and through your experiences, you begin to develop a greater sense of self-identity.[2]

As you become self-aware, you pay attention to what is happening to you. You focus on your perception of yourself, your place in the world, how you influence your world, and how the world impacts you. Start to notice your feelings and thoughts, and the sensations they bring up in you. As you become more curious and observant, it will increase your self-awareness.

Bodily Awareness

Bodily self-awareness is an awareness of your body. It is your ability to direct your focus inward to the internal sensations you experience. Bodily self-awareness is also your ability to notice the sensations you experience on your skin through touch, pressure, and vibration, but also through energy. (I'll discuss more on touch and energy in Chapters 7 and 8.)

Awareness of your body's sensations happens through proprioception and interoception. Proprioception is sensing your body's movement, and the position of your body in space.[3] Interoception is feeling into the internal state of your body.[4] (I'll discuss these more in Chapter 7.)

You relate to your body by perceiving it, sensing it, controlling it, and recognizing how it is affected by your experiences. As you become more aware of your body, you will start to notice, understand, and experience feelings and sensations you may have never felt before. It's normal to not have words for what you feel in your body. Sometimes your body is speaking so loudly that you don't want to listen; it is too uncomfortable to handle complicated feelings and sensations such as fear, anxiety, or pain. Difficulty feeling emotions and sensations in the body is why people disconnect from their body—it is too unbearable.

As you increase bodily awareness, you will begin to experience what is happening inside and outside your body. There is a phenomenon known as *touchant-touché*. It is the duality of the body's awareness from the inside and the outside. "When we touch our knee with our hand, we have a tactile experience of our knee from the outside (*touché*), but we also have a tactile experience of our knee from the inside (*touchant*), and the same is true of the hand."[5]

As you start to listen to what your body is saying, keep an open mind and perspective of your feelings and sensations. Don't discount what you feel, and brush it off as your imagination. Your body speaks to you all the time. Increasing bodily awareness allows you to understand your experience, and more quickly work through your feelings and sensations.

Why It's Important to be Self-Aware

When you become self-aware, you understand yourself better and recognize your unique individuality. When you know yourself, you become empowered to build on your strengths for growth and transformation. Here are some benefits to becoming self-aware:

- Understand all aspects of yourself.
- Have a strong sense of self-identity.

  - Who you are.
  - What you stand for.
  - How you react to situations.

- Acceptance of self.

- Feel comfortable being with your whole self—not only your mind.
- Not be ruled by your mind, or your emotions.
- Make healthy decisions that are in your best interests.
- Set and maintain healthy boundaries.
- Make changes to support emotional overwhelm, or decrease unwanted behaviors.

Embodied Exercise

Take 30 seconds to become self-aware. You don't need to do anything with the information. It's for you to recognize that you can become self-aware. Do not judge your experience—state it.

Find a place to sit quietly with no distractions. If that's impossible with children, lock yourself in the bathroom. Turn off your phone, the TV, or your computer. Take a couple of deep breaths until you feel calm and settled in your body. Choose a recent event that is disturbing or troubling to you. Then, close your eyes, turn inward, and ask yourself the following questions:

- What are my thoughts?
- What emotions do I feel?
- What sensations do I notice in my body? (If you have difficulty connecting with sensations in your body, that's okay, we will explore this more in Chapter 7.)

Write down what you noticed, including any new insight or clarity, so that you can explore it further at another time.

How was the exercise? Were you surprised by how easy it was to check in with yourself, and become more self-aware? Was it difficult? If yes, don't worry. It will become easier with practice and completion of the other exercises in this book.

What is Mindfulness?

Now that you understand the differences between consciousness, self-awareness, and bodily awareness, let's look at mindfulness. Mindfulness, or being mindful, is a hot topic in therapy, yoga, and other healing modalities. You may have already heard a lot about mindfulness, or have read numerous articles or books on this topic. For some, this may be a new concept. What exactly is mindfulness? Mindfulness is a "state of being conscious and aware of something…by focusing one's awareness on the present moment, while calmly acknowledging and accepting one's feelings, thoughts, and bodily sensations."[6] Mindfulness is staying present in your current experience from moment to moment while not focusing on the past or the future.

Unfortunately, being human means we've experienced wounds, trauma, or situations we wish we could change. No matter how often you go over these types of situations in your brain, you can't change the past. If you stay stuck in regret, it doesn't support you. Regret keeps you stuck in ongoing suffering. The past is the past. To find acceptance of your wounds or trauma doesn't mean you forget what happened to you. It is a chapter in the story of your life. If you haven't done so already, it's a chapter you may need to open and read, and explore with the help of a counselor. Then, when you're ready, it's a chapter you can close, as it will no longer affect you. Your past does not define who you are. It is something you experienced. It has shaped the person you've become. If that person is someone you don't like, you can learn, change, and grow into the most meaningful expression of yourself. Don't let your past keep you stuck in your story. You are the author of your story, and you get to write who you are and what happens to you. Be your own heroine!

For others, there may be a tendency to stay stuck in the future. Fear and worry keep you focused on things that haven't transpired, and will likely never come to pass. Fear of the future is fear of the unknown and loss of control. You don't have a crystal ball, you don't know what the future holds. The future is non-existent. Therefore, to feel less fearful, and gain back control, you need to stay in the present. Suppose your brain takes you to fear or worry about the worst-case scenario. (Remember the cognitive distortion of catastrophizing in Chapter 3?) In that case, look at the truth of the situation at that moment. Is that situation happening now? If not, then you need to get out of the future and stay focused on what is happening in the present moment.

Mindfulness is consciously being present in the current moment as you notice your thoughts, emotions, body sensations, and your environment. What are you currently doing? Whatever it is, that is where your attention needs to be. For example, if you are washing the dishes, then stay focused on washing the dishes. Feel the suds as they bubble up on your hands and the texture of the sponge. Feel the effort it takes to clean the plate. Feel how your fingers and muscles contract, and the pressure your hand exerts on the sponge. Feel the temperature of the water as you rinse the plate.

How Do You Become Mindful?

Have you ever tried yoga? If you have, have you ever experienced being in a specific pose, and then, out of nowhere, you get emotional? When you participate in yoga, you experience mindfulness as you focus in silence on your body, and feel into a pose. When you are mindful, you engage the right side of your brain. You can have an ongoing connection to your left brain as you notice your thoughts, but you don't want to get stuck in your analytical and rational brain. Think of it as being awake and self-aware as you engage in your present experience. You don't want to be on automatic pilot where you engage in behaviors out of habit. You can practice mindfulness anytime, and anywhere, with whatever you are doing.

In Dialectical Behavior Therapy, Dr. Marsha Linehan addresses mindfulness through *what* and *how* skills. There are three critical components to *what* skills when you practice mindfulness.

1. **Observe**—Consciously choose to pay attention to the present moment. Notice your body sensations without using words, but instead, feel them. As thoughts come into your mind, let them go as quickly as the rise and fall of your breath. Focus your attention on your experience. Don't try to push it away, but don't try to hang onto it either. Observe what is happening both inside and outside of you. Remember—no words. This practice is more challenging than it appears. You can observe using your five primary senses of sight, sound, smell, taste, and touch. (I'll discuss this more in Chapter 7.) For example, physically connect with a tree, and notice the tree's different characteristics with all of your senses. Remember, don't use words. Observe.

2. **Describe**—Acknowledge, and put words to, your experience as any thoughts, emotions, or sensations arise. Label what you observe with your senses. You can label a thought, emotion, sensation, or action. Do not include opinions or interpretations—only the facts of who, what, where, and when. For example, "I notice I feel sad. I notice that sadness as a sensation of heaviness in my chest."

3. **Participate**—Let yourself be thoroughly involved in the current activity, and be one with whatever you are doing. Intuitively engage in whatever way is needed. Go with the flow and let yourself be spontaneous. Become one

with your experience and forget yourself. For example, if you are dancing, then dance, feel the vibrations and let your body move to the music's rhythm.[7]

Practice each skill one at a time. Practice observing daily for a week. Then, add in describing for another week, and finally, participating until you have mastered all three at once.

There are three critical components to *how* skills as you observe, describe, and participate in mindfulness.

1. **Nonjudgmentally**—Do not describe things as good or bad, only the facts. Accept each moment and everything you notice. You can acknowledge if something is harmful, helpful, safe, or dangerous, but do not judge whatever comes up. You can also recognize how you reacted emotionally, what values it bumped up against, or what your wishes were, but again, do not judge them. For example, "I missed the bus, got to work late, and my boss commented on the importance of being on time." As opposed to "The bus driver doesn't know how to do his job. He intentionally left while I was running for the bus, which made me late for work. I am so stupid for not leaving earlier. My boss is so mean. I hate this job."

2. **One-Mindfully**—Be completely present in the moment. Only do one thing at a time. Do not multi-task. If any thoughts, emotions, or other actions distract you, let them go over and over again. For example, if you are taking a shower, focus on each task. Focus on soaping your body. Focus on washing your hair. Focus on the sensation of the water hitting your skin. Focus on the water rinsing the soap and shampoo as it slides off your body. If your mind wanders to other thoughts, emotions, or actions, bring yourself back to the current task.

3. **Effectively**—Do whatever is necessary to help you achieve your goals for that particular situation. Focus

on what works, and let go of emotions that derail your efforts. Engage with the skill set you have, and follow the rules to the best of your ability. Let go of willfulness, stubbornness, disobedience, or choosing to be idle and sitting on your hands. "Willfulness is refusing to do what's effective and closing yourself off from the possibilities."[8] For example, notice if you are willful in a situation. If you are, ask yourself, "Is this effective?"[7]

When you engage in mindfulness, and utilize the *what* skills, ensure you apply all three of the *how* skills together—always nonjudgmentally, one-mindfully, and effectively.

Mindfulness Practice

As discussed above, engage in mindfulness and mindfulness skills anytime, anywhere, and with anything you are doing. You can be mindful in a moment as you focus on your breath, or you can engage in mindfulness for several minutes or longer with your thoughts, emotions, body sensations, or an activity. Engage in a mindfulness practice by focusing on the moment without judgment, or a need to hold onto your experience. Here are some examples:

- Be mindful of something using one of your five senses: what you see, hear, smell, taste, or touch.
- Notice thoughts as they come in and out of your mind.
- Focus on your breath.
- Be mindful while doing an activity like singing, dancing, running, jumping, walking, cleaning, swimming, or playing.[8]

Meditation

Meditation derives from the Latin word *meditari*, which means to think, reflect, ponder, or concentrate. Meditation is when you deliberately and consciously take the time to cultivate mindfulness. Meditation is the practice of disengaging your mind as you focus on a particular thought, object, or activity for a specific period. It allows you to train your mind to bring attention and awareness to your experience. Meditation can either open or focus your mind.[7,9]

When you think of meditation, does it conjure up images of sitting cross-legged on the floor for hours at a time with incense burning, and complete silence? It can be this, but it doesn't have to be. You can engage in meditation while sitting, standing, lying down, or moving. It can be done in complete silence, with music or sound, or guided. You can do it while sitting still, focusing on an object, or engaging in an activity. It can be done with intention, like prayer, or being in the moment with whatever transpires.

History of Meditation

Meditation appears to have originated in India approximately 5,000 to 3,500 BCE. The estimation comes from dating wall art that depicts people seated in meditative postures with their eyes half-closed. In 1,500 BCE, the Vedas, which are ancient Indian religious texts, mention meditation. However, the Vedas were passed down through oral traditions for centuries long before written down. Mostly religious people, or wandering ascetics—someone who practices severe self-discipline and restraint from indulgences—engaged in the practice of meditation.

In the 6th century BCE, Siddhartha Gautama learned meditation and philosophy to attain enlightenment. Dissatisfied with what he had learned, he created his methodology, achieved enlightenment, and became Buddha. He spent his life teaching meditation and spiritual awakening to thousands of people. Through his teachings, Buddhism spread throughout Asia.

During the same *golden century*, three other religions created approaches to meditation:

1. **Jainism**—was founded by Mahavira in India. Meditation techniques focused on breath, mantras, gazing, visualizations, and self-inquiry for self-purification, self-discipline, contemplation, and non-violence.

2. **Taoism**—was founded by Lao Tzu in China. It emphasized the union of living in harmony with nature and cosmic life, or Tao. This meditation focuses on the generation, transformation, and circulation of inner energy. Its purpose is to quiet the body and mind, unite body and spirit, obtain inner peace, and harmonize with Tao.

3. **Confucianism**—was founded by Confucius in China. It focuses on self-contemplation, self-improvement, morality, and community life.

The philosophies of meditation culturally influenced Greek philosophers due to Alexander the Great's military exploits of India from 327 to 325 BCE. Greek philosophers practiced navel-gazing (*omphaloskepsis*) to aid in philosophical contemplation. Later philosophers developed meditation techniques involving concentration.

Meditation in Christian mysticism involved the repetition of religious words or phrases along with silent contemplation of God. The Jesus Prayer is one form of Christian meditation developed in Greece some time in the 10th to 14th centuries.

Zen is a popular school of Buddhism founded by Bodhidharma in the 8th century. Zen or Zazen meditation aims to regulate attention, which involves *thinking about not thinking*, and focusing the attention inward. In Japanese, Zazen means seated Zen or seated meditation.

The Sufis, or mystics of Islam, were influenced by Indian contemplative traditions, and developed meditation practices that include breathing, mantras, and gazing. Some state that it originated in the 7th century after Mohammed's death, while others believe it emerged between the 8th and 10th centuries. The goal of Sufi meditation is to connect with Allah.

The Jewish tradition of Kabbalah developed a form of meditation based on the deep contemplation of the names of God, philosophical principles, prayers, symbols, and the Tree of Life in the 13th century.

In the 18th century, meditation began appearing in the Western world. Europeans translated Eastern philosophies and spiritual texts like the Upanishads, Bhagavad Gita, and Buddhist Sutras. Swami Vivekananda introduced yoga and meditation to the United States in the early 20th century. The Transcendentalist movement was also well received. Several famous Indian spiritual teachers migrated to the United States. Paramahansa Yogananda founded the Self-Realization Fellowship in 1920. Maharishi Mahesh Yogi taught Transcendental Meditation. Swami Rama founded the Himalayan Institute in 1969. Swami Rama was the first yogi to be studied by Western scientists. He demonstrated how he could control his bodily processes—such as blood pressure, heartbeat, and body temperature—which scientists thought were involuntary. These early experiments sparked five decades of scientific research and studies on the effects and benefits of meditation. In the 21st century, meditation has become mainstream and secularized for its mind, body, and wellness benefits.[10]

Meditation spread throughout history and the world as a means for purification, discipline, contemplation, transformation, enlightenment, and harmony with oneself, nature, the Universe, and God. Although rooted in spiritual and religious beliefs and philosophies, you don't need to adhere to a specific spiritual or religious belief to benefit from the practice of meditation, or seek spiritual enlightenment. Meditation supports you to get out of your mind, and into your body, as you connect with your inner self, and become more deeply embodied.

Misconceptions of Meditation

Some people may have preconceived notions or misconceptions about meditation—how to do it, its purpose, how long you have to do it, and the goal. Let's look at five common misconceptions.

Misconception # 1

The first misconception is that you need to sit cross-legged in the lotus position on the floor with your back upright for meditation to be effective. You do not need a specific meditation pillow or bench, nor do you need to sit on the floor. Many people may need back support. You can meditate while lying down, or sitting in a chair. The goal is to be comfortable. If it isn't comfortable, you will likely stop doing it and miss out on the benefits of connecting with yourself, your Higher Self, and your body. If you lie down, you may be more likely to fall asleep. As such, I would suggest sitting upright in a chair with your feet firmly on the floor. You can experiment to see which meditation posture feels the most comfortable, supportive, and effective.

Misconception # 2

The second misconception is the belief that the goal of meditation is to clear and empty your mind of thoughts. As I stated in Chapter 3, we have 50 thousand to 80 thousand thoughts per day. You can't stop your thoughts from happening. During meditation, you may be free of thoughts, and other times, thoughts will present themselves. You are not failing meditation if you have thoughts. When thoughts arise, just notice them, acknowledge them by stating *thought*. Observe any judgments that may arise, let go of the thought, and gently return to your point of focus—your breath, a candle flame, a mantra, or guided meditation. The longer you engage in a meditation practice, the less frequently your thoughts will arise, and your thinking mind begins to slow.

Misconception # 3

The third misconception is that meditation needs to be in complete silence. Meditating in silence may be unrealistic if you live in a busy household with children running around, or on a busy street with traffic sounds. Allow the sounds to be part of your meditation practice to increase your self-awareness skills and mental resilience. Notice the sounds, and then gently bring yourself back to your focus point. You may notice thoughts around wishing your environment or the experience to be different. Acknowledge any thoughts and let them go.

Misconception # 4

The fourth misconception is the belief that the goal of meditation is to be calm. If you choose to engage in a meditation practice, you will start to feel good and relaxed in your body. Your SNS will become less activated by the stress and fight-flight-freeze response. Meditation will allow you to stay within your Window of Tolerance, and engage the PNS in a state of restfulness. But that's not the only goal. Meditation gets you out of your thinking brain, and helps you reconnect with your body and become embodied. It allows you to become consciously and mindfully aware of your body, and increase your level of self-awareness to the emotional states and physical sensations housed in your body.

Misconception # 5

The fifth misconception is the belief meditation goes against or impedes religious practices. Meditation is supportive of one's spirituality because it doesn't subscribe to any one type of religion. Meditation can deepen and enhance your connection to God, Spirit, Creator, the Universe, or whatever belief system you hold. Meditation allows you to clear your mind, and disengage from your extraneous thoughts so you can listen to God. As I discuss later in this chapter, prayer is a form of meditation practiced in most religions. Historically, many cultures throughout the world engage in some form of meditation practice, and it goes hand in hand with their religious beliefs.[11]

Types of Meditation

Below you will find several different types of meditation you can engage in to discover the style that aligns with you best. Meditation takes practice. It is not about perfection. Meditation is about taking the time to increase your awareness, engage and connect with your body, and release your mind from thoughts. Meditation is both calming and insightful. You get to support mental, emotional, and physical distress, while also obtaining new knowledge and understanding of yourself, and your connection to others, your Higher Self, and God or the Universe.

Start with five minutes a day, and slowly increase the time up to 20–30 minutes. Other than movement meditation, you can sit or lie down for any of the meditations listed. Find the most comfortable position for your body.

Find the best time of day to meditate. Many enjoy meditating first thing in the morning to start their day feeling calm, and a reminder to be mindful throughout the day. Others may prefer to meditate after work, or later in the evening before bed to release tension and stress, help the body unwind, and improve sleep.

Meditations can either be guided or unguided. In a guided meditation, someone leads you through a series of steps. Guided meditation can be helpful for beginners to get the most out of the meditation practice. In an unguided meditation, you sit alone in silence and no one explains the process to you. Many of the types of meditation below will be unguided.

If you feel frustrated with one kind of meditation, choose another. The list below is not exhaustive. Choose at least one form of meditation. Be consistent with it; do it for several months so it becomes habit-forming. I'll discuss the benefits of mindfulness and meditation at the end of the chapter. For now, I want to impart that mindfulness and meditation are essential to increase your self-awareness. A mindfulness or meditation practice will allow you to recognize and feel what is happening in your body, reduce and quiet unwanted and unsupportive criticizing thoughts and untruths, and help you connect with your body and become embodied.

Body Scan or Progressive Relaxation

Body scan or progressive relaxation meditations promote relaxation, and decrease stress and tension in the body. When you do a body-scan meditation, start either sitting or lying down. Close your eyes, take a couple of deep breaths, and let your body soften into a comfortable position. Start at the top of your head, and slowly move your mind's awareness down your face, back of your head, neck (front and back), shoulders, arms, forearms, hands, fingers, chest, back, stomach, hips, buttocks, legs, calves, feet, and toes. Notice whatever body sensations are present in these parts of your body. In your mind, describe the body sensations you notice in different parts of your body, for example, throbbing temples. (See Chapter 7 for various body sensation descriptors.) Breathe in white light, or visualize calming waves, directly into the affected body part. On the exhale, breathe out any tension or body sensation you feel. If your attention wanders, bring it back to where you left off.

In progressive muscle relaxation, you will address each of your body parts, but this time you will engage your muscles by squeezing as hard as you can, holding for four to ten seconds, then releasing them. Imagine you are breathing out all the tension on the exhale. Close your eyes, squish and tighten your face muscles, squeeze, squeeze, squeeze, and then release. Then tighten your neck, shoulders, and back, and release. Then your arms and forearms, and close your fingers into tight balls, and release. Then tighten your chest and stomach, and release. Finally, clench your buttocks, tighten your legs, calves, and scrunch up your toes, hold, hold, hold, and then release. You may wish to squeeze all parts of your body simultaneously, and release them after several seconds. Do this two or three times. When you release your muscles, you will feel waves of energy letting go. You can also shake out your body parts afterward. As the muscle contracts and releases, it disengages the body from holding tension and storing stress. It allows your body to get out of the SNS's stress response and return to the PNS's response of rest-and-digest. This meditation is a great tool to relieve stress and anxiety before bed.

Expanding Awareness

Expanding awareness meditation is when you expand your awareness from one area of the body to the next. You start by focusing on your breath—your inhalation and exhalation. After a minute or two, bring your focus to your body. What sensations are you experiencing in your body from one moment to the next? Notice this with curiosity. Then shift to noticing the sounds in the room or outside. Are there people talking, do you hear the furnace or air conditioner, are there birds chirping, wind blowing, or traffic sounds? If there is only silence, be present with the silence. Now bring your awareness to your thoughts; notice them come up, then let them fade away. Allow your thoughts to come and go without judgment or attachment. Next, notice your emotions. What emotions are coming up, and where in your body do you experience those emotions? Notice this with open curiosity, nonjudgmentally, and with acceptance—name them, feel them, and notice as they pass. Finally, without choosing, have a spontaneous awareness of whatever comes up, whether it be your breath, body sensations, sounds, thoughts, or emotions.[12]

Focused

Focused meditation involves concentrating on one of your five senses: sight, sound, smell, taste, or touch. You want to focus on the *experience* of engaging with the sense, not your *thoughts*. How does it feel? Sit upright in a chair, and allow yourself to get comfortable by moving your body into a relaxed position. Choose one of your senses to be your focus. With sight, you could focus on a candle flame, a serene picture, a spot on the wall, or your hand. With sound, you could repeat a mantra (such as *Om*), or listen to singing bowls, tuning forks, drums, or chanting. With smell, light a scented candle, burn an essential oil, or light sage, sweetgrass, or palo santo. With taste, place a piece of chocolate, candy, or other food on your tongue, and notice the textures and flavors as you slowly savor it. With touch, you could caress your pet or a soft blanket, hold a rock or gemstone, or place your hand lovingly on a part of your body, such as your cheek, belly, or heart. You can also focus on your breath as it moves through your body. Notice your body's sensations with each inhale and exhale. Notice the cool air as it comes in your nose, the rise and fall of your belly, and the expansion of your ribs. If your mind wanders, gently let those thoughts go without judgment, and bring your attention back to the sense.

Touch may be difficult and triggering for some people who have experienced physical or sexual trauma. Take it slow. Start with another sense until you feel more comfortable with increased awareness and connection with your body. When you feel ready to engage with touch, start with a stone in your hand, or stroke your pet or a blanket. When you feel comfortable and ready, move your hand to a part of your body where you may feel less triggered. Imagine sending yourself love and compassion, and let yourself feel comforted and soothed. You may only be able to do this for a few minutes at a time, and that's perfect. Stay present in your body and do not get out of your Window of Tolerance. Be gentle with yourself. There is no hurry.

Loving-Kindness

In loving-kindness meditation, you direct love, compassion, kindness, acceptance, and forgiveness toward yourself first, and then toward others. It can be for people you know or don't know, people you love, are struggling with, or have been harmed by, or for whole groups of people. It can be for all living beings, including animals and Mother Earth. Imagine you are receiving unconditional love from Mother Earth, Source, Creator, or the Universe. Breathe love into every cell in your body and let it fill your heart. Then, emit love out from your heart to whomever you wish. Feel your emotions and body sensations as you engage in this meditation.

Mantra

Mantra meditation uses repetitive sound to clear the mind through a word, phrase, or tone. The mantra can be spoken silently in your head or out loud. Some people find it easier to use mantras instead of sitting in silence, or focusing on the breath or an object, as the mind is less likely to wander, or get distracted by other thoughts.

Mantras can be self-affirming statements to help calm mental, emotional, and physical distress, and to increase self-confidence and strength to face the world. When you meditate on an intentional mantra at the beginning of your morning, you set your day up for success and positivity. It can also return you to a mindfulness state and calm center by speaking the mantra throughout the day. Later in this chapter, I discuss the power of your intentions. For now, ensure your mantras are positive, and you speak words in the present tense as if they have already come to fruition. Here are some examples:

- My body is healthy.
- I am calm.
- I am at peace.
- I am love.
- I listen to my body and give it what it needs.
- My potential is limitless.
- I speak with confidence.

Chakras are energy centers that run along your spine. There are seven main chakras. The root chakra is at the base of your spine. The sacral chakra is just below your belly button. The solar plexus chakra is in your stomach area. The heart chakra is located in the center of your chest. The throat chakra is located in your throat. The third eye chakra is located between your eyebrows. The crown chakra is located at the top of your head. (I discuss chakras in detail in Chapter 8.) For now, focus a mantra on a specific chakra that is blocked, and manifesting mental, emotional, or physical disturbances in your mind and body. When you chant for a particular chakra, it resonates as a specific sound. For the crown chakra, there is no chanting—you listen. In the italicized words below, the *a* is pronounced as *ah*. Here are some examples of phrased mantras you can repeat or sound mantras for each chakra:

- Root Chakra—I am safe or *Lam*.
- Sacral Chakra—My emotions flow freely or *Vam*.
- Solar Plexus Chakra—I accept myself or *Ram*.
- Heart Chakra—I am compassionate or *Yam*.
- Throat Chakra—I speak my truth or *Ham*.
- Third Eye Chakra—I trust my intuition or *Om*.
- Crown Chakra—I am connected to the Universe.[13]

The Universe is comprised of particles in motion that create energy. Humans emit energy and vibrations from the frequencies of our thoughts, words, and actions. The vibrational frequency of chanting *Om* is the same frequency found in all things throughout nature and the world. Om is considered a sacred word because of its mystical power. When you chant Om, it creates a vibration that resonates and connects you with the frequency of your Higher Self and the Universe. Om is pronounced AUM. The "A" originates deep in the back of the throat. "It equates to the conscious mind—the doer of all actions."[13] The "U" resonates in the upper palate along with vibrations in the throat. "It equates the subconscious mind—the planner of all actions."[13] The "M" "resonates the deep silence of the infinite," or the "unconscious state—the state of deep sleep."[13] When you speak a mantra out loud, your body gets the added benefit of the vibrational energy. It enriches your mind and nourishes every cell.[14]

When you chant Om, sit up straight in a chair with your eyes closed. Take a deep breath; exhale slowly while chanting AUM, focusing on each vowel and consonant sound until you run out of breath. Then, take another deep inhale and repeat. Do this for several minutes. There are several videos online you can chant along with Om, or the other chakra mantra sounds.

Mindfulness

Mindfulness meditation is when you pay attention to whatever thoughts arise as you focus on an object or your breath. When you just *notice* your thoughts, you allow them to pass through without judgment, or getting caught up or involved with the thought. Observe the thought, and note any patterns around the type of thoughts that arise, then let them go. Mindfulness meditation focuses on concentration, and increases your awareness of your thoughts, emotions, and body sensations. When thoughts arise, notice them, then return to your breath or the object of focus.

Movement

Meditative movement is a type of exercise that combines movement with meditative awareness of your body sensations. Meditative movement can include many different forms, such as yoga, martial arts, or spiritual dance. However, you can incorporate any form of movement into a meditative movement practice. For example, walking, jogging, hiking, gardening, or horseback riding.[7]

Below, I give a brief description of five types of meditative movement exercises you can explore. These are not all-inclusive types of meditative movement, and again, any form of movement can become your meditative movement practice. If you feel called to learn more about one of these meditative movement practices, check out a book, search more information, follow along with videos online, or attend a class in your area.

Labyrinth

A labyrinth walk is an ancient spiritual practice used in many cultures and different faiths for prayer, contemplation, and to center oneself spiritually. "The labyrinth symbolizes a journey to a predetermined destination (such as a pilgrimage to a holy site), or the journey through life from birth to spiritual awakening to death."[15] You can usually find a labyrinth in most cities—likely in a park, garden, next to a church or monastery, or at a spiritual retreat center.

Labyrinths are similar to mandalas. A mandala is a geometric design enclosed in a circle. The circle represents the entire Universe. "Like mandalas, labyrinths are archetypal collective symbols that transcend all cultures because they are grounded in consciousness itself."[16] What does that mean? It means that while you engage in a labyrinth walk, you increase awareness and perception, and awaken to the connection between your mind, body, surroundings, and the world at large. A labyrinth is a symbolic representation of you and your inner harmony.[16]

A labyrinth is not a maze; mazes have dead ends or forks to offer directional choices. A labyrinth has only one way to the center and back out. A labyrinth uses rocks, stones, or cut-out sections of grass to form an intricate path of winding passages that go back and forth until you reach the center. When you get to the center, you turn around and retrace your steps until you reach the exit.

Before you enter a labyrinth, become mindful, centered, grounded, and turn inward. (See more about grounding in Chapter 6.) You can focus on a prayer that you repeat, or create an intention to receive answers or insight about a particular question you are contemplating. If you ask a question, don't focus on it. Clear your mind. As you begin, walk slowly and calmly. You may notice your footsteps, or your thoughts, emotions, or body sensations. As these arise, acknowledge them and let them go. Stay present with your experience. When you reach the center, take the time to pause and reflect. You may pray, or listen for answers, profound revelations, or insights. When you exit the labyrinth, take some time to journal your experience and any insights that arose.[15]

Qigong

Qigong originated in China around 4,000 years ago. *Qi* (pronounced chee) means breath, or air, and refers to the universal energy or spirit that flows through your body. *Gong* (pronounced gung) denotes cultivation, or work achieved through practice, skill, and mastery. Qigong is the cultivation of vital life-force energy. It utilizes coordinated body postures, slow-flowing movement, deep rhythmic breathing, a calm meditative state, guided imagery and visualization, and chanting or making sounds for health, fitness, spirituality, and martial arts training.

There are 56 contemporary, and 75 ancient, qigong forms, but these are by no means an exhaustive list. Most qigong forms fall under five categories: medical, martial, spiritual, intellectual, and life-nourishing. Qigong focuses on the following four principles:

1. Soft gaze and expressionless face.
2. Solid stance through firm footing and an erect spine.
3. Relaxation through slightly bent joints and relaxed muscles.
4. Balance and counterbalance as you move over your center of gravity.

The three advanced goals of qigong are:

1. Equanimity through fluidity and relaxation.
2. Tranquility by emptying the mind, and heightened awareness.
3. Stillness by performing smaller and smaller movements, decreasing them until you achieve complete stillness.[17]

Qigong's gentle, slow movements and calm breathing is supportive for all ages and levels of health. It promotes mental, emotional, physical, and spiritual well-being. Check out a beginner qigong class in your community or online.

Sacred Dance

Sacred dance occurs during religious rituals and ceremonies, and has been present in most religions throughout history. Liturgical, worship, praise, or gospel dance are specific to Christianity. Sacred dance was a way to give thanks, and worship gods, goddesses, or deities. The Hawaiian hula is a dance to the volcano goddess, Pele.

In Sufism, whirling is a form of ecstatic dance as a means of worship.[18] In ecstatic dance, dancers don't necessarily follow specific steps. They abandon themselves to the rhythm of the music, and move freely to invoke a trance state and feeling of ecstasy. This type of dance allows the dancer to become connected to themselves, others, and their body and emotions, as a way to cope with stress and attain a level of serenity. Ecstatic dance incorporates healing, ritual, and spirituality. In shamanism, spiritual practices utilize ecstatic dance, and rhythmic drumming, to alter consciousness. Shamans use dance, and repetitive music, along with fasting and hallucinogenic drugs, to induce ecstasy. Gabrielle Roth created 5Rhythms, a modern form of ecstatic dance. There are five different rhythms to connect the dancer with their fear, anger, sadness, joy, and compassion. You will likely find a 5Rhythms class in your city.[19]

Indigenous cultures throughout the world have used sacred dance to honor their ancestors, as part of their rituals, to give thanks to Mother Earth, and as part of healing ceremonies. North American indigenous people celebrate their culture at powwows, and perform several different dance styles in a circle. "For all dancers, the spiritual center of a powwow is always the Circle—a revered area blessed by a spiritual leader."[20] Dancers enter the circle from the east to walk in the same direction as the sun's daily journey through the sky. The circle represents the circle of life, and its connection to all things in the world. The different dances represent some aspect of the Spirit or natural world.[21]

These are a few of the different sacred and spiritual dances that occur throughout the world. If you want to incorporate meditative movement through dance into your life, you don't have to engage in a specific religious, cultural, sacred, or spiritual dance. Close the blinds, turn off the lights, or go into a private room. Turn on your favorite music, let yourself go, and become one with the music and your body. Let your body move as it feels called. Turn up the volume on your stereo, or put on headphones or earbuds to feel the vibration as it reverberates throughout your body. Shut down your brain. It's only you and the music, and the movement of your body. To release negative beliefs about your body, dance in the nude. Set yourself free!

Tai Chi

Tai chi is a Chinese martial art practiced for health, meditation, and defense training. Tai chi is a "mind-body exercise that integrates slow, gentle movements, breathing, and a variety of cognitive components, including focused attention, imagery, and multi-tasking."[22] There are five traditional schools of tai chi:

1. **Chen-Style**—utilizes silk reeling, which is twisting, spiraling, and rotating the body and limbs, alternating fast and slow motions with bursts of power.
2. **Yang-Style**—incorporates slow, steady, expansive, and soft movements.
3. **Wu (Hao)-Style**—utilizes small, subtle movements focused on balance, sensitivity, and internal development.
4. **Wu-Style**—focuses on small circle hand techniques, pushing hands, weapons, parallel footwork, and horse stance.
5. **Sun-Style**—uses small circular hand movements, that are smooth and flowing, with gentle postures.

Each style has its nuances, but they all focus on slow, deliberate orchestrated movements that flow from one to the next. They may incorporate crouching, twisting, and moving hands, arms, and legs forward, up, or side to side. These precise movements help to build muscle strength and concentration. Warm-up exercises help to prepare the musculoskeletal system, and encourage deep breathing and relaxation. After a warm-up, several sets of postures engage different parts of the body. The spiritual component of tai chi focuses on balance through yin-yang, and *qi* (chee), or life-force energy.

Since tai chi is slow, and low-impact, it is ideal for those with disabilities, suffering from illness or disease, or the elderly. Healthy people of all ages will also benefit from this form of meditative movement.[22] Check out a beginner tai chi class in your community or online.

Yoga

Yoga is a spiritual discipline that focuses on achieving harmony between the mind and body. In Sanskrit, yoga means to join, to unite, or oneness. Through the practice of yoga, there is a union between individual consciousness and Universal consciousness. You attain harmony between mind and body, and man and nature. You are not separate from, but an inclusive part of, Universal energy.

Yoga can be traced back over 5,000 years ago to sacred Indian texts. One of these holy texts, the Bhagavad Gita, states, "Yoga is the journey of the self, through the self, to the self."[23] The aim of yoga is self-realization. "**Self-realization** is the truth of who we are, what we are—the realization that we are not the physical body, the physical form that we believe ourselves to be, but the energy within that physical form that gives us life."[24] Through self-realization, one overcomes suffering to create a state of liberation (*Moksha*) or freedom (*Kaivalya*).[25]

In Pantanjali's book, *Yoga Sutras*, he discusses the *Eight Limbs of Yoga*, which is a step-by-step approach to prepare the body to reach the ultimate goal of truth, ecstasy, and bliss.

1. **Yama (Morality)**—stresses the importance of conducting our lives with honesty and integrity, treating others as we wish to be treated, and following a path of non-violence, truth, and self-control.

2. **Niyama (Discipline)**—is achieved through spirituality by recognizing and praying to the supreme energy, and stresses contemplation and thoughtfulness.

3. **Asana (Physical Exercise)**—yoga focuses on the human body. It considers the body as sacred, and it needs to be cared for and nurtured. Asana prepares the body for meditation, and a spiritual journey through discipline and concentration.

4. **Pranayama (Breath Control)**—focuses consciously on the inhalation and exhalation of breath to connect your mind, body, and soul. Breath is pranic energy. In Sanskrit, prana means vital life force. By filling your body with breath, you become powerful and energetic, to support the body to heal.

5. **Pratyahara (Detachment)**—is turning inward to concentrate on, become aware of, and observe your inner self without the clutter of outside stimuli. It is detachment from the outside world.

6. **Dharana (Concentration)**—is training the mind to focus on a single object, thought, or mantra. It diminishes the control of your mind's incessant chatter, and supports a calm state.

7. **Dhyana (Meditation)**—the mind is aware without focus. The goal is to stay still with minimal or no thoughts, and no concentrating.

8. **Samadhi (Self-Realization)**—through self-realization, you create a state of ecstasy and oneness with all living beings. It promotes bliss, peace, happiness, and freedom, and an experience of enlightenment.

There are eleven styles of yoga:

1. **Anusara**—focuses on alignment in the *asanas*, or poses, and the mind-body-heart connection.

2. **Ashtanga**—utilizes a set of poses through conscious breathing to build internal heat. It builds core strength and increases flexibility.

3. **Bikram**—utilizes 26 body postures and two breathing exercises in a heated, humid room for 90 minutes. It supports the release of toxins from the body and improves blood circulation.

4. **Hatha**—is a gentle introduction to yoga that focuses on the basic postures and breathing techniques. The poses are practiced more slowly and include more static posture holds.

5. **Iyengar**—utilizes props, such as ropes, blankets, blocks, and chairs, to ensure the precision and alignment of poses and breath control. It improves balance and coordination, and alleviates neck and backaches.

6. **Jivamukti**—combines physical asanas with meditative and spiritual concepts to promote non-violence, devotion, and scripture contemplation. It increases balance, flexibility, and blood flow within the body. It flushes out toxins and strengthens the body.

7. **Kundalini**—utilizes physical and meditative practices to awaken the latent coiled energy in your sacrum, which is the base of your spinal column connected to your pelvis. It enhances awareness and connection with your inner self.

8. **Power**—is fast-paced and strenuous, moving quickly from one asana to the next. It lowers blood pressure, and improves heart health.

9. **Restorative**—is slow, and utilizes props, such as ropes, blankets, and blocks, to support the body to stay in each pose for a longer time to achieve its full effects. It relaxes and calms the body and is helpful for insomnia and anxiety.

10. **Vinyasa**—is fast-paced movement from one pose to the next utilizing the breath in a specific pattern. It builds lean muscles and calms the mind.

11. **Yin**—is slow-paced movement with seated postures held for 45 seconds to two minutes. It is also a meditative practice to help find inner peace.[23]

Yoga is an incredible form of meditative movement that can support the connection between your mind, body, and spirit. Do yoga on an empty stomach. When done in the morning, it can energize and rejuvenate your body for the rest of the day. If you're not a morning person, find a time to practice yoga for a minimum of 20 minutes a day. Choose one of the styles above that resonates with you. Find a yoga class in your community, an online course, or purchase DVDs to do it from home.

Embodied Exercise

Choose a form of exercise to engage in meditative movement, and be present and aware of your body's experience. I will discuss the different senses and sensations you can experience in your body in Chapter 7. For now, notice the movements you make, or the times when your body is still. Use all of your senses to attune to your experience.

- What do you see? Look around, take in your environment as you engage in the meditative movement.
- What do you hear? Be at one with the music, or feel the peacefulness in the silence.
- What do you smell? If outdoors, smell the air. If inside, notice any particular scents, or the scent of your body.

- What do you taste? If outside, you may taste the earthiness, saltiness, or dampness in the air. If inside, you may taste the sweat on your lip or humidity in the room.

- What sensations do you feel? Does your body feel light or heavy? Is there pain or discomfort, or ease and freedom? Do you feel strong or weak? What kinds of sensations are you experiencing—shaky, tingling, or throbbing? (Check out Chapter 7 for a list of sensations.) What temperature do you notice in and on your body?

- Is your body in balance? Do you feel grounded in your core, or do you feel off-center? (See Chapter 6 for more on grounding.) Does one side of your body dominate?

- What are the different movements in your muscles, joints, digits, limbs, or torso? Notice how you feel when you bend or straighten.

- What automatic sensory receptors become engaged while you do this meditative movement? Are you hungry or thirsty? Notice if your heart rate and respiration have increased. Notice if there is pain, temperature change, pressure, or stimulation in or on your body. Notice your emotions. How do you feel as you participate in this meditative movement—happy, sad, or angry? (Utilize the emotions list from Chapter 4.)

You are being informed and influenced by all your senses as you engage in meditative movement. Ensure you breathe deeply into your belly and exhale fully as you engage in meditative movement. Journal your experience, and include what you noticed in your body, your emotions, and any insight or clarity that arose.

Prayer

Contemplative prayer is a spiritual, meditative practice.[7] Prayer is speaking to Spirit and meditation is listening to Spirit. The bible references stillness and silence in a number of its verses. Psalm 46:10 states, "Be still, and know that I am God."[26] Many interpret this verse as a directive to quiet your mind through meditation. Christianity is not the only religion to incorporate prayer. All religions engage in some form of ceremonial prayer to commune intentionally with God through worship.

As you commune with God through prayer, you connect with yourself, and embody your wishes, dreams, or suffering. You need to feel it in your body. With a desire or longing, you plant a seed through prayer, water and care for it, and it becomes manifested. When you experience mental, emotional, or physical upset, prayer helps you process your distress and release it.

Prayer can be purposeful through praise, thanksgiving, or requests for help. People pray to address their needs, hopes, and wishes for themselves and their loved ones. It can involve faith healing for those who are sick. People pray for their communities, cities, and countries. They pray for those suffering due to famine, disasters, or war. You can pray to Mother Earth, giving thanks for all she offers, and to help her heal. You can pray for the world and humanity at large. There is no limit to prayer.

Prayer can take the form of mantras, incantations, hymns, creeds, or whatever heartfelt words come to mind. People pray with objects such as *malas*, rosaries, or other forms of prayer beads to keep count of repetitions. Many light candles and incense, and have images of idols and icons.

Prayers can be done individually or in groups. Places of worship can include shrines, synagogues, churches, monasteries, mosques, and temples. Creating a sacred place of worship within your home, or outside on Mother Earth, is no less intentional, meaningful, powerful, or devotional. You can pray anywhere at any time.

As I discussed at the beginning of this chapter, with my experience creating a despacho in Peru, prayer is a full-bodied experience. Be present with your body in prayer. You may have an image of prayer as being still and quiet, with people reverently prostrating themselves before God. For many, this is their experience of prayer, but it is not the only way. People may sway their arms, do the Sign of the Cross, join their hands together, or place a hand on their heart. Some people raise their hands to the sky, while others have their arms out to the side with palms up in the shape of the cross. Some people place them on the ground. Some may kneel, bow deeply, place their foreheads on the ground, or lie flat, face down on the ground. You can pray when you dance, or walk in your garden or a park. People pray on a pilgrimage as they walk El Camino, or at Mecca or other holy sites. Notice, and engage in, movement through prayer as you feel called.

If you've never prayed before, or don't follow a specific religion, you may feel unsure or overwhelmed. Please don't. You do not need to follow a particular religion, or engage in any of the above ritualistic practices. You can pray to God, Creator, the Universe, Mother Earth, or other higher power. Find your way to pray. In prayer, be present with your words, intentions, and body movements. Speak from your heart about your worries, fears, hopes, or goals. You can silently speak the words in your head, but there is power and energy to words when vocalized. Let your emotions flow when you pray—sadness, anger, or joy. Feel the sensations in your body as you pray, feel your prayers with your whole body. You can pray daily, or when a need arises.

Spiritual

Many Eastern religions and Christianity practice spiritual meditation. As discussed above, prayer is a form of spiritual meditation, but isn't necessary to becoming spiritually attuned. The focus of spiritual meditation is to sit in silence to seek a deeper connection to God, Creator, or the Universe. When you engage in spiritual meditation, you develop a greater understanding of yourself through your relationship with a higher power as a means of spiritual growth. It isn't necessary, but essential oils or incense can help heighten the spiritual experience. These can include, but are not limited to:

- Cedar
- Frankincense
- Myrrh
- Palo Santo
- Sage
- Sandalwood

Transcendental

Maharishi Mahesh Yogi founded Transcendental Meditation (TM). The technique is effortless because there is no need to empty your mind, monitor thoughts, concentrate, or control the mind. The practice consists of utilizing a silent mantra for 20 minutes, twice per day, while sitting comfortably with eyes closed. Certified teachers teach TM. You receive personalized one-on-one instruction over four consecutive days. If you are interested in learning TM, and finding a teacher in your city, check out their website (ca.tm.org/en).

Visualization

During a visualization meditation, you utilize your imagination to focus on a person, picture, object, or future goal. Imagine the outcome of your goal becoming a reality. Use all of your senses—sight, sound, smell, taste, and touch—to heighten the experience of what it will be like when you achieve the goal. For example, if you have a dream of going on vacation to Hawaii, visualize the sights you will see, the sounds you will hear, the smells in the air, the foods you will taste, the things you will touch, and what body sensations and emotions you will feel. A visualization meditation can be self-directed, as in the recent example, or guided by someone else. There are hundreds, if not thousands, of guided visualization meditations online. They can guide you through a forest, along a beach, or into space. Create your own, or choose a guided visualization that feels compelling.

Power of Intention

In shamanism, which you will learn more about in Chapter 9, intent is everything. Intention allows the shaman to manipulate reality for healing and manifestation. Intention provides purpose and direction. What you think and speak is what you create in the world. Be intentional. Your words have power, so think before your speak. Your intentions and desires are the seeds you plant in your consciousness toward your destiny. The Upanishads, a series of Hindu sacred texts, have this to say about intention, "You are what your deepest desire is. As your desire is, so is your intention. As your intention is, so is your will. As your will is, so is your deed. As your deed is, so is your destiny."[27]

Intention is about focusing your mind on a specific aim or goal. Become self-reflective and decide what you want. When you focus on achieving what you want, you first need to know your why. *Why do you want what you want?* When you are clear on your why, it gives greater power to your intention.

When you write down or speak your intentions, talk about them positively as if they have already come to fruition. Connect with God, Creator, the Universe, or a higher power, and give thanks for your desires already being fulfilled. For example, let's say you are currently struggling with ill health. Don't speak the words, "God, please remove this cancer from my body." Instead, state, "Thank you, God, for my body's perfect healed state."

Now you have a map to get you where you want to be. You can use intention-based exercises like meditation, prayer, or visualization to get you there. Don't hold onto your intentions for dear life. Like actual seeds, they need to be released, planted, placed in the sun, and watered to help them grow. Use prayer or meditation to go beyond your ego state, and into the stillness and silence of pure consciousness. Pure consciousness is the ideal state to plant your seeds of intention.

Speak your intentions aloud, or in your mind, during prayer or meditation. Don't focus on the how, or the details, of it transpiring. Once you've set your intention, let it go, and stop thinking about it. Stay positive, and know your intention has been heard, that everything will be alright, and that it will happen at the right time. Don't focus on a specific outcome or result. Allow yourself to be detached, and know the best outcome will happen with your best interests in mind. For example, if you focus only on getting a specific job at a particular company, you limit yourself from other possibilities. When I state my prayers or intentions, I always say at the end, "For whatever is for my highest good." Let the Universe handle the details. Your job is to set your intentions, and know that you've "set the infinite organizing power of the universe in motion."[27]

Benefits of Being Mindful

When you incorporate a daily mindfulness practice, such as meditation, prayer, or movement, you will experience several mental, emotional, and physical benefits.

- Increase concentration, decision-making, planning, and problem-solving.
- Increase focus, mental clarity, memory, and learning.

- Ability to recognize and let go of negative thinking, rumination, cognitive distortions, and future thinking.
- Deeper connection with yourself and your body.
- Increase spiritual connection with a higher power.
- Access inner knowing or Higher Self.
- Increase self-awareness, insight, and intuition.
- Ability to feel internal and external sensations in your body.
- Improve well-being and quality of life.
- Increase self-esteem, self-compassion, and self-acceptance.
- Increase empathy.
- Increase happiness, confidence, hope, and a positive outlook on life.
- Increase relationship satisfaction.
- Reduce stress and psychological distress.
- Decrease fight-flight-freeze response.
- Decrease anxiety, depression, and mood disorders.
- Reduce fears, anxiety, or worry.
- Ability to feel your emotions and let them go.
- Cultivate strength.
- Obtain forgiveness of self and others.
- Reduce anger and aggression.
- Boost immune response.
- Reduce chronic pain or addiction.
- Reduce inflammation.
- Improve muscular strength.
- Open and stretch joints and muscles.
- Increase balance and flexibility.
- Increase blood flow and energy.
- Increase relaxation.

- Improve arthritic symptoms.
- Improve cardiovascular health.
- Lower blood pressure.
- Improve sleep.
- Improve breathing.
- Strengthen and heal internal organs.
- Increase life span.[28,29,30]

———

I hope this chapter about self-awareness, bodily awareness, mindfulness, and meditative practices has been insightful. Pick and choose whichever meditative practice calls to you, or try them all to find the right fit, but pick at least one. Meditation will give you the stepping stone to be present with your body, learn to listen to your body, and feel your experiences.

———

Join me in the next chapter as I discuss the concept of grounding—what it is, the different ways you can ground, and how it can support a deeper connection to your body.

6

GROUNDING—
BECOME ROOTED

*"Get yourself grounded and you can navigate
even the stormiest roads in peace."*

Steve Goodier

The concepts of grounding and centering are often used interchangeably, but there are slight differences. When you are centered, you are "anchored in both spirit and mind, logic and emotion, physical reality and the ethereal world."[1] When you are not centered, you feel lost, disconnected, and out of touch with yourself. This can occur if you externalize your experiences and fixate on the stories as if they are continually happening to you. This keeps you hyperfocused on your thoughts and emotions in relation to the narrative and perpetuates suffering. Alternatively, one can also stay stuck in the ethereal world by meditating excessively. You are living a human existence within a human body. You cannot keep yourself in a checked-out, blissful, dream-like state, as it keeps you disconnected from your physical reality and responsibilities. When you are centered, you are present and in balance with your thoughts and emotions, and feel calm and at peace—in the core of your being—with whatever is going on around you.

Have you ever heard someone say, "I feel ungrounded," or "I wish I were more grounded?" You may have thought this was an odd expression, but it is what your body instinctively is seeking. There are two ways you can be grounded. First, to be grounded means being true to yourself and comfortable and confident with who you are. It is being present, in tune, and connected with your body, while also connected to your external environment. Second, grounding, or earthing, connects you energetically by placing your bare feet or full body on the Earth. (See more on this later in the chapter.) Grounding allows you to clear your mind, calm your emotions, and recharge your body.[2]

Do you remember being a kid and running around barefoot in the dirt, and wiggling your feet into the grass? There is nothing like it. One of my favorite things to do is bury my feet in the sand, then feel the water rush up from the surf and cover my toes. As the water mixes with the sand, it squishes my feet deeper into the sand. This activity is not only pleasing to the senses, but it's beneficial. You are connecting more deeply to Mother Earth energetically. Mother Earth gives you strength and provides nourishment when you place your bare feet on her. When you ground, you feel fully embodied, stable, and a part of the greater Universe.

When someone first asked me to ground, the concept felt foreign to me. What do you mean *ground*? Sit on the ground? How is that going to help? For most of my life, I felt grounded but didn't know what it was or how to label it until I started seeking alternative therapies and teaching modalities. It was something that came naturally to me without knowing it was a *thing*. My body intuitively engaged in this way on its own. As a Virgo, I embody the earth sign. I know I've lived on Earth for several lifetimes. I have always felt a sense of maturity, deeper connection, and wisdom, even as a young child. I felt disconnected from my friends, and thought the things they did or said seemed immature or frivolous. I knew I was different. I felt more at home being by myself out in nature, with my feet on the ground, swimming in a body of water, and connecting with animals.

Before I discuss the science of grounding and the different ways you can ground, let's look at how we became disconnected from our body and Mother Earth.

Disconnection

To ground is to connect, yet we are often disconnected. When you have become disconnected from your body, especially if you have experienced dissociation, you are not fully present in the world. Some people have their head in the clouds. When you are with these types of people, they flit about, and you feel like you need to tether them. They may have difficulty forming complete sentences or staying on topic. They are go, go, go, but they are not grounded in their body. For some, this is their normal personality, or their elemental sign from birth—the air element. (See more on this later in this chapter.) For those who have experienced trauma, their body feels foreign or unsafe, so they disconnect. This state goes against their body's natural flow, and they have become disembodied, or separate from their body.

We have lost our connection to Mother Earth—to the ebb and flow of nature, to animals, to the plants and trees, the sun and moon cycles, the tides, and the seasons. We have lost our symbiotic relationship with Mother Earth. As she breathes, we breathe. She lets us know when it's time to eat and sleep, when to plant and when to sow, and her beauty shows the way toward connection and meaning in our life. Her knowledge and wisdom are endless. We cannot thrive, or survive, without her.

We rarely go barefoot anymore. Our feet are covered in socks, and tied up in shoes with rubber soles. We walk on pavement. Shoes and pavement interfere with grounding. We live and work far removed from nature in homes and office buildings.

For those of us living in colder climates, it's insanity to think about putting our bare feet on the ground when it's covered with snow. As such, for the majority of our life, we miss out on this necessary connection and healing modality.

There is also a spiritual connection to Mother Earth, which I will explore in Chapter 9. For now, think about how you can incorporate grounding into your life—when the weather is warm, or through the exercises in this chapter when you can't plant your feet on the ground.

Science of Grounding

Our body is electrical. We need Mother Earth's energy to fill up our energetic body with healthy negatively-charged healing electrons. By putting your bare feet on the ground, you absorb these electrons. It's like taking a handful of antioxidants—like Vitamins C and E.

The average human body contains around 37.2 trillion cells.[3] Yes, I said trillion! Grounding supports tissues and organ systems right down to the cellular function of the entire body. Your cells are made up of atoms that are either positively or negatively charged. Healthy atoms have more negatively-charged electrons. Atoms can become damaged when electrons are *stolen* from them. Damaged atoms become unstable and are known as free radicals. Damaged atoms can result from trauma, stress, infection, cell damage, inflammation, and from our toxic environments. You may have heard about free radicals. They cause damage because they race around in search of an electron to complete themselves, leading to a decline in your health. One way to repair the damage is by ingesting neutralizing antioxidants, like Vitamin C or Vitamin E, or large doses of negatively-charged electrons through grounding.[4]

Ways to Ground

How can you ground yourself when you can't get out in nature? Companies make shoes, wrist bands, bed sheets, and mats that support you to ground. You receive the same electrons as you would by putting your bare feet on the ground. Leather moccasins are good conductors; however, most people prefer more structured footwear. The cost of grounding items may be prohibitive as they can run in the hundreds of dollars. If you are interested in grounding products, search online, or check out Earthing.com or EarthingCanada.ca.

Instead, why not try something free and accessible to everyone. When it's warm, I urge you to take off your socks and shoes, and be a kid again. Feel your bare feet on the Earth. As moisture provides better-quality conduction, place your bare feet on wet dirt, wet sand, or damp grass to offer the best grounding experience. Lay your whole body down on the ground and rest. Feel the connection and energetic pull. Feel supported, held, and nurtured by Mother Earth. Being close to, or in, a body of water also increases negatively-charged electrons in your body. Stand next to a waterfall, place your feet in a river, or immerse yourself in the ocean for healing and nourishment.

Grounding—Not Only Electrons

Yes, I want you to get your bare feet on the grass to support increased negatively-charged electrons coursing through your body. More importantly, I want you to feel connected, centered, and embodied, which means performing grounding exercises in your home, especially when you feel separate from, or out of, your body.

Other Ways to Ground

Aromatherapy

Aromatherapy can support you to be grounded, centered, and connected with your body in the present moment. Find a store where you can sample some of the essential oils listed below. Choose one or several that you resonate with the most. Place a couple of drops of essential oil onto your hands and rub them together. Place your hands in front of your nose for a minute or two and breathe in the fragrance. Notice any shifts in your mood or body. Rub a couple of drops into the soles of your feet. Add a couple of drops to a footbath or full bath, along with Epsom salts (see more on this below), to help you ground. You can also put a couple of drops of essential oils in a diffuser, and meditate with the smell as you connect with Mother Earth.

Grounding and other essential oils can support all of your chakras. (See more details on chakras in Chapter 8.) To energetically support the root chakra, located at the end of your tailbone, apply a couple of drops to the back of your neck and rub down your spine to your coccyx (tailbone). When the root chakra is open, and not blocked, it is the seat of your safety and security, and supports your identity in the world. It is where you energetically ground and anchor yourself to Mother Earth.

Be conscious of allergies. Someone with severe allergies in spring or autumn may have a reaction to Chamomile. Also, stay away from scents that you know may trigger negative emotional reactions—scents that were in your immediate environment when something negative happened to you. For example, being sexually assaulted or abused in a lavender field or by someone wearing a specific cologne.

It is easy to search online to find essential oil blends to promote grounding. Some common singular grounding essential oils include:

- Angelica Root
- Benzoin
- Black Spruce
- Cedarwood
- Cinnamon
- Cypress
- Frankincense
- Myrrh
- Patchouli
- Petitgrain
- Roman Chamomile
- Rosewood
- Sandalwood
- Vetiver
- Ylang Ylang[5]

Deep Breathing

As previously discussed in Chapter 1, a stress response or trauma can accelerate lung function in the ANS as it regulates breathing. The SNS activates during inhalation, and the PNS activates during exhalation. As such, practicing two-to-one breathing can help to soothe the nervous system during times of stress or hyperarousal. This type of breathing involves exhaling for twice as long as you would take to inhale. For example, if you inhale for a count of four, you will exhale for a count of eight.[6] Start practicing the two-to-one breathing, or try some of the breathing exercises below.

Deep breathing can be grounding when done correctly. Being mindful of your breathing will allow you to break away from the automaticity of your breathing—which is usually shallow. In these exercises, you will inhale through your nose and exhale through your mouth. Feel the cool air enter your nose, go down your windpipe, expand your belly, expand your diaphragm and ribs, and fill your lungs up to your collar bone. Place your hand on your belly to ensure you breathe in the air first into your stomach, and then into your lungs. If you see your hand rise, you know you've gotten a full breath into your belly.

People tend to be mouth breathers, and breathe only into their chest. Shallow breathing can also result when a person is out of their Window of Tolerance, and in a fight-flight-freeze response. Continual shallow breathing can result in increased:

- Anxiety
- Blood Pressure
- Cardiovascular Problems
- Dry Mouth
- Fatigue
- Headaches
- Heart Rate
- Hyperventilation
- Illnesses and Infections
- Neck, Shoulder, and Back Pain
- Panic Attacks
- Respiratory Problems
- Stress[7]

People who have experienced intense, stressful events or trauma, and are out of their Window of Tolerance, can undergo anxiety or panic when being mindful and focusing on their breath. Try to breathe as naturally as possible while doing the breathing exercises, and don't exaggerate breathing. If you start to hyperventilate, go back to your normal breath, then continue trying the two-to-one breathing, or the breathing exercises below.

Earth Breath

Use the earth breath to ground and reduce stress.

- Find a quiet place where you can sit comfortably with your feet on the floor.
- Place one hand over your chest, and one hand over your belly.
- Breathe in through your nose to a slow count of four.
- Notice your belly expand, and then your diaphragm and rib cage. Finally, your chest lifts as you fill your lungs up to your collar bone.
- Pause before you exhale.
- Exhale slowly to a count of four.
- Pause before inhaling again.
- Complete ten full breaths.
- If thoughts, feelings, or memories come up, let them go, and return to the breath.[8]

Water Breath

Use the water breath to help you ground, to feel calm, and soothe emotions.

- Find a quiet place where you can sit comfortably with your feet on the floor.
- Breathe in through your nose and, as you do, imagine the air is silently and slowly streaming in like water over stones.
- Feel the breath flowing in and filling every cell in your body.
- Pause before you exhale.
- Release the breath silently and slowly in a steady stream out your mouth, envisioning it washing away any tension.

- Pause before inhaling again.
- Complete ten full breaths.
- Notice how your body feels now.[8]

Tree Breath

Use the tree breath to help you ground.

- Stand up straight and relaxed with your arms at your side.
- Imagine your body and legs are the trunks of a tree, and your feet are growing roots that connect you to Mother Earth.
- As you breathe in, imagine life-force energy coming up through Mother Earth into the soles of your feet.
- With each inhale, draw up the energy into your legs and the core of your body.
- As you feel the energy rise into your hips, extend your hands straight out to the sides of your body and raise them until they reach above your head.
- Imagine your arms as the branches of the tree.
- See them reach over your head as they draw in energy from the sun's rays.
- Pause at the top of the inhale.
- As you exhale, imagine the sun's energy coming down your body.
- Let the sunshine fill your body, legs, and out your feet into Mother Earth.
- Pause before inhaling again.
- Complete ten full breaths.
- Notice your body feeling more grounded and stable.[8]

Epsom Salt Baths

For those who are sensitive, and take on other people's energy, grounding is a way to clear those energies. If you have a history of trauma, and your Window of Tolerance is smaller, you may experience more heightened emotions, and a need to be more hypervigilant in the world. Epsom salt baths not only relax muscles and help detoxify the body, but are also calming and grounding. The warm water soothes the SNS (your fight-flight-freeze response), and the magnesium relaxes muscles and supports the proper function of electrical nerve impulses. You need to have efficient electrical nerve impulses in your brain. One acute stressor can affect the cerebellum's performance, a part of the brain responsible for motor movement and emotional and cognitive functioning.[4]

Sitting in the bath is an excellent opportunity to incorporate mindfulness. Focus on your breath, and notice the sensations in your body as your skin interacts with the water. Feel the temperature of the water on your skin. Glide your hand and legs through the water to notice the different sensations and pressure you feel. Incorporating this form of grounding into your life will support your mental, emotional, and physiological well-being.

Food

Food is also grounding. However, for some, if they feel anxious, they may not feel hungry, or the thought of food makes them feel nauseated. I do not expect you to have a huge meal, but it can help you feel more grounded and connected to your body if you eat something small. It's essential to choose the right type of food—nothing sugary or sweet. A handful of nuts, roasted chickpeas, a small cube of cheese, or other protein, would be ideal. Some types of fruit, like bananas, can be grounding for some people. For others, it may result in an insulin spike leading to more heightened energy in their body. Those who can eat a full meal, think of what gave you an emotional hug as a child. Maybe something your mom made—thick soups, stews, or Shepherd's Pie. Be conscious of your reaction to various foods. It will help you see what works best for your body. Food can help bring comfort, grounding, and connection with the body as long as it's not a coping strategy to ignore uncomfortable thoughts, emotions, sensations, or experiences. Food is not to be used to disconnect from your body, or soothe emotions. It is to ground you, and return you to the state of rest-and-digest.

Gemstones

Grounding stones and crystals are also connected with the root chakra, and help drain unwanted energies from the body into Mother Earth. They support you to feel calm, balance energy levels, provide stability, and ground. You can carry the crystal in your pocket, place it in your office or a room in your home, or wear it as jewelry in the form of a bracelet, necklace, or earrings. A few common grounding crystals include:

- Apache Tears
- Black Obsidian
- Black Tourmaline
- Bloodstone
- Carnelian
- Hematite
- Jade
- Red Calcite
- Red Jasper
- Ruby
- Smoky Quartz
- Tiger's Eye[9]

Embodied Exercise

This exercise will help you ground using a gemstone.

- Have a pen and paper handy to write down anything that comes up.
- Find a quiet place where you can be alone for several minutes.
- Notice how you feel in your body before you begin.
- Take a crystal or a stone from Mother Earth and place it in the palm of your hand.
- Sit upright in a chair and plant your feet firmly on the ground.
- Close your eyes. Take a couple of deep breaths in through your nose, down your chest, into your belly, and out your mouth.
- Feel the sensation of the crystal or stone in your hand.
- Move the crystal or stone around, and notice the texture. Is it smooth or rough?
- How big is it? How much room does it take up in your palm?
- Does it have a temperature? Is it cold or warm?
- What is the weight of the crystal or stone? How heavy or light does it feel?
- Does it have energy? Does it vibrate?
- Hold the crystal for several minutes, and notice any shifts in your body as you hold it.
- When you feel ready to return to the room, slowly take your time, and move your fingers and toes.
- Then take another couple of deep breaths and open your eyes.

Write in your journal what came up—thoughts, memories, or images. Did you notice any shifts in your body's energy? Do you feel more grounded? If not, keep practicing and you will start to feel slight energetic shifts in your body.

Meditation

I discussed mindfulness and meditation in Chapter 5 in great detail, but I wanted to give you a couple of exercises for using meditation to ground. Guided meditations can help you explore your body so you can feel more grounded and connected. A guided grounding meditation can allow you to focus on yourself, and your natural rhythms, as you connect with the energies of Mother Earth. Below is a meditation to help you ground, and connect to your body and Mother Earth.

Embodied Exercise

You can do these meditations while sitting somewhere comfortable inside your home. If you are outside, you can do this while standing barefoot on the grass, lying on the ground, or with your back leaning against a tree for even deeper connection and grounding.

Tree Meditation

- Take a moment to notice how you feel in your body.
- Close your eyes. Place your hand on your stomach and take a couple of deep breaths.
- Feel your breath enter through your nose, down your chest, and into your belly.
- Feel your hand on your belly rising with each deep inhalation.

- After several breaths, imagine your feet growing roots that connect deep into Mother Earth. Big, thick roots that curl around each other, and go down deep into Earth's core.

- Allow yourself to release any uncomfortable feelings (sadness, anger, frustration) or sensations (pain, stress). Let them flow out of your body down through the roots into Mother Earth.

- Now imagine life-giving energy from the magma deep in Mother Earth's core coming up through the roots into the heels of your feet.

- Let it co-mingle with your blood and fill every cell in your body. Breathe it into every cell.

- Now, let it come up your ankles, calves, thighs, and into your hips. Then, up through your torso and back. Up into your shoulders, down your arms, and out your fingertips. Up into your throat, face, and head, and shooting out the top of your head like a geyser.

- Feel the warmth, connection, and unconditional love pour into you from Pachamama.

- Take in the feeling of being supported and grounded.

- Take two more deep healing breaths.

- When you are ready to return, wiggle your toes and fingers.

- Take your time opening your eyes.

Mountain Meditation

- Take a moment to notice how you feel in your body.

- Close your eyes. Place your hand on your stomach, and take a couple of deep breaths.

- Feel your breath enter through your nose, down your chest, and down into your belly.
- Feel the hand on your belly rising with each deep inhalation.
- Envision a majestic mountain with all its trees, rocks, and peaks. Are there waterfalls? Is there snow?
- Feel into its weight—unmovable, solid, stable, and deeply grounded with Mother Earth.
- Imagine you becoming the mountain. Feel the mountain within you.
- No matter what happens around you, you feel calm, secure, peaceful, strong, stable, and unwavering.
- As seasons or storms pass, observe, but do not engage.
- No matter what internal or external experience you have, you can live in the stillness, and feel grounded.
- Before opening your eyes, feel how calm and centered you are now.
- When you are ready, let yourself return to the room and open your eyes.[10]

Notice how it feels in your body now. Did anything shift? Do you feel more solid or grounded in your body? Are you more relaxed or calm? If not, that's okay. It may take further practice, or for you to incorporate some of the other grounding techniques.

Did you get any thoughts, messages, images, or memories? If so, take a few moments to journal about what came up during this experience.

Return to these grounding meditations as often as you like to help you feel more embodied and grounded.

I discussed body-scan meditation in Chapter 5. It is a grounding meditation that incorporates a body scan of all parts of your body. This meditation provides grounding energy within your body so you feel more connected and embodied.

Smudging

Smudging is the burning of a sacred plant, typically sage, to help cleanse and purify negative energy from a person or place. Think of smudging as an energetic bath, similar to using water to clean your body in a bath or shower. Smudging incorporates four elements:

1. The first element is the shell, typically an abalone shell, which represents water.
2. The second element involves four sacred plants: cedar, sage, sweetgrass, or tobacco, which are gifts provided by Mother Earth.
3. The third element is fire from the lighting of the plant.
4. The fourth element is the smoke from the burning plant, which represents air.[11]

Sage often comes in pre-tied bundles, and can be lit intact. If you have loose sage, form it into a small ball with your hands, and place it in an abalone shell or a ceramic bowl. Light the sage, preferably using a wooden match, and then fan it over your body with your hands or a feather. Typical areas to focus on include:

- Top of the head
- Eyes, ears, and mouth
- Neck
- Heart center
- Stomach
- Down the arms and legs

- Under the feet
- Around the back

It's also supportive for those with long hair to let the smoke filter through the hair, as it can carry stuck negative energy. Gently breathe in the smoke as it cascades around your body. Feel yourself become relaxed, calm, centered, and grounded.

You can also smudge your living area or workspace. Ensure all cupboards and closet doors are open, and close any windows. Start from the left side of the front door. Move in a clockwise manner throughout all the rooms returning to the front door, and pushing the smoke out the front door. You can use your hand or a feather. Focus on corners and closets as this is where negative energy can get stuck. If you are intuitive or sensitive to energies, you will likely know when a place feels heavy. If you move into a new space, or argue with someone, this is an excellent way to remove the negative energy. Listen to your body, and when an area doesn't feel clear, smudge it to return to balance. Notice how your body feels in the space before and after it has been smudged. There will likely be a noticeable difference.

The ashes absorb negative thoughts, feelings, and energy. Immediately dispose of the ashes outside on the land, don't keep negative energy stored in your home.[11] By returning the ashes to Mother Earth, you let her compost the negative energy as fuel for re-growth and, in so doing, transform yourself to a healed state.

Your home is a mirror and representation of your body. If your home is cluttered, there will be more places for energy to get stuck. Take the time before you smudge to clear the clutter. As you remove the clutter in your home, you also clear away the negative thoughts and feelings stored in your body.

To clear away the clutter, set up three boxes—one for the garbage, one for donation, and one for things you need or want but don't know where to put. Go through each room, placing wanted items in their proper place and unwanted items in the appropriate box. Take the box of garbage outside and dump it into the bin. Place the donation box in your car to take to a local shelter, or call someone to pick it up. Go through each item in the third box and decide where it best belongs. Don't keep damaged, unwanted, or never-to-be-used stuff in your home.

Smudging also supports the release of negative ions allowing you to feel grounded without stepping on the land. Our electronics, appliances, and furniture are filled with positive ions, along with dust, odors, bacteria, viruses, dust, mold, pet dander, pollen, and cigarette or marijuana smoke. The sage's negative ions attach to these positively charged particles rendering them too heavy to stay airborne. They fall to the floor, or attach to nearby surfaces, where they can no longer be inhaled.[12]

Along with feeling more grounded and centered in your body, smudging with sage has several health benefits:

- Achieve a healed state.
- Anti-aging effects from the negative ions as they fight off free radicals.
- Antidepressant effects similar to prescription antidepressants.
- Antimicrobial and antibacterial properties, which can help to remove bacteria, viruses, mold, fungi, and common allergens.
- Boost energy level, and increase positivity.
- Calming and relaxing effects.
- Cleanse objects (such as second-hand items), or empower objects (such as crystals or healing stones). (See more in Chapter 9.)

- Connect spiritually.
- Dispel negative energy from others, troubling experiences, wounds, and trauma.
- Enhance intuition.
- Improve cognitive functions for memory and focus.
- Improve your mood, and eliminate negative thoughts and feelings.
- Increase well-being.
- Lower blood pressure and normalize breathing.
- Reduce stress and alleviate pain.
- Soothe anxiety and improve sleep.[12,13]

Sound

Sound healing is believed to date as far back as Ancient Greece. Vibrational waves from sound are felt in the body, and can heal and release blocked energy. There are several different types of sound modalities to help you ground.

Chanting and Mantras

There are many chants and mantras used in Buddhist teachings for bringing in peace, compassion, enlightenment, gratitude, and devotion. As discussed in Chapter 5, a simple mantra used for grounding is to chant *Om* repeatedly. By chanting Om, you recognize your connection to everything in the world and the Universe.[14]

Embodied Exercise

This is an exercise for chanting Om for grounding.

- Sit in a chair, or cross-legged on the floor, and close your eyes.
- Touch your pinky to your thumb on each hand, and gently rest your hands with your palms facing up on your thighs or knees. There are several hand mudras to draw you mindfully inward, and reinforce healing states of mind. "The thumb symbolizes space; the index is air; the middle finger is fire; the ring finger is water; and the pinky stands for earth."[15]
- Repeat Om as many times as you are able. As a reminder:

  "When pronounced correctly, *Om* has four syllables and is pronounced AUM, beginning in the solar plexus and sending vibrations up into the chest. The second syllable – U – moves the sound up into the throat as the sound moves forward along the upper palate. The third syllable – M – is a prolonged syllable and brings the vibration through the upper chakras as the teeth come together to touch gently. The final syllable is the deep silence of the Infinite as the overall vibration rises through the body and into the Universe."[14]

Dancing

Grounding and connecting with your body through dance can be a freeing and euphoric experience. Allow yourself to feel fully into the rhythm of the music. Let your limbs and body move to the sound of the music as it feels called to express itself. Don't hold back. Let go of judgment, criticism, and inhibitions. Take a deep breath, and shake out your limbs. Become centered by feeling into your core, and connecting with the lower half of your stomach—your center of gravity. Feel the strength of your thigh muscles, and let your feet sink deep into the floor as you move. Don't just move your limbs—move your hair, neck, shoulders, wrists, fingers, body, hips, and toes. Let go of every part of you, and let the music move through you. Feel the vibration as it fills every cell in your body. Let go of your thoughts. Be one with the sound of the music and the movement of your body.

Check out the album *Drumsex* by Brent Lewis. *Dinner at the Sugarbush* is my favorite to get your body moving and to feel grounded. You won't be able to stop every part of your body from moving to the drum and rhythm.

Drumming

During drumming, the left and right hemispheres become synchronized by transmitting rhythmic energy—thus, strengthening your intuition. Whether you drum or listen to drumming, you generate new neural pathways in the brain, which leads to a more accurate sense of self-awareness. Drumming can increase alpha brainwaves, helping you feel relaxed and calm. Drumming can align your body and mind, help you feel more connected, and ground you to the natural rhythm and flow of Mother Earth.[16] If you don't have a drum, check in your community for drumming circles you can attend.

Singing Bowls

Crystal or Tibetan singing bowls promote healing through the vibrational frequencies generated by the sound. "Healing processes are initiated through entraining our brainwaves to synchronise with the perfect resonance of the bowls."[17] Sounds from the bowl entrain the brain—moving the brain into theta brainwave frequencies. These frequencies induce relaxation, increase intuition, mental and emotional harmony, optimize energy flow, self-healing, and increase self-awareness of the mind-body connection.[17] If you don't have a singing bowl, listen to a grounding meditation that uses a crystal or Tibetan singing bowl.

Sound Therapies

Below are several different types of sound therapies for reference:

- Vibroacoustic therapy has the person lie on a recliner, mat, or mattress with speakers embedded in them to transmit music and sound vibrations directly to their body.
- Guided meditations help a person meditate through voiced instruction, and include chanting, mantras, or prayers.
- Neurologic music therapy includes listening, singing, creating, or moving to music.
- Bonny method uses guided imagery and classical music.
- Nordoff-Robbins treats the person with familiar music, creates new music together, and then puts on a performance.
- Tibetan monks use singing bowl therapy for rituals and meditation.
- Tuning fork therapy is similar to acupuncture, and uses sound frequencies to stimulate meridian points on a person's body.
- Brainwave entrainment uses pulsing sounds to align brainwaves to the frequency of the beat.[18]

—◦◦◦—

Incorporate chants, mantras, drumming, crystal or Tibetan singing bowls, or other sound therapies (like singing) into your grounding practice to feel more connected, relaxed, and energetically cleansed. Remember to be mindful as you incorporate these practices. Focus on being present in the moment. Hear the sounds coming into your ears, or the sounds coming from your lungs and mouth. Feel how the vibrations interact and resonate with your body. You may experience thoughts, emotions, body sensations, images, or memories. Note anything that comes up, and journal about it afterward.

Aikido

When I did my Master's degree in Counseling Psychology, we were required to take Aikido classes. Aikido is a Japanese martial art. The founding father of Aikido, Morihei Ueshiba, created this martial art with the philosophy that a person should protect themselves while not bringing injury to their attacker. Aikido often translates to "the way of unifying [with] life energy,"[19] or as "the way of harmonious spirit."[20] This martial art doesn't use force. It uses fluidity of movement to disable the attacker. You use the attacker's energy and center of gravity in such a way that by slightly moving to the side, along with specific hand movements, you can propel them onto their back with little exertion. If you've never seen it, I suggest you check out a video online. It's quite impressive.

In my Aikido class, we looked at how people present differently in their body according to a specific element. We *became* the elements physically in our body. For example, when I was the earth element, I practiced feeling solid, heavy, and grounded in my body. We all moved around the room and interacted with other elements. We experienced what it was like for earth to connect with another earth, air, fire, or water element. Some element relationships were harmonious, and other elements were harder to connect with.

When connecting with another earth element, it felt easy, comforting. Both of us took up our natural boundary and held our space, not trying to inflict ourselves on the other person.

When trying to connect with the person who represented the air element, it was difficult because they were out of their body. I couldn't solidly connect with them. It was difficult to make and keep eye contact. The water element was fluid, and went with the flow; ever moving, it was hard to stay connected with them. The fire element crossed my personal boundary. They stayed close to my body and were in my face; it felt hard to manage that much intensity.

Elements

Each person's astrological sign is associated with a specific element. For Taurus, Virgo, and Capricorn, the element is earth. For Gemini, Libra, and Aquarius, the element is air. For Aries, Leo, and Sagittarius, the element is fire. For Cancer, Scorpio, and Pisces, the element is water.

By understanding your and other people's core element, you will discern why people display certain qualities, and why they interact and view the world from this perspective. This understanding can help you be less judgmental of yourself and others, and more open to other people's viewpoints.

Earth

Someone who has earth energy presents as calm, compassionate, loyal, dependable, resilient, and supportive. They are rooted in the earth element, and present as stable. Being rooted allows them to support those they come into contact with. The earth element is about growth, and they do this by taking one step at a time in a constructive manner. Because changes are slow, they tend to be permanent. You feel yourself relax around them. Instinctively, you let out a breath of air that you feel you've been holding. It feels like they are anchoring you to this world. It feels as if you are being enveloped or wrapped in a warm blanket. This person is typically unwavering in their way of being. Their opinions, ideas, and standards are constant. They don't get easily ruffled or shaken by other people's demands or energies. They feel trustworthy, and you feel safe and secure around them. They are self-sacrificing, want to be of service, and do anything to support their friends and family. They may be good listeners, and you may find yourself going to them for guidance and support. However, they can be boring, conservative, and rigid with rules and regulations. Once they make up their mind about something, it is difficult to change it.[21,22]

You may not be an earth element that can naturally connect to grounding energies, but that doesn't mean you can't take time daily to feel grounded.

Air

Have you ever met someone who flits around from one thing to the next? They seem elusive, and you can't quite hold them down. They seem to be living in the stars. People born under the air element can change and shift. However, they want the change to happen immediately, and can use manipulation to get their way. They are always in motion, mentally, emotionally, and physically. They are extremely intelligent, express their ideas well, effectively problem solve, and come up with several practical solutions. The air element transforms, and contains the breath of life. These people are always full of new ideas and plans, and can transform the details of projects. However, like the wind, they can also uproot things from their foundation. They have no attachment to anything, and may appear devoid of emotion. They have hyperactive minds with endless thoughts and ideas that are hard to keep track of. If crossed, they can blow you right over. It can be hard to feel connected to this completely detached and ungrounded elemental energy. You may feel ignored or overlooked around an air person. Staying grounded around these individuals can help to anchor you, so you don't start to drift away from your core.[21,23]

Fire

The fire element is exactly what you'd expect. People born in this element glow and radiate the energy of the sun. Their energy is constantly burning within them. They are doers, and always seem to be involved in starting a new project. They are incredibly enthusiastic and go-getters. There is an urgency to everything they do. They are leaders, and enjoy being center stage. Intuition is a big part of the fire element, and they can perceptively know things. They have an inner knowing of what they need to do, but have difficulty finding rational words to explain it to others. They can be charming and witty, and make friends easily. They are straightforward with their opinions, which can sometimes feel harsh and critical. They have strong egos that need to be acknowledged. They are good communicators, but insist on people acknowledging their point of view. They don't like to be ignored, and crave attention. Their overconfidence can sometimes alienate them from groups if it is perceived as an inability to cooperate. It can sometimes be difficult to deal with the almost overbearing force of the fire element. As such, grounding before being in the presence of a fire sign can support you to speak your mind, and have your opinions acknowledged, and not brushed aside.[21,24]

Water

People with the water element display characteristics of flowing, changing, and renewing. Water is fluid, as are the emotions of people born with this element. As such, they are guided by their emotions, and make decisions influenced solely by their emotions. Their hearts feel everything deeply, and they are great empathizers. Water is healing, and people with this element have a natural healing gift. They are observant, and emphasize attention to detail. They are creative, and can bring new life to projects. They are often artistically inclined. They are governed and affected by the moon and its cycles. They perceive things more instinctively, and react that way too. Being extremely sensitive, they have difficulty controlling emotions, which results in emotional highs and lows from one minute to the next. Strong emotion leaves little room for logic and reasoning. They need to feel secure in relationships, which can often feel overly possessive. Being grounded with these individuals can help you not take on their emotional energy as your own, and hold your physical boundary from their emotional needs.[21,25]

Maybe through your astrological sign, or by the descriptions listed above, you already connect to one of these elements. You may feel like, "Yes, that's totally me, I'm a water element." Of course, there is so much more to astrology, than your sign's element, that makes up the type of individual you are and the personality you have. Sometimes, the result of trauma, neglect, abuse, lack of attachment, lack of boundaries, being stuck in your head, or being emotionally overwhelmed, influences your natural way of being in the world. Maybe you were the element associated with your sign, but it no longer resonates with you due to your experiences.

Becoming more embodied requires you to connect with the earth element, even if your sign is air, fire, or water. To feel more grounded and connected to your body, connecting with the earth element is critical. How can you bring the earth element into your life as a means of support?

Embodied Exercise

The following are some questions to consider about your element:

- How does your element show up in your life? How does it influence the way you are in the world?
- Does it feel natural to you?
- How does it support you?

- How does it hinder you?
- Does it help you to connect with your body? With other people? If not, what needs to change for you to do so?

The earth element, and being grounded, is not the only way to be. It's not about changing your personality or being inauthentic. It's about noticing areas where you may not be as connected or grounded, and using the earth elements' traits in your life to help you feel more connected to your body and others.

Mother Earth

In my shamanic teachings, we honor all the elements, but especially Mother Earth. Ceremonies take place in nature, on the land where you can connect to its power and be grounded. Being energetically connected to Mother Earth, and all of nature, is a profound experience. Mother Earth is a living, breathing entity. Connecting with Mother Earth allows you to feel connected to something beyond yourself. It is how nature and Mother Earth can inform you—to see yourself in a different light. It is a powerful and beautiful experience. Nature is awe-inspiring.

Have you ever felt so connected to nature it felt like a euphoric or spiritual experience? Have you ever been mesmerized by a rainbow, rays of light coming through the clouds, a perfectly bloomed flower, or the expanse of a valley with all the trees, water, and mountains surrounding it? See how infinitely abundant the world is with all its majesty. As you connect and ground with nature, it makes you smile, lifts your heart, and moves you in a profoundly emotional way. Existential thoughts may have you feeling insignificant or small, but they can also bring you to a knowing that we are all connected, all revered, all one being. It lets you know there is more than you, and your experience, on this planet. The world is vast. There is so much beauty that it can bring you to tears.

For me, this was the one thing I didn't realize was missing from my life. Growing up in a traditional religious household, I missed out on the spiritual connection to Mother Earth, and what she offers us—unconditional love and support. Being connected to the land was a deep longing, and I found that connection through ceremonies and shamanic teachings. A spiritual connection to Mother Earth is rewarding. I feel supported, held, nurtured, and unconditionally loved by Pachamama.

Mother Earth provides unconditional love, nurturing, and healing. When you walk in nature, speak your worries, your cares, your concerns, or whatever is troubling you to her. Feel every step as you walk. Feel that deep connection as you breathe in and out. Imagine Mother Earth taking your words, and mulching them into fertilizer to feed the soil. You are not harming her in doing so. You are releasing what no longer serves you. Feel the negative energy you've been holding onto drain out with every word you speak. Don't worry about whether or not there are people around. If there are, you can whisper, but it's important to vocalize your worries, not just keep them in your head. Most people have Bluetooth earbuds or headphones, and it looks like they are talking to themselves, but they are talking to someone on the phone. No one knows or cares what you are doing or saying. When done speaking what needs to be released, look around you and breathe in the beauty and nourishment Mother Earth provides. Breathe in her love and feel restored and grateful.

Benefits of Grounding

There are several benefits to incorporating grounding into your life:

- Calm the nervous system from a fight-flight-freeze response (SNS) to a rest-and-digest response (PNS).
- Connect you to your body.
- Connect you to the present moment.
- Connect you spiritually to Mother Earth.
- Cope with dissociation, flashbacks, nightmares, or other PTSD symptoms.
- Decrease anxiety, racing thoughts, emotional overwhelm.
- Decrease chronic health conditions.
- Decrease inflammation.
- Release toxins.
- Improve immune function.
- Improve sleep.
- Increase energy.
- Manage pain.
- Normalize cortisol and reduce your stress response.[3]

—◦◦◦—

How can you feel like you are a part of something greater than yourself, and connected, when you don't have adequate support systems or resources in your life? Engage in grounding techniques and spend time in nature to feel supported by Mother Earth. You are not alone. You are one with Mother Earth and the Universe.

I hope you utilize the exercises in this chapter to allow your body to unite with Mother Earth, and become grounded. These exercises will bring you a greater connection to your body and a sense of calm and peace in your whole being.

—◦◦◦—

In the next chapter, I explore the different senses and sensations you can feel in your body, and I discuss intuition and extrasensory perception.

7

SENSES—
FROM THE PHYSICAL
TO THE MYSTICAL

"Lose your mind and come to your senses."

Fritz Perls

*"One of the most useful and important ways to be able
to use your psychic gifts is to learn how to read
what's happening in your very own body."*

Catherine Carrigan

Reiki is a light-touch spiritual practice that connects you to Ki (also known as chi or qi) energy, or universal life-force energy. (See Chapter 8 for more on Reiki.) When I provide Reiki for a client, I connect with all my senses. I engage with the sensations I feel in my body, my intuition or inner knowing, and extrasensory perception.

Self-awareness is crucial. I become mindful and present in the moment. My mindfulness state is obtained, first, by smudging myself and the room using sage. As stated in Chapter 6, smudging is a traditional indigenous ceremony done to cleanse yourself and your space from negative energy, thoughts, and emotions. Second, I open sacred space to set the intention for the Reiki treatment, and to connect with Spirit. (See Chapter 9 on how to open sacred space.) When I connect with Spirit, I open my intuition and extrasensory perception.

These processes set the stage for me to get out of my ego, and to connect beyond myself to see what is happening physically, energetically, and spiritually for my client. I become an open vessel for whatever needs to transpire in the session. Being open doesn't mean I detach from myself or my experience. On the contrary, I become hyperaware of what I see, hear, feel, and know beyond rational thought. These are the four *clairs*, which will be discussed later in this chapter. Whether in words, images, or knowing, whatever comes up is what I impart to my client so they can understand what is happening in their body and world.

A big part of Reiki is being attuned to the energies I experience in my hands as I move them over my client's body. Either I lightly touch certain points, or hover my hands over these same points, being conscious of my client's personal boundaries. Being mindful and connected in the present moment allows me to discern the subtle energy shifts and sensations I feel, and where to place my attention. It enables me to engage with all my physical and spiritual senses to discern my client's experience.

Your Eight Senses

Most people are familiar with the five senses: sight, sound, smell, taste, and touch. However, I wanted to include three more: vestibular, proprioception, and interoception. Knowing these will give you a more well-rounded understanding of how your senses play a part in connecting with your body.

Visual

The visual system is responsible for seeing. Visual information can include color (unless you are color blind), shape, orientation, and motion.[1] Light reflects off an object to the eye. Then the lens of the eye bends the light, and focuses on the retina, which is full of nerve cells. These cells include cones and rods. Cones translate light into colors, central vision, and details. Rods translate light into motion and peripheral vision.[2]

Auditory

The auditory system is responsible for hearing. "Sound is produced when an object vibrates, creating a pressure wave."[3] Sound waves can only travel through a medium, such as air, water, or a solid form. You measure sound through frequency and amplitude. Frequency, also known as pitch, is the speed of vibration. Frequency units are called hertz (Hz). Humans can hear sounds ranging from 20 to 20 thousand Hz. Anything above 20 thousand Hz is considered ultrasound. Dogs can hear ultrasonic frequencies as high as 45 thousand Hz. As such, some sounds are inaudible to the human ear, like a dog whistle. Anything below 20 Hz is known as infrasound. Low-frequency sounds travel farther, and are ideal for long-distance communication. Amplitude is the size of the vibration, which determines the loudness or volume. You measure amplitude in decibels (dB), which is the sound pressure level or intensity. A normal speaking voice is around 60 dB, while a rock concert, about 125 dB, can cause damage to the human ear.[3,4]

Olfactory

The olfactory system is responsible for processing smell. Humans have over 400 smelling receptors, and researchers suggest we can detect over one trillion scents.[2] Wow, that's a lot of smells! Humans are about as good as dogs when it comes to a sense of smell. The olfactory bulb transmits smell from the nose to the brain. The olfactory bulb has four functions:

1. To distinguish between odors.
2. To increase your ability to detect odors.
3. To filter out background odors.
4. To allow higher brain areas related to arousal and attention to modify their ability to distinguish and detect odors.[1]

Memories may come to the surface as you engage with your senses. Smell, being the most primal sense, is the strongest when it comes to evoking memories, but not the only one. There is a close connection between taste and smell. Have you ever tasted something, and it took you back to your mother's cooking? Senses are powerful for evoking memories.

Gustatory

The gustatory system is responsible for your sense of taste. A part of your survival system, it helps you to differentiate between safe and harmful foods. You can distinguish four different tastes: sweet, salty, bitter, and sour. Humans prefer sweet and salty over bitter and sour. Salt is critical for regulating your internal body processes. Sweet taste signals carbohydrates. They are high in calories, and were needed for survival back in our caveperson days when we likely experienced long periods of food scarcity. The ability to detect bitter and sour foods could signal that a plant was poisonous or rotten. If you're like me, and like watching the Food Network, then you have likely heard of the fifth taste—umami or savory. Some examples of umami include: meat, aged cheese, seaweed, mushroom, or kimchi. Although spicy food is not always hot or painful, it is not considered a taste. It is a pain signal. You sense taste mostly through taste buds on your tongue. However, your sense of smell is also involved, as they both use the same types of receptors in the brain. If you lose your sense of smell, your sense of taste will not function and food will become tasteless. Adults have roughly two thousand to four thousand taste buds. The tongue's sides are more sensitive than the middle, but you can sense all five tastes anywhere on the tongue.[1,2]

Tactile

The tactile system is responsible for processing touch. You receive touch sensations in the somatosensory cortex part of the brain from the neurons on your skin. "The body sends tactile information to the somatosensory cortex through neural pathways to the spinal cord, the brain stem, and the thalamus."[1] The somatosensory cortex integrates touch, pressure, temperature, light touch, vibration, and pain through different skin receptors.[1,2]

Vestibular

The vestibular system is responsible for balance and the orientation of your head in space. It informs you about movement, and the position of your head in relation to gravity. Movement allows you to detect rotation and linear directionality through acceleration and deceleration. The vestibular system helps keep you upright, and controls your eye movements. It contains three semicircular canals in each ear.

1. The horizontal canal detects rotation around a vertical axis, like doing a pirouette.
2. The anterior semicircular canal detects movement in the forward and backward plane, like nodding your head.
3. The posterior canal detects movement in the frontal plane, like doing a cartwheel.

The vestibular system has several functions:

- Movement of head, eyes, and posture.
- Allow eyes to stay fixed on a moving object, while staying in focus.
- Adjust circulation and breathing when the body moves to a new position.
- Quick reflexes with balance.
- Control head and body motor responses.[1]

Proprioception

The proprioception system is responsible for sensations and movement of muscles and joints. It understands where your body is in space. It senses position, location, orientation, and movement. Neurons receive sensory information in the inner ear to help detect motion and orientation. Proprioception can become impaired if you are overly tired, from an overdose of vitamin B6, chemotherapy, or brain injury. People with poor proprioception may be clumsy or uncoordinated. There is also spiritual proprioception, which is the ability to hold your center when you are in higher forms of consciousness. In spiritual proprioception, you sense your connection to God and the Universe. Typically, you do not notice your proprioception sense because you become habituated, desensitized, or adapted to sensory stimuli that are continuously present. This ability is advantageous because it allows you to focus on other concerns while sensations continue unnoticed in the background.[1,2]

Interoception

The interoception system is responsible for processing sensations related to the physiological or physical condition of the body. Interoceptors, or internal sensors, allow you to sense how your internal organs are feeling. For example, hunger and thirst. It detects responses to guide the regulation of your heart rate, hunger, respiration, and elimination. It incorporates the vestibular and proprioception senses to determine how you perceive your body. For example, if you can detect a hunger sensation, it prompts you to eat, but you will not die if you don't eat immediately. It can create "distinct feelings from the body including pain, temperature, itch, muscular and visceral sensations, vasomotor activity, hunger, thirst, and the need for air."[1] It also provides the basis for subjective feelings of one's emotional awareness. Interoception is the foundation for subjective feelings, emotion, and self-awareness.[1]

Things to Notice When You Engage With Your Senses

As I ask you to be more mindful and present with your senses, there are some things you need to keep in mind—your thoughts, emotions, and body sensations. Sometimes your experience will be positive. Other times, it may not. Being mindful and present with your senses is an essential part of connecting, and becoming embodied. When you become self-aware, you will attune to your body's experience with people, objects, and events. You will start to recognize how informed and affected your body is, whether positively, negatively, or neutrally.

Check in with your thoughts. What are you saying to yourself as you engage with the sense? Notice if there is judgment. If there is, try to remove your judgment. Say something factual about your experience instead. Something may be displeasing to you, but you can notice it without criticism. You don't have to degrade something to make it relevant. For example, "Rap music causes me to have a headache." Instead of, "Rap music is the worst music ever." For many, rap music is appealing, but for African-American youth, it can be life-affirming.

Also, check in with your thoughts to see if there is judgment toward yourself. For example, "I'm so stupid I can't feel sensations in my body." Be compassionate toward yourself. You are learning something new. Disconnection from your body has occurred for many years. As such, it will take time to connect with your body, and to understand what you are experiencing. Don't give up—the rewards are well worth it.

Check in with your emotions. What emotions arise in you as you engage with the sense? When you start to pay attention to your senses, you will experience sensations in your body, which will likely evoke emotions. Notice which emotions you feel as a result of your experience with a particular sense.

Check in with the sensations in your body. (See the next section for more detail.) As you engage with your senses, you will experience sensations in your body. Notice the sensation, state the sensation you are feeling, then let it go, and continue being mindful of your experience. For example, "My heart is racing as I watch this scary movie."

Be present with the sensation, and notice if it supports you. If it does not, then ask yourself why you are engaging in an uncomfortable situation. Give yourself permission to remove yourself from a troubling situation. If you can't remove yourself from the situation, how can you shift your experience to support your body's comfort? When you gain a deeper connection with your body, you will quickly know when something is off for you. Ask yourself, "What is going on here? Is it something I am experiencing in this moment?" If so, you have the power to alter your experience to support yourself.

Using Your Senses to Become More Embodied

I realize the above description of the senses is relatively dry and technical. You may be thinking, "Why discuss the technical part at all? How does that relate to my ability to connect with my body? Who cares that the light reflects off the object and goes through the lens to hit the retina, and you can see through cones and rods?" Not having to think about automatic processes is precisely the point. The body does these things automatically, and you don't have to think about the process. You don't have to pay attention to the senses in your body because they just happen. Here is where mindfulness comes into play. You need to become present with your senses, understand them, feel them, and engage with them in a more meaningful and impactful way so you can find an authentic sense of connection. You have to take a moment to feel into a sense, and the sensations that arise to connect with your experience thoroughly. Below, I discuss how to engage and connect with each of the different senses more fully.

Sight

When you stop to take the time to see something, and deeply connect with the sense of sight, look at it mindfully and thoroughly—as if you are seeing it for the first time. What are the colors? Where is the light source? Are there shadows at play? What are the contrasts? Notice all the different shades. Look at the scene, object, or person from all sides. Give a full description, with detail. For example, go for a walk in the park, or sit on a park bench, and be present with what you see. What are your thoughts, emotions, and body sensations as you engage with your sense of sight?

Sound

Sound can be pleasant or unpleasant, loud or soft, musical or noise, or audible or inaudible. When you listen to something, notice the different tones or pitches. What is the amplitude—soft or loud? Is the sound pleasing, distracting, irritating, or annoying? Notice the sound pressure or intensity of the sound. Do you experience any vibration in your body? Choose some music to listen to, and feel the experience of the sound with your whole body. Notice your thoughts and emotions, and feel your body's sensations as you listen to the music.

Smell

There are ten different categories of smell: fragrant (e.g., cologne or floral), woody or resinous (e.g., fresh-cut grass or mold), fruity (non-citrus) (e.g., apple or watermelon), lemon or citrus (e.g., limes or oranges), mint (e.g., eucalyptus or camphor), sweet (e.g., chocolate or vanilla), toasted or nutty (e.g., popcorn or almonds), chemical (e.g., gasoline or paint), pungent (sweat or garlic), and decay (e.g., sewage or rotting meat).[5]

What is the aroma you smell? Is the smell pleasing to you or not? Is it irritating or harmful? For example, put on some lavender essential oil, and breathe it in fully. How does it make you feel? What sensations arise in your body? (See the next section.) Sometimes our experience with smell can be irritating, harmful, or unpleasant. For example, maybe you hang out with friends who smoke cigarettes, but you have asthma. By being connected and embodied, you attune to your senses, and recognize your body's response to the harmful smell. Notice the different smells in your environment, how they make you feel, what you experience, and what this means to you and your well-being. Choose a smell, become mindful of your experience, and notice your thoughts, emotions, and body sensations.

Taste

We live in a world with such a vast array of food choices. Yet, we barely take the time to be present with our food, or savor the food we eat. Some people scarf down their food like they've been fasting for months. Others eat while working, watching TV, surfing the Internet, or browsing their social media. (I'm guilty of this.) We have lost the art of just sitting down to a meal and being present with our food. As such, there is a disconnect between accurate hunger signals and feelings of fullness and satiety.

Take the time to eat mindfully, and savor the food you eat. Sit at a table with no distractions. Put your phone or computer away. If possible, remove other distracting sounds. Make the table pleasing to you. Put away clutter, or work that can distract you from being present with your food. Do you have a sense of being hungry? When was the last time you ate? If it wasn't that long ago, then you may be eating for emotional reasons, or out of boredom. What kind of taste are you experiencing—sweet, salty, bitter, sour, or umami? How do you feel when you eat the food? Was it what you wanted or expected? Can you sense when you are full?

Start with something small, like a taste test—for example, a piece of chocolate. Look at the chocolate first, and then smell the chocolate. Place the chocolate in your mouth, and move it around. Let it settle on your tongue, and let it slowly melt. Notice your thoughts, emotions, and body sensations.

Touch

When you touch something, feel the texture. What does it feel like? Is it smooth, rough, or coarse? Use different examples to feel the effect of different textures on your skin. Notice how you experience the different textures outside your body, and what sensations it evokes inside your body. Are some soothing and calming? Are others irritating or agitating to your skin? Is there a temperature to the touch—cool, cold, warm, or hot? Use different degrees of pressure to notice the subtle effect on the skin. For example, take a feather, and lightly move it across your skin. Then take a heavy rock, and move it across your skin, or hold it in your hand. Notice your thoughts and emotions. Then, compare the two experiences.

We are so fortunate that our body has this remarkable ability to connect through touch. In the section on clairsentience—in this chapter and Chapter 8—I'll go even further. You don't have to touch things to feel them in your body and experience a response. Energy, in and of itself, can be felt in your body, and on your skin. You can feel energy both internally and externally.

Balance

Balance is about your body in relation to your head's movement. It moves in a way that allows you to find equilibrium. Being in balance enables you to be present, engaged, and connected with your body. When you are balanced, you are stable, and not off-kilter. What does it mean if you do feel off-center? Is that a result of a physiological issue or trauma? Do you step outside of your body or dissociate? Is your body out of alignment?

Are you balanced between your head and your body? Move your head around, and feel into your body at the same time. For example, let your eyes fix on an object slightly off-center and notice if this feels comfortable. You may prefer to face an object or person head-on to feel balanced in your body. Notice your posture. Are you able to stand tall, or are you slumping or cowering? A straight posture will allow you to feel more grounded and present in your body, and be balanced when engaging with the world. As you engage with an object or person, notice the balance between your head and body along with your thoughts and emotions.

Movement

There are several different movements your muscles, joints, digits, limbs, and the rest of your body can make. You can bend or straighten. You can move things away from your midline, or bring things closer to you, like spreading or bringing your fingers and toes together. You can move your body forward or backward. You can rotate items away or toward the midline.

Play with different body movements. How does it feel as you place a part of your body in a specific position? Does it feel comfortable or uncomfortable? Is there tension or pain?

Notice if you can orient the rest of your body with this new position and movement. Notice if you are flexible or stiff. Do you have full mobility, or is the range of motion limited? Do you feel strength and power, or do you feel weak? What is your endurance capability? Do you feel stable in your movement and your body? For example, go for a walk, notice your thoughts and emotions, and the sensations you feel in your body as you engage with the movement.

Physical Sensations

Interoceptors, or sensory receptors, respond to five types of stimuli. Chemoreceptors are sensitive to chemical stimuli. "Our heartbeat and respiration rates are also controlled by chemoreceptors that detect carbon dioxide, oxygen, and pH levels in the blood."[6] Tissue damage stimulates pain receptors. Temperature changes activate thermoreceptors. Changes in pressure or movement stimulate mechanoreceptors. Finally, light energy stimulates photoreceptors.[7]

You can't sense a chemoreceptor in your body, but you can recognize hunger, thirst, increased heart rate, or increased respiration. Notice if you experience any form of pain, temperature change, pressure, or light stimulation. For example, go outside and look up toward the sun without blinding yourself, and feel into the sensations that arise as the light enters your eyes, and heat penetrates your body. Notice your thoughts and emotions. Also, as stated above, interoception provides the basis for subjective feelings, emotions, and self-awareness. When you engage in self-awareness to notice your feelings and emotions, you become more embodied, and have a deeper understanding of your experience.

Embodied Exercise

Take one of the senses above, and practice engaging with it more mindfully. It doesn't have to be for a long time. You can do this for five minutes or so. Be fully present with the sense.

- Find a quiet space to be present with one of your senses.
- Take a couple of deep breaths. Feel the air coming in through your nose, and down into your belly. Exhale any tension through your mouth.
- Be mindful of sight, sound, smell, taste, touch, balance, movement, or physical sensations.
- Be one with the sense, and your experience of it.
- Observe everything about that sense you can.
- Describe your experience in detail.
- Notice your thoughts. Judgment may show up. For example, *this is a stupid exercise, the music is boring, this painting is ugly,* or *this tastes gross.* Acknowledge the judgment, and state only what is factual about the sense.
- You may experience self-judgment. For example, *I hate my body,* or *I'm not capable of doing this.* Be kind and gentle with yourself. This exercise may be a new way of exploring your senses. With time and practice, you will do so easily and quickly.
- Check in with your body. How does your body feel while you experience this sense?
- Do a mental scan of your entire body. What are the sensations you feel? (See the next section for more information on sensations.)

- What emotions, if any, arise as you engage with this sense? Name them and let them go.
- Memories may come up as you become mindful of the sense. Experiencing memories is normal. Acknowledge the memory, let it go, and return to being aware of the sense.
- When you feel complete, slowly return to the room, and your body, and open your eyes.
- Journal anything that came up.

Different Types of Sensations

Now that you have a deeper understanding of connecting and embodying your senses, you might wonder how to describe your experience's sensations. There are many different types of sensations your body can experience and feel. Some people may struggle, and find it challenging to capture their body's experience in words. Below is a list of words to help you describe the sensations you feel in your body. The greater the clarity and accuracy you can assign to what you feel, the more you will gain a deeper understanding of what is happening in your body. It will allow you to become more familiar with your experience and accept it without judgment.

This is not a complete list of words to describe sensations, but hopefully it captures the majority. Feel free to add to this list as you gain greater insight into your sensations.

Aroused: nervous, anxious, jittery, nauseated, queasy, jumpy, shaky, agitated, uneasy, startled, shocked.

Blah: dull, blocked, dense, wooden, congested, frozen, thick, heavy, suffocated, numb, closed, hollow, empty, closed, contracted, dark, bland, dim, dreary.

Comfortable: calm, dreamy, relaxed, eased, comforted, relieved, soothed, reassured, free, invigorated, softened, revitalized, consoled.

Disconnection: scattered, disembodied, disconnected, shattered, broken, detached, separate, muddled, disjointed, jumbled, garbled.

Inaction: halted, stopped, dead, idle, ceased, decreased, declined, inert, stagnant.

Movement: shaking, fluttering, shivering, dizzy, wobbly, bubbly, trembling, rattling, rocking, shuddering, convulsing, swaying, shivering, restless, spacey, breathless, waves, agitated, jerking, palpitating, quivering, vibrating.

Nerve Quality: prickly, twitching, tingling, electric, buzzing, itching, burning, radiating.

Pain: jabbing, stabbing, throbbing, achy, twisting, tearing, ripping, knotted, irritated, sore, spasm, twinge, pricking, stinging, cramping, tender, tense, tight, constricted, clenched, slashing, gouging, sensitive, bruised, dull, pounding, sharp.

Temperature: warm, cool, hot, cold, frigid, tepid, lukewarm, icy, chilled, frozen, shivery, glowing, flushed, sizzling, sweaty, scorching, roasting, melting, toasty, burning.

Well-Being: calm, centered, whole, peaceful, light, airy, freeing, energized, relaxed, open, spacious, releasing, expansive, flowing, floating, quiet, settled, relieved, soothed, steady, composed, tranquil.

For some of you, when you start to explore and sit with the sensations in your body, it may feel overwhelming, scary, confusing, and challenging to stay present. The sensations may bring up negative thoughts of self, uncomfortable emotions, or disturbing memories. If negative thoughts or memories come up, notice the thought or memory, continue to breathe, and let it go. Allow yourself to be mindful of the task at hand, explore sensations in your body, and stay present with those sensations.

As you start to explore your body's sensations, you will likely tap into emotions stored in parts of your body. Although you may not believe it, this is a great thing to happen. As discussed in Chapter 4, there are several reasons why you may not have been able to feel your emotions fully. For example, it wasn't safe to do so because a parent or caregiver yelled at you if you cried. Whatever the reason, your brilliant brain recognized it needed to shut down your emotions to survive. As you tap into sensations in your body, you will likely tap into repressed emotions that need to be processed and released. If an emotion comes up when you explore a particular sensation in a specific part of your body, name the emotion, and let yourself feel the emotion along with the sensation. For example, "I feel tightness around my heart, and I feel sad." Explore the tightness, and its nuances, in and around your heart, and let yourself feel sad.

Allow yourself to titrate, or slowly ease into sitting with the sensations for extended periods so as not to take yourself out of your Window of Tolerance. Listen to your body's intuition about what feels right for you. If you feel uncomfortable, ask yourself if you can sit in the discomfort for one more minute. Breathe normally as you explore the sensations in your body. If you become highly triggered, or feel yourself becoming distant from your body, you are out of your Window of Tolerance. Stop and take some deep breaths. Do a grounding exercise to ensure you are back in your body, and no longer dissociating or checking out.

Many of you will be able to explore the sensations in your body without being triggered. Either way, stay mindful, and have an open curiosity about what you notice in your body.

Embodied Exercise

Think about exploring your body's sensations as a road map to learning and understanding more about your body, how you feel in your body, and how your body expresses itself with sensations. You are on a journey of self-exploration that can be insightful and revealing. You are opening up a whole new world. Get excited!

- Find a quiet place where you can sit and explore your body.
- Shake out your limbs, and get comfortable in your chair.
- Close your eyes. Take a couple of deep breaths to relax and center yourself.
- Breathe in through your nose, and down into your belly. Exhale any tension through your mouth.
- Focus your awareness on your body.
- You can do a scan from the top of your head to your toes, or you can sit and breathe and wait for a sensation to make itself known.
- You may notice several sensations.
- Choose one to focus on more in-depth.
- Focus on the sensation in that particular body part. No judgments. Only the facts.
- What sensation are you feeling? Name it.
- What is the sensation's intensity on a scale of zero to ten—where zero is neutral, or no intensity, and ten is the strongest intensity?
- How much space is the sensation taking up? Is it the size of a dime or the size of a dinner plate?
- Is it on the surface of the skin or deep inside your body?

- Is there a specific movement? Does it radiate or stay in one part of your body?
- Is there a color associated with it?
- Is there a temperature associated with it?
- Are there thoughts, emotions, or memories coming up? If yes, let the thoughts and memories go. Name the emotion, and feel the emotion associated with the sensation.
- You can ask the body part what it wants from you. Sit and wait for an answer. Take whatever comes to your mind as truth, don't brush it away. It may be a word or image. Then ask the body part what it needs from you. The answer will be completely different—a deeper, more profound truth. For example, "I want you to play more," and "I need you to love yourself." If nothing comes up, that's okay. The longer you practice, and sit with your body and your inner knowing, the more easily it will reveal itself to you. (I talk more about your inner knowing in the next section.)
- As you sit with the sensation, notice if it shifts or ebbs. When you start to pay attention to a sensation, it will likely increase in intensity, and eventually fade away.
- If that sensation has disappeared, you can check out another sensation or stop.
- Thank your body for helping you listen and connect, and for all it provides.
- When you are ready, slowly let yourself return to the room, and open your eyes.
- Journal anything that came up.

Instinct Versus Intuition—Your True Inner Knowing

People often use the words *instinct* and *intuition* interchangeably, but they are two different sensations. Neither of these comes from your rational brain. In Chapters 3 and 4, I discussed Hermes Trismegistus' Seven Hermetic Principles. I will focus on *as above, so below* from The Principle of Correspondence to distinguish between instinct and intuition.[8]

"Instinct refers to impulses that come from below."[9] Below is referring to your physical body. When you experience a sensation or stimulus in your body, you have an innate, or inborn, response to the trigger with a predetermined behavior. Instincts are not learned behavior. You inherit them through your genes for your survival. For example, when a baby is hungry, it cries. Unable to feed itself, a baby has an innate instinct to express an emotional state in response to hunger's physical stimulus so its mother will provide sustenance for its survival upon hearing the communication. A baby instinctively responds to get its needs met.

"Intuition refers to impulses that come from above."[9] Above is referring to Spirit, or your Higher Self, or inner knowing. There is no rational, analytical thought process when you connect with your intuition. You have immediate recognition and understanding of some knowledge or information. "Above is the realm of conscious intention."[9] To be conscious means to be aware or awake. As such, you awaken, and engage with your intuition. There are four levels of intuitive awareness: mental, emotional, physical, and spiritual.[10]

Mental Intuition

Mental intuition is about knowledge. There are three kinds of knowledge: imagination, reason, and intuitive knowledge. Intuitive knowledge is the most powerful of the three. Have you ever known something to be truthful, but wondered how you knew? This experience is called intuitive knowledge. Intuitive knowledge doesn't come from conscious reasoning. Intuition involves both intuitive judgment and intuitive insight. Intuitive judgment provides information about *what to do*, whereas intuitive insight *produces knowledge that did not exist before*.[10]

Your brain is constantly processing your experiences to provide meaning and understanding. When you connect to your intuitive knowledge, it helps you know what to do in a way that may not have existed before. Let's discuss problem-solving as an example. You tend to rationalize and analyze your way through a problem. You access your intuition to help you solve problems that are beyond your reasoning. If you let go of the problem, and go about your daily life, your subconscious will continue working to solve the problem by connecting with your intuition. Then, all of a sudden, you get the answer most unexpectedly.

Emotional Intuition

Emotional intuition means you can discern the feelings and emotions other people are experiencing—you are empathic. Empaths are highly sensitive and, as such, take on the sensations and feelings of others, sometimes to the detriment of their own well-being. You know things about people without them telling you, or without witnessing their behavior. For example, you may know when someone is lying to you, or trying to deceive you.

Physical Intuition

Intuition comes from above, but it resides below. There is a place in your body where your inner knowing lies and expresses itself. For me, this is mainly my stomach—a gut feeling. For others, depending on the situation, maybe your skin tingles or shivers, your heart feels light or dense, or perhaps you feel it in your throat as an inability to speak, or speak words you know to be accurate, but don't know where they came from. This experience happens to me often. I speak words to my clients I know to be true, and what they need to hear.

Think of it as being on a stage. The spotlight is focusing on that part of your body where your intuition lies. Do you have a sense of where your intuition, inner knowing, or inner guidance lives in you? You may be unsure, and that's okay. Don't despair. We all have intuitive abilities. Think back to an experience where you physically knew something to be true. Where did you feel that sensation in your body? That body part is your go-to physical intuition.

Spiritual Intuition

With spiritual intuition, you access *knowing* through the Divine—God, angels, or spirit guides. You also can connect with your Higher Self to support decision-making for your highest good. Spiritual intuition can present through psychic abilities for information that goes beyond conscious reasoning. For example, maybe you have a feeling something terrible happened to your mom. You call, and found out she fell and hurt herself. Perhaps you've experienced something similar. If so, you have accessed your spiritual intuition. Later in the chapter, I'll discuss the different forms of psychic abilities. These include clairvoyance, clairaudience, clairsentience, and claircognizance—the four clairs.

Repair Your Relationship With Your Intuition

When you quiet your mind and turn inward, you connect to your inner knowing to incorporate understanding and acceptance, and reveal messages for your well-being. The ability to repair your relationship with your intuition takes time, practice, and increased self-awareness of your emotional feelings, and the physical sensations you experience in your body. Increased self-awareness allows you to discern information from the truth and your inner knowing, instead of coming from a place of negativity and fear. Below are some ways to improve your intuition:

- Practice the exercises in this book to increase self-awareness, and become more connected to your body and embodied.
- Quiet your mind, stay in the present moment, and become mindful.
- Engage in a meditative practice.
- Be quiet, still your body, and listen.
- Feel your emotions, and notice where you experience them in your body.
- Become more attuned to the sensations in your body.
- Quiet your negative self-talk, limiting beliefs, judgment, and fear.
- Set and maintain healthy boundaries.
- Work through and release past wounds and traumas.
- Listen and trust your gut feeling.
- Let go of negative people who drain your energy.
- Be aware of your environment.
- Notice the subtle messages you receive when you interact with others—their body language, voice, tone, mannerisms, or gestures.
- Pay attention to your dreams, and the messages they provide.
- Trust what you receive.

Different Ways of Knowing—The Four Clairs

The four clairs are: clairvoyance, or clear seeing; clairaudience, or clear hearing; clairsentience, or clear feeling; and claircognizance, or clear knowing. These abilities allow you to go beyond the normal senses. One of the preceding clairs will be your primary clair, and the others will help support and strengthen this primary means of connecting beyond yourself. Think about the way you like to learn and connect with your world. Some may be more visual, while others may prefer auditory, kinesthetic, or intellectual processes.

If you are visual, you have a discerning eye, and can pick up on the smallest of details in your environment. You notice what people are wearing, or if they've changed their hair. You enjoy things that are pleasing to the eye, such as the beauty of nature or architecture. You notice things in your surroundings before anything else, and have a way of putting things together that creates harmony.

If you are auditory, you may be sensitive to unpleasant sounds and noise. You notice the sound of a person's voice, and take pleasure in their laughter. You enjoy the crunching of snow or leaves under your feet, the sound of the ocean and waves as they crash into the surf, or birds chirping. You become moved by, and derive meaning from, music. You also appreciate silence.

If you are kinesthetic, you engage with the world through emotional feelings and physical sensations. It is vital to feel comfortable and safe around people, and in your environment. You notice how people make you feel. You are moved emotionally and physically by your experiences. You may be highly sensitive, and have difficulty dealing with crowds, noises, and smells. You may take on other people's feelings as your own. You are compassionate and need to help others.

If you are intellectual, you engage through facts, ideas, and knowledge. You likely do not enjoy small talk, but prefer meaningful conversations. You like people who are interesting to you, and who can appreciate a mutual subject of interest. You appreciate cultural and historical information. You see situations and experiences through of lens of learning, life lessons, and growth.[11]

Clairvoyance (Clear Seeing)

Clairvoyance is when you see with your mind's eye—inside your mind. However, it can also be external. There are people with clairvoyance who can physically see things beyond the eye's capability. Your eye refracts light, but there is nothing to refract. They can physically see things that are not present. They can see the unseen, such as energy, spirits, or angels.

For example, when I do Reiki on people, I get images; whether my eyes are open or closed. I may see people, animals, or objects. It comes into my mind's eye, and I know this is relevant for the person. I then impart that information to the client. It is important to note that what I visualize, or what you will visualize, may not represent the actual thing. It is symbolic. For example, if I see a horse, it may not be that an actual horse will show up in that person's life. A horse has a symbolic meaning. It could be strength or power. What does it mean for the person or you?

When you witness something, and start to pay attention to going beyond your regular sight, you may experience something in its symbolic form. You can then search online the symbolic meaning of what you see. When you read the meaning, choose the message that feels right for you and discard the rest. You tap into your internal knowing, and a higher sense of self, to determine this is the message for what you witnessed. For example, if you saw a horse, and it resonated that the message was around strength, where do you need to have more strength in your life? Where do you lack strength? How can you physically embody strength? It can also be a reminder that you are strong and capable, and it is revealing a connection with the resource you already have inside you. Here are some ways you may experience clairvoyance:

- See visions either mentally or with your physical eyes.
- See visions in dreams.
- See signs or symbols.
- See imagery during guided meditation.
- See things that feel surreal.
- See lights, colors, sparkles, flashes, or orbs.

How do you become more clairvoyant? You can start by looking from the periphery of your visual field—from the corners of your eyes. You will begin to see shadows, images, or movement. Don't discount what you start to experience. Trust it. The more you do it, and pay attention, the more you will see and encounter. You can practice journeying, which I discuss in Chapter 9. Journeying will start to open up a new world of vision for you so you can see beyond your eyes. Some people will be able to see auras, colors, or images around people. When you look at someone, don't look at them directly. Soften your gaze and expand it to the peripheries, the edges of their physical body. We have several energy bodies, which I discuss in Chapter 8, and this is where you direct your extrasensory sight.

Clairvoyance correlates with your third eye chakra, which is slightly above the space between your eyes. You can heighten your clairvoyance by placing an amethyst, clear quartz, or moonstone on your third eye chakra while meditating to open up your third eye and clairvoyance.[11,12,13]

Clairaudience (Clear Hearing)

Clairaudience is hearing beyond the physical human ear's ability. You may hear a noise, sound, or voice in your mind, or you may physically hear something in your environment, or next to your ear when there is nothing in your environment producing sound.

In the beginning, it may be hard to discern which words are usual chatter and which are intuitive messages from your Higher Self or Spirit. In clairaudience, the messages will be neutral, there will be no judgment or emotion, and it will not come from a place of fear. Pay attention to how you receive messages through clairaudience. Here are some ways you may experience clairaudience:

- Hear messages in your mind, or outside your ear, related to your concerns.
- Hear someone speaking to you, even if it's in your voice.
- Hear the sound of your name when no one is around, or upon awakening.
- The voice is loving and positive, even when warning you of danger.
- The voice is blunt and to the point.
- Hear high-pitched ringing.
- Hear music out of nowhere.

Embodied Exercise

You can ask questions about any area of your life that you require guidance for, and Spirit will respond to you through clairaudience. The answer may come immediately, or it may come at a later time. Spirit does not work with the human concept of time. Be patient, and have faith that you will receive an answer.

- Take some time for quiet reflection.
- Take a couple of deep cleansing breaths. Breathe in through your nose, and down into your belly. Exhale any tension through your mouth.
- In your mind, ask God, Spirit, the Universe, or your angels, your question.

- Hold the intention your question has been received, and have faith Spirit will answer you.
- You may get an immediate response.
- If you do not get a response, thank Spirit for hearing your request and return to the room and your body.
- Note that messages may not necessarily come from inside your mind in your voice, or outside of you from a disembodied voice. You may receive messages in the following ways:

  - You may get messages from a song on the radio. If a song stands out to you, look up the lyrics. The lyrics' meaning will resonate in your body as truthful.
  - You may overhear people talking about the thing you need an answer to.
  - You may come across a TV show or Internet video with your answer.
  - A book you need to read may fall off the shelf. Randomly open to a page, and read the first section you see.

- Sometimes Spirit provides solutions you don't want to hear. You may be unwilling, or are not ready, to make the decision or change being asked of you. God gave us free will. As such, it may take a while before you are willing to act.

Many people experience tinnitus, which is ringing in the ears due to a disturbance of the auditory nerve. With clairaudience, you may hear ringing in your ear, but it is not a physical problem. The ringing is Spirit's way to connect with you and give you messages. Suppose you experience a high-pitched ringing in one ear that increases rapidly. In that case, it is an indication that a spiritual being is next to you, and downloading messages to you through electrical impulses. You may not hear a message, but know it is being downloaded into your subconscious to help you take positive action.

You can increase your clairaudience by paying attention to the ringing in your ears. You can listen for voices when you first awake in the morning. You can sit in meditation, and notice if you hear any messages. Clean up judgmental and negative self-talk as this is toxic to increasing your clairaudience. Increase your sensitivity to sound by becoming mindful each day, and notice all the sounds in your environment. What do you hear—voices, laughing, birds chirping, a dog barking, the TV, the heater, the tapping of keys on a keyboard, the flipping of pages as you read a book, the whistle of steam releasing from the kettle, or your stomach rumbling? As you increase your clairaudience, you may experience more sensitivity to sound. If this happens, protect yourself and your ears from harsh noises in your environment.

Clairaudience correlates with the ear chakras. Yes, there are ear chakras. They are located above each eyebrow. You can heighten your clairaudience by placing phantom quartz or garnets above each eyebrow while meditating with the intention of opening up your clairaudience.[11,12,13]

Clairsentience (Clear Feeling)

Clairsentience is your ability to sense something internally or externally without experiencing actual physical touch. It is like a tingling spider-sense that comes over you. It is knowing that something either feels right or wrong. You physically feel it in or on your body. The sensations you experience will feel warm, loving, comfortable, and safe. You are not experiencing clairsentience if you feel fearful, cold, or uncomfortable.

Highly sensitive and empathic people typically experience clairsentience as their primary clair. These people attune to the energy in their environment. They tend to take on other people's feelings and emotional states as their own. Therefore, you must learn to discern what is yours, and what is someone else's so you don't carry it; instead, release it. Clairsentience can provide wisdom and insight about your environment. As you increase your intuition and self-awareness, it will help you discern what is yours, and not yours, to ensure healthy boundaries. Here are some ways you may experience clairsentience:

- Emotions such as love, compassion, joy, or bliss that come out of the blue.
- Physical sensations not a result of your environment.
- Temperature or air-pressure change.
- You smell a scent not coming from your environment.
- Feel something touch you.
- Feel calm or at peace in stressful or traumatic situations.
- Sense someone next to you when no one is there.
- Feel a spiritual presence.
- Feel a sense of familiarity.
- Gut feeling.

Embodied Exercise

Below is a way to test for clairsentience in your body. Bring up a query you are unsure of to complete this exercise. For example, "Should I take this job offer?"

- Find a quiet place to sit for several minutes.
- Take a couple of deep breaths. Breathe in through your nose and expand your belly. Release the breath through your mouth and let go of any tension in your body.

- Bring up your question in your mind.
- Notice the emotions that come up. Are you sad, angry, joyful, excited, or some other emotion(s)?
- Notice the sensations that arise in your body. Do you feel your heart opening, are you relaxed, do you feel light, or do you feel tight, uncomfortable, or nauseous?
- If the emotions and sensations are unsupportive and uncomfortable, then the decision is not in your best interests.
- If the emotions and sensations are supportive and comfortable, then it is the right decision to make.
- Your emotions and physical sensations are a gauge to your Higher Self, soul's desire, and Divine will.

You can increase your clairsentience by engaging in the exercises in this book to help you become more sensitive, and in tune with your emotional feelings and the physical sensations. Increase the practices where you mindfully connect through physical touch. For example, close your eyes, and feel your pet's fur, or take objects from your environment and feel the different textures, details, and sensations that arise in your hand and body. If you are exhausted, heavy, or sluggish, it will be harder to discern emotional feelings and physical sensations in your body. You can take a nap, soak in an Epsom salt bath, engage in some form of physical exercise, and eat light, healthy meals to feel less dense and heavy, and allow for heightened sensitivity to your gut feelings.

Clairsentience connects to your heart chakra, which is approximately in the middle of your chest. You can heighten your clairsentience by placing pink tourmaline, rose quartz, or smithsonite on your heart chakra while meditating with the intention to expand your heart center and clairsentience abilities.[11,12,13]

Claircognizance (Clear Knowing)

Claircognizance is the ability to think clearly. It is your inner knowing. You know something is true even though you have no rational or logical knowledge to back it up. You connect with what feels right and true for you, or about other people and the world. It feels like knowledge that you don't know you have. Have you ever spoken words to someone, or written something down that seems profound, and beyond your knowing? This experience is claircognizance.

The messages you receive are consistent, repetitive, uplifting, motivational, and familiar to your interests, passions, and gifts. The messages provide you with information for ways to improve your life, or the lives of those around you. For example, when I try too hard to make connections, and nothing comes to me, I get out of my way, and I instantly tap into my claircognizance abilities. I become connected to my higher knowing, and what comes through is what I speak to my clients. Here are some ways you may experience claircognizance:

- Know something without knowing how you know.
- Know something to be true or false.
- Experience an *aha* moment.
- Express wise words through speech or writings that don't feel like your own.
- Know details of a person you just met.
- Knew something was happening or was going to happen.
- A premonition that something was going to turn out okay.
- Lost something, but knew where you could find it.
- Ability to fix something without instruction.
- Ideas that come to you out of nowhere.

Claircognizance can happen subtly as a thought or idea. The best way to increase your claircognizance is to start paying attention to your repetitive thoughts and any inspired ideas. Sometimes this may feel like a fleeting thought, or it can come as a light-bulb moment with flashing neon signs. Don't second guess or dismiss what you know to be significant and relevant. Keep a daily journal of your thoughts and ideas to notice patterns, and as a means to gauge their accuracy.

Claircognizants tend to be rational people who focus on their work. As such, you need to experience balance in your life. Get out of your routine and get out in nature. Nature can bring you closer to the Divine, inspire you, and heighten your psychic abilities.

Journaling your thoughts is another way you can connect with your claircognizance. When you begin journaling, you are in your rational, left-side brain. If you write long enough, your writing starts to change. You stop editing your thoughts and write more freely. Your hand may move randomly on its own. It starts to feel more profound, more truthful, and sometimes you write words or thoughts that are not your own. You are writing automatically, and have tapped into your right-side brain, and the subconscious mind. When you access your subconscious mind, you connect with your Higher Self and inner knowing.

You can go even further by connecting with higher states of consciousness to channel messages from the spirit world through spirit guides. Channeling allows you to commune with Divine energy. When you channel Spirit, you put your mental and physical self to the side, and become embodied by your spirit guide for them to communicate. This process can be through written or spoken words. Channeling is a powerful way to achieve spiritual awakening and conscious enlightenment. Through meditation, you shift out of your rational mind and physical state to connect with a higher state of consciousness.

Probably the only time I will suggest that it is okay to be slightly disembodied is while channeling. As you meditate with the intent to channel a spirit guide, you will feel present, but somewhat out of your body. If you tend to dissociate, my suggestion is to not engage with channeling until you can stay fully present in your body at all times. It is helpful to have someone record what you say if you are not able to write it down yourself. They can also help bring you back to present reality when the channeling ends.

Embodied Exercise

Set aside five minutes, three days a week, for channeling—to connect with Spirit, and hear the voice of your soul.

- You can use a pen and paper, tablet, or laptop.
- Take a couple of deep breaths to center yourself. Inhale through your nose, deep into your belly, and exhale out any tension.
- When you channel, the frequency of your vibration is elevated, so ensure you ground before engaging in this exercise.
- At the top of the page, write the following, "What does my soul want to tell me today? I choose to allow my soul to speak to me from the highest light."
- Begin writing whatever comes up.
- Your mind may drift when channeling—this is normal.

Claircognizance connects to your crown chakra, which is on the top of your head. You can heighten your claircognizance by placing sugilite on the top of your head while meditating with the intention to expand your consciousness and inner knowing.[11,12,13,14]

—◁◁◁◁▷—

We all have the ability to experience the four clairs. It is your birthright. Do you need the four clairs to be able to connect with your body and become embodied? No, but it will heighten your senses and connect you to your inner knowing, Higher Self, and Spirit for your highest good.

I added the section on the four clairs for two reasons. The first is to give you some knowledge of something you likely have already experienced, but brushed off as your imagination or your mind playing tricks on you. Your experiences were real. Secondly, I wanted you to understand that your senses and sensations go beyond your physical ability. This understanding will set the stage for the ideas and exercises in Chapters 8 and 9.

Benefits of Connecting With Your Senses

There are several benefits to engaging and connecting with your senses:

- A more profound connection with your body.
- Feel more embodied.
- Feel comfortable in your body.
- Understand your physical experience.
- Understand your emotional experience within your body.
- Ability to communicate your experience with others.
- Feel calm.
- Feel more comfortable in social situations.
- Reduce anxiety and depression.
- Improve mood and physical well-being.
- Access memories.

- Improve daily functioning.
- Ability to experience knowing beyond your human senses.
- Achieve higher levels of consciousness beyond yourself.
- Engage in transpersonal (beyond the self) experiences.
- Increase intuition.
- Ability to set and maintain healthy boundaries.
- Mental, emotional, and physical healing.
- Understand your environment and how you interact with it.
- Increase enjoyment and pleasure.

———

I hope this chapter gave you some tools to understand and engage with your senses, provide language to feel into your body's emotional feelings and physical sensations, and the skills to tap into your intuition and extrasensory perception.

———

Join me in the next chapter as I explore energy. I discuss what energy is, your body's energy centers and energy bodies, how to give yourself energy for healing and release, and how to clear energy from your body and your environment.

8

ENERGY—
THE ESSENCE OF YOUR BEING

"Energy is the living, vibrating ground of your being, and it is your body's natural self-healing elixir, its natural medicine. This medicine, this energy medicine, feeds body and soul, and attending to it restores your natural vitality. Energy medicine is the science and the art of optimizing your energies to help your body and mind function at its best."

Donna Eden

In 2009, I contracted H1N1 and, in less than five days, I had bi-lateral pneumonia. It all started on a Monday, a regular workday. During our weekly staff meeting, I couldn't stop coughing. My boss, fearful of me passing on whatever I had, sent me home. I figured I had the flu, but by Friday, I knew I was in severe decline. I got my family doctor to see me urgently. She immediately took a pulse ox measurement of my blood oxygen, and it was eighty-something, extremely low. Normal pulse ox is between 95 and 100. The ambulance came and took me to the hospital.

I was quarantined in a dark, freezing room immediately upon arrival at the hospital. I received a dose of Tamiflu, was hooked up to an IV, and had to get a blood oxygen measurement—of my oxygen saturation level. Unlike the painless pulse ox, taken from the pulse on the outside of a finger, getting an oxygen saturation level is an extremely painful needle inserted into the wrist. Besides getting x-rays, the nurses pretty much forgot about me except to help me pee in a bedpan once.

I was transferred onto a ward the following day and quarantined alone for a week. As I was bedridden, the nurses put air circulation pads on my lower legs to decrease the possibility of blood clots. The machine that pumps the air was so loud I barely slept. The nurses had my IV fully open to hydrate me, which resulted in me wetting myself because I was coughing so violently, and couldn't move away from the circulation pads to get to the bathroom.

I remember nurses coming into my room only to change my IV bag. When I'd ring the bell to ask for water, and a nurse would finally bring it, I could tell by her tone that attending to me had put her out. Because I was in quarantine, the nurses had to get gowned up, and put on a mask and gloves, to come into my room. No one asked how I was feeling or if I needed anything.

My hair was greasy and my head itched. I felt disgusting, and smelled sickly sour from my sweat, and my nether regions weren't a bed of roses either. As no nurses came to help me go to the bathroom, I took it upon myself to wash. I unhooked my circulation pads, unhooked my oxygen cannula, and dragged my IV to the washroom. My breathing was labored from the lack of oxygen. I could barely stand. I knew I couldn't have a shower, so I washed my hair, armpits, and privates from the sink. It took all my energy to stand there for what was likely only five minutes.

One day, when my mom was visiting, the nurse came in and gave me shit because I wasn't wearing a mask—fearful I may infect my mom. I complied, while I thought, "My mom has visited me every day, and now three or four days later, you're worried about her health?" Why was I not informed from day one to wear a mask around others?

I saw a doctor on the first day only. He said I had H1N1 and bi-lateral pneumonia. I was placed on the highest level of oxygen intake, which was a ten. The doctor said I needed to be at zero oxygen use before I could leave the hospital. He gave me a spirometer to use several times a day to strengthen my lungs and oxygen intake. As no nurse or doctor ever returned to instruct me on reducing my oxygen from ten to zero, I did it myself. Every day, I would decrease the input a couple of points until I finally reached one on the day of my discharge. Even though I still had labored breathing, I was discharged.

At home, I was still extremely weak and sick. My breathing was shallow, and without the oxygen, I felt panicked. I hardly slept. Lying flat in my bed made me feel like I was drowning and I couldn't catch my breath. I tried to get out and move around, but I could barely walk to the corner and back to my house without feeling like I'd run a marathon. I was off work for an entire month.

So, why am I telling you this story in a chapter on energy? First, this experience is an excellent example of the different layers of trauma. I not only experienced a big "T" trauma, which was the illness itself, but several little "t" traumas, including isolation, lack of care and compassion, shaming, blaming, bullying, and a betrayal of my body.

Secondly, that year, I was constantly sick. My immune system was tanked, and I knew I needed help. I already had my fill of the medical system in action, and didn't want any more. So, I turned to what I knew would help my immune system reboot—Reiki. But before I discuss Reiki, let's talk about energy.

What is Energy?

We are all comprised of energy particles bouncing around through time and space. We are infinitely connected to each other, to inanimate objects, to animals, to plants, to trees, to the planet we live on, and to the stars and galaxies beyond our reach. We emit energy from our thoughts, feelings, and interactions, and we store our experiences as energy in every cell in our body. Our body informs us on how to be in the world.

Since the end of the 17th century, science has followed Newton's theory that the Universe and humans are all made up of matter, and nothing else. He believed light was made up of particles. Science now recognizes the entire Universe, which includes us, is made up of energy.

Quantum physics is a branch of physics that looks at the smallest scales of energy levels of subatomic particles and atoms. "The quantum behavior of atomic objects (electrons, protons, neutrons, photons, and so on) is the same for all, they are all 'particle waves.'"[1]

If you look deeper into the atom's workings, you will see nothing there but energy waves. "An atom is actually an invisible force field, a kind of miniature tornado, which emits waves of electrical energy."[2] Since we are all made up of atoms, we, in turn, are energy—or electricity. For every hour, humans roughly produce as much energy as a 100-watt bright incandescent light bulb.[3] Whether we are awake or asleep, we are continuously absorbing or giving off light and energy. Every cell in our body is a miniature battery that holds 1.4 volts of energy. This voltage is not a lot until you multiply all of the cells in our body (50 trillion), which results in a total voltage of 700 trillion volts of electricity in our body. That's intense! "This energy is what the Chinese call 'chi,' and is also the energy used in hands-on healing."[2]

Embodied Exercise

This exercise will help you feel your body's energy.

- Be free of any distractions, and take a moment to center yourself.
- Get comfortable in your chair, and take a couple of deep inhalations.
- Breathe deep into your belly through your nose, and exhale fully through your mouth.
- Now rub the palms of your hands together back and forth for about 10–20 seconds.
- Then slowly pull your hands apart, and keep your fingers slightly separated.
- Imagine holding a ball between the two palms of your hands suspended in space.
- Slowly pull your hands apart, and bring them back together, as if you could grow or shrink this energy ball between your hands.
- Take your time, and play with this energy.
- You may rotate your hands, or place one hand slightly above the other to feel the energy penetrating the skin.
- Alternatively, focus on one of your hands. More specifically, become hyperfocused on the spaces between your fingers, or the edges alongside your hand. It is not the hand itself that you'll feel the emitted energy, but the empty spaces around the fingers and hand.
- Sensations may include heat, cold, tingling, light pinpricks, or pulling.

Your body, and the whole world, are made up of this energy. We are all interconnected on an energetic level.

How was that exercise? Were you able to feel the energy? You may be thinking, "Well, of course, I felt the energy, Vicky. The friction from rubbing my hands together created the sensations." True, but you don't need to rub your hands together to create and emit energy. This exercise was a helpful way for you to start to discern energy, and have a tangible way to feel it.

My Introduction to Reiki

I was introduced to energy work, specifically Reiki, in my mid-20s. I was curious and interested to find an alternative form of healing. When I tried it, I found it relaxing and peaceful, but didn't think it did anything more. It wasn't until later in my life that I truly understood how the energy transformed me, especially after my immune system crashed from H1N1 and bi-lateral pneumonia.

That was the most challenging year of my life in regards to my health. My breathing was shallow and raspy. I couldn't take full deep breaths from all the coughing as my diaphragm had become tight and constricted. I was extremely weak and lethargic, and I constantly got sick. I knew I couldn't continue this way of life without long-term harm to my health. So I did what I always do—I turned to an alternative form of healing.

I instinctively knew I needed to get some Reiki. My friend was seeing a practitioner, so I contacted her for their name. Karine Schipper is a Usui and Karuna Ki Reiki Master and Teacher. She has studied many healing therapies and modalities. She is highly knowledgeable and skilled; I knew my health was in good hands.

To say Karine transformed my life is an understatement. Not only did she improve my health in many ways, but she became a dear friend, taught and trained me to be a Usui Reiki Master, and instigated my path to becoming a psychologist.

Reiki Beginnings

A Japanese priest, Mikao Usui, discovered Reiki in the 19th century. During a 21-day meditation and fast on a holy mountain, Usui entered into a state of awakened consciousness. He received a powerful healing energy force along with information and meaning of symbols and mantras. He injured his toe while returning from the mountain; after placing his hands around his foot, the bleeding stopped and he experienced spontaneous healing. It wasn't until he miraculously cured several people that he realized the connection between the symbols he received, and the life-force energy that passed into him. He opened a Reiki clinic in Tokyo in 1922, provided hands-on healing to thousands of people, and provided workshops to share his knowledge.[4]

When you break down the word *Rei-Ki*, *Rei* refers to "mystery, gift, holy, and nature spirit, or invisible spirit."[5] In Japanese, there are several names for energy, but typically it is known as *Ki*. Ki means life-force energy. Rei-Ki refers to guided life-force energy that is universal. It is a "healing energy that has wisdom, guided by Spirit."[5] William Lee Rand, founder of the International Center for Reiki Training, states, "Reiki is Ki guided directly by a higher power, also known as God, the Supreme Being, The Universe, The Universal Mind, All That Is, Jehovah, Krishna, Buddha, The Great Spirit, etc."[6]

Before his death, Usui passed on his knowledge to Dr. Chujiro Hayashi. In Hayashi's records, he noted, "Reiki reaches the source of the physical symptoms, fills the body with the required energy and restores it to wholeness."[4] Hawayo Takata, a young woman suffering from several disorders including a tumor, decided not to have an operation, and instead sought treatment at Dr. Hayashi's Reiki clinic. She was cured after several months of treatment. She asked Hayashi to teach her Reiki and he agreed. After her training, she returned to Hawaii, where she became a successful Reiki Master. She traveled throughout the USA and Canada, teaching Reiki to others. She trained 22 Reiki Masters, which is how Reiki spread throughout the Western world from Master to student.[4]

How Reiki Works

Reiki has three levels or degrees of training. The Reiki Master passes down the symbols and teachings through four different attunements. In an attunement, you are initiated and attuned as an open channel for universal life-force energy.[4] Once you receive an attunement, you have activated the Reiki energy and flow throughout your body. You are now a conduit for channeling universal life-force energy. The universal life-force energy is channeled into your body, out your hands, and to the person or animal you are working on. When I perform Reiki, I imagine the energy as a white light coming from God in through the top of my head, down my arms, and out my hands.

Ki flows through your chakras, meridians, and aura layers. The body is in optimal health when Ki flows freely, and in balance, throughout the body's organs and cells. Illness results from a disruption in the flow of Ki. "When a person receives a Reiki treatment, the Rei or God-Conscious part of the energy assesses where the person is blocked and then directs the healing energy."[7] Reiki raises the vibrational energy to release stored negative thoughts and feelings that attach to the body. Reiki heals the energy pathways and allows healthy Ki to flow naturally.

The Reiki Master or practitioner, either methodically or instinctively, places their hands above, or on various parts of the body, to provide universal life-force energy. The universal life-force energy is activated for the client's highest and greatest good. There is no physical manipulation of the body as in massage. It is powerful, gentle, safe, and non-intrusive.

A Reiki Master or practitioner is not a healer. It does not matter where the practitioner places their hands, as the Ki energy is intelligent—it flows to where it needs to go to support the body's innate healing capability. A Reiki Master or practitioner senses the blockages in the body and places their hands in the appropriate areas. However, even if I place my hands on the person's head, the Ki will go where it needs to go in the body to restore wholeness. As a Reiki Master, I am the conduit for the Ki.[8]

Reiki is holistic as it supports mental, emotional, physical, and spiritual healing. It can also "encourage personal and spiritual awareness and growth."[7] Reiki is a spiritual practice, not an energy practice, because the practitioner brings awareness to their body (a spiritual act) to sense what is out of balance with their client.[8] Ki energy is all around us. When I tap into my spiritual self-awareness, I access my higher knowing, and am able to direct the Ki energy to my client.

Does Reiki Energy Really Exist?

As previously discussed, everything in the Universe is comprised of energy. There are several unseen energies, such as light, sound, radio waves, or radiation. You can't see Reiki energy with the naked eye, unless you are clairvoyant (clear seeing), but it is there. Similarly, you can't see sound, but you can hear it and feel it in your body if it is loud enough to create vibrations.

Semyon Kirlian, a Russian scientist, developed a machine that allows unseen energy to be visible through a photograph. Kirlian photography captures the energy waves of the object. Kirlian photographs taken before and after a Reiki treatment revealed the energy emitting from the body was stronger after Reiki, and formed harmoniously balanced patterns.[4]

Reiki is effective because of Ki. Remember, Ki is life-force energy that is everywhere. It is all around us, within every *thing*, and accessible to everyone. It is limitless, abundant, forever flowing, and omnipresent.[5] All you have to do is connect to it, and use it.

Reiki, and other forms of energy work, may appear to be a time to quiet the mind, and relax the body from a busy life. Reiki is definitely relaxing, but, more importantly, it works on a deep cellular level. Some people feel an immediate shift. They feel lighter, grounded, have more insight or clarity about their life, and behave differently. For others, the shifts happen subtly, and a year may pass until they realize they are different—mentally, emotionally, physically, and spiritually. Past wounds or trauma seem less disturbing. Limiting or negative thoughts arise less frequently, and are quickly squashed, and there is an ability to replace them with more truthful statements, positivity, and compassion. I love practicing Reiki, and connecting with the body, because the receiver can feel the shifts. You can feel your body release tension and stuck energy. You feel more deeply, are more in tune with yourself, and more whole. It's like a light switch that turns on your body's innate healing ability.

Chakras

Chakra means wheel of light in Sanskrit; they appear as wheel-like vortices of energy. Along your spinal column are seven energy centers, or vortices, of the etheric body. The etheric body is the first layer of your aura after your physical body. (See more information on the different energy bodies later in the chapter.) Chakras are present in the front and back of the body, except for the root and crown chakra, which have only one entry point. These energy centers spin and vibrate to maintain homeostasis within the body. Each chakra is associated with specific organs and glands. Energy can become blocked in your chakras from wounds, trauma, and negative beliefs. When your chakras are blocked, you experience imbalances—mentally, emotionally, physically, spiritually.

There are also smaller chakras on the palms of your hands and soles of your feet. These chakras help to move energy. These smaller chakras feed you essential life-giving positive energy, and release unwanted negative energy through the endocrine glands and the lymphatic system.

When you connect, and channel Reiki energy, it flows in through the crown chakra, and out through the chakras in the soles of your feet. The Reiki energy then flows out of your palm chakras and into the person you are working on.[7] On the next page, is a chart of the different chakras.

	Root	Sacral	Solar Plexus
Purpose	Vitality, Life Force, Safety, Security, Survival, Ground to Physical World	Sexuality, Creativity, Intuition, Emotions	Personality, Personal Power, Will in the World
Principle	Physical Entity	Reproduction of Being	Formation of Being
Location	Base of Your Spine Between Your Genitals and Anus	Below Your Navel	Base of the Sternum
Body Parts	Base of Spine, Anus, Adrenal Glands, Legs, Feet, Bones, Immune System	Sexual Organs, Bladder, Pelvis, Large Intestine, Hips	Abdomen, Stomach, Pancreas, Kidney, Liver, Gallbladder, Spleen, Small Intestine, Middle Spine
Color	Red (Secondary Color Black)	Orange	Yellow
Element	Earth	Water	Fire
Gemstones	Ruby, Garnet, Obsidian, Bloodstone, Red Jasper, Smoky Quartz, Black Tourmaline	Carnelian Coral, Amber, Agate, Orange Calcite	Amber, Citrine, Gold Topaz, Yellow Calcite, Tiger's Eye, Gold
Essential Oils	Cedar, Clove, Cypress, Marjoram, Myrrh	Sandalwood, Petitgrain, Ylang Ylang	Chamomile, Lemon, Thyme, Ylang Ylang
Blocked	Fearful, Anxious, Insecure, Self-Centered, Greed, Frustrated, Anger	Difficulty Expressing Feelings or Emotionally Dysregulated, Envy, Manipulative, Sexual Difficulties, Purposeless, Jealousy, Lack Energy	Low Self-Esteem Self-Confidence, Sensitive to Criticism, Worry What Others Think, Feel Taken Advantage of, Anger, Fear, Distrustful
Symptoms	Obesity, Anorexia, Tension in Spine, Constipation, Knee Problems	Urine and Bladder Problems, Impotence, Stiff Lower Back, Muscle Spasms, Constipation	Poor Digestion, Liver Issues, Diabetes, Nervous Exhaustion, Food Allergies
Balanced	Connection to Mother Earth, Manifestation, Grounded, Individuality, Security, Courage, Patience	Friendly, Open, Kind, Emotions Flow Freely, Ability to Reach Out to Others, Desire, Pleasure, Sexual or Passionate Love, Work Creatively with Others	Will, Personal Power, Energy, Cheerful, Outgoing, Acceptance of Self and Others, Inner Calm and Peace, Wholeness

Heart	Throat	Third Eye	Crown
Unconditional Love, Compassion	Communication, Express Individuality	Insight, Psychic Ability, Intuition, Vision, Clarity, Spiritual Understanding	Divine, Pure Consciousness, Enlightenment, Spiritual Connection to the Universe
Loving Beyond the Self	Expression of Being	Knowing of Being	Pure Being
Center of Chest	Between Inner Collarbone	Between the Eyebrows	Top and Center of the Head
Heart, Lungs, Circulatory System, Shoulders, Arms, Upper Back, Chest, Ribs, Breasts, Thymus Gland	Throat, Neck, Trachea, Mouth, Jaw, Teeth, Lungs, Thyroid, Parathyroid, Hypothalamus	Face, Left Eye, Nose, Ears, Lower Brain (Cerebellum), Pituitary Gland, Nervous System	Right Eye, Upper Brain (Cerebellum), Cerebral Cortex, Pineal Gland, Muscular and Skeletal Systems
Green (Secondary Color Pink)	Light Blue	Indigo	Violet, White, Gold
Air	Ether	Light	All Elements
Emerald, Green Jade, Rose Quartz, Kunzite, Green and Pink Tourmaline, Malachite	Aquamarine, Blue Topaz, Turquoise, Azurite, Chalcedony, Celestite, Chrysocolla	Amethyst, Lapis Lazuli, Sodalite, Indigo Sapphire, Opal	Amethyst, Clear Quartz Crystal, Topaz, Alexandrite, Sapphire, Diamond
Geranium, Bergamot, Rose, Clary Sage	Lavender, Sandalwood, Neroli, Sage	Jasmine, Vetiver, Basil, Patchouli, Rosemary	Frankincense, Lotus, Olibanum, Oakmosss
Self-Pity, Bitter, Hatred, Paranoid, Resentful, Grief, Anger, Afraid of Letting Go, Afraid of Getting Hurt, Unworthy of Love, Loneliness	Difficulty Expressing Self, Hold Back, Timid, Quiet, Fearful of Judgment and Rejection, Ignorance, Addiction Feel Weak	Non-Assertive, Inadequate, Fearful of Success or Stuck in Ego, Fearful of Intuition, Reject Spirituality, Focus on Science and Intellect	Lack of Inspiration, Confusion, Lack of Joy, Frustration, Destructive Feelings, Stuck in Anxiety and Fear, Depressed, Unsatisfied
Heart Problems, High Blood Pressure, Circulation Problems, Difficulty Breathing	Thyroid Issues, Ear or Throat Infections, Skin Irritations, Back Pain, Inflammation	Headaches, Eyestrain, Blurred Vision, Blindness, Bad Dreams, Detached from the World	Migraines, Depression, Senility
Peace, Divine and Unconditional Love, Empathy, Forgiveness, Understanding, Harmony, Nurturing, Compassion, Acceptance, Openness, Contentment	Balance of Expression, Centered, Listens to Inner Voice, Trusts Intuition, Peace, Truth, Wisdom, Knowledge, Reliability, Loyalty, Faith, Honesty, Kindness	Unafraid of Death, Non-Attachment to Materialism, Clairvoyance, Astral Travel, Connection to Past Lives, Intuition, Wisdom, Insight, Peace of Mind	Knowing Self Reflects the Divine, Unity, Connecting to Divine, Trust, Spiritual Will, Inspiration, Wisdom, Faith, Abandon Individual Ego for Universal Ego[7,9,10]

Embodied Exercise

This exercise can detect any blockages or stagnation in the spinning of your chakras, and deepen your connection with your body's energy.

- Find a place to sit where you won't be disturbed.
- Get comfortable in your chair.
- Breathe in through your nose. Take several deep breaths into your belly, and exhale slowly through your mouth.
- As you feel more centered, return to your normal breath.
- State an intention to explore your chakras.
- Start with one chakra at a time from the root to the crown, and incorporate the appropriate color for each chakra.
- As you sit with the root chakra, observe the color red. Is it nonexistent, faded, or bright?
- Is it spinning? At what rate? Slowly or quickly? Clockwise or counter-clockwise?
- Ask your chakra if anything is blocking it.
- Ask if any repressed emotions need to be released.
- If emotions arise, allow yourself to feel and express those emotions.
- Ask if there is anything your chakra needs from you to work more effectively.
- Sit patiently, and wait for any response, whether through thoughts, images, symbols, or an internal knowing. Trust whatever comes up.
- If any memories come up, let the memories play out in your mind, and notice if any emotions arise that need to be released.

- Notice any limiting beliefs you are holding about yourself or the world.
- If there are blockages, ask your guides or angels to help heal and release any blocks.
- When nothing else comes up, take the time to recharge your chakra.
- Imagine yourself breathing in the color red. (Other than the root and crown chakra, let the color fill the chakra on both the front and back of your body.) As you breathe out, exhale the color red. Do this for a minute or two.
- Then, imagine increasing the spin rate of your chakra in a clockwise fashion. Not too fast.
- Ask for any final insight into how you can work with this chakra in your daily life, and what action steps you can take to keep it open and spinning effectively.
- Thank the chakra, guides, and angels for the information and assistance in connecting, and healing any blockages.
- Continue onto the next chakra, or end the session by returning to your body.
- Feel your hands, feet, and heart. Move your fingers and toes. Stretch. Take several deep breaths.
- Feel yourself back on the chair, and in the room, and slowly open your eyes.
- Journal your experience. Write or draw any thoughts, images, symbols, or memories that came up. Write out any emotions or negative beliefs. Write out any new insights or action steps you can take, and start to incorporate those into your daily life.

Over the next several weeks or months, you can continue to work with a specific chakra. For example, with the root chakra, wear the color red, eat red foods, wear or carry red gemstones. Engage in the disclosed action steps. Challenge any limiting beliefs. Rewrite them as positive beliefs and repeat them several times a day. Do a daily meditation to inhale and exhale out the color red. Continue to let yourself feel the emotions you repressed, that need to be released from the revealed memories.

Human Energy Bodies

Your body is comprised of a subtle energy system where life-force energy flows. Seven energy bodies, the layers of your aura, surround your physical body. These energy bodies help you process emotions and thoughts. Your aura is continuously changing as you grow and evolve through your life experiences. Listed after the physical, are the seven energy bodies that make up the aura, or human energy field:

1. **Physical**—helps you be present in the here and now, and allows you to be conscious of everything you do.

2. **Etheric**—is the first layer above the body, approximately an inch thick. It reflects energy when it flows through the meridians and chakras. It is connected to the root chakra.

3. **Emotional**—reflects your emotions and feelings. If emotions are stuffed down or not processed effectively, they become stuck in the emotional body. Later, blockages can appear that can create dis-ease in the body. It is connected to the sacral chakra.

4. **Mental**—reflects your conscious, logical mind and thinking. It teaches you self-knowledge. It is connected to the solar plexus chakra.

5. **Astral**—expresses unconditional love. It is a bridge between the physical world and spiritual realm. It is connected to the heart chakra.

6. **Etheric Template**—expresses Divine will. Thought processes and memories are mirrored here. It stores the present and all possible futures. It is connected to the throat chakra.

7. **Celestial**—mirrors the subconscious part of your brain. It is where you connect to your intuition. Your consciousness is expressed as universal love. It is connected to the third eye chakra.

8. **Causal (Ketheric Template)**—your soul communicates with the conscious mind via the subconscious mind. It is connected to the crown chakra.[7]

The etheric, emotional, and mental bodies constitute the physical plane. The astral body is the bridge to the astral plane. The etheric template, celestial, and causal (ketheric template) bodies constitute the spiritual plane.

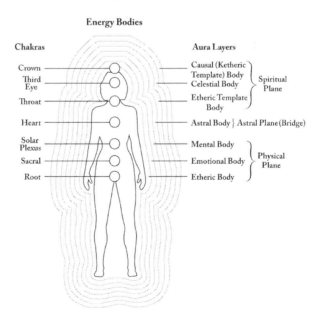

Energy Bodies

How Reiki Supports You

You don't *heal* people with Reiki. The Ki triggers the body's natural ability to heal itself. You don't manipulate Reiki or Ki energy. The energy goes to where the body needs it.[8]

Physically, Reiki helps strengthen the immune system. It can break energetic blockages, remove intrusions, and help cleanse toxins from the body. It is a tremendous stress and pain reliever. People often report deep restorative sleep after a Reiki session.

Emotionally, Reiki is calming and relaxing, and supports emotional balance. Since you store everything in your body, Reiki can open up emotional blockages ready to be released. As such, emotions often flow during a Reiki session. Do not be alarmed by this. Enjoy the release, knowing your body is letting go of emotions that were repressed and got stuck in your physical body. You may have stuffed down feelings due to an inability to express them, or because they were too intense and uncomfortable to feel.

Mentally, Reiki helps to calm down an overactive mind from overthinking, worry, rumination, or negative thoughts or beliefs. During a Reiki session, you can experience new insights into life stressors, or clarity about creating change and improving your life.

Spiritually, Reiki allows the receiver and the giver to connect with Source and unconditional love. It increases your awareness of yourself, and connects you with your inner knowing and "true Divine essence."[7]

Reiki has the inherent wisdom to give the body what it needs.

Intention

If you already incorporate energy work into your life, that's fantastic. It's a great way to connect with your body, and become more embodied. As this book is about helping *you* connect with your body, I don't expect you to get energy work from another individual. When you receive Reiki from someone else, you may be limited by finances or time. What if you could give yourself daily energy whenever you needed to? Below, I provide information on how to give yourself energy.

When you connect to universal life-force energy, intention is key. Without intention, you are like a feather blowing in the wind. You are being torn and pulled from different directions—swirling back and forth. You need direction. Your intention is your direction for where you want to go. Your intention is about honing information, not only for yourself, but to put it out to the Universe to provide whatever you require. Before you give yourself this energy, set an intention. For example, "My intention is to provide unconditional love to my body through universal life-force energy."

Giving Yourself Energy

Have you ever placed your hand on a friend or loved one when they were upset? The act of putting your hand on someone can physically reduce the physiological and chemical reactions flooding their body. A friendly touch increases the release of oxytocin, known as the *cuddle hormone*. But it is more than that. It provides a deep level of connection with another human being. We crave physical contact, and if we don't get it, our body can feel depleted emotionally and physically.

What we seem to forget is that we can also provide this physical contact to ourselves. You don't have to seek out comfort and physical touch from another. You can bring energy, care, and comfort by placing your hands on your body.

Embodied Exercise

Below is an exercise to give yourself energy, unconditional love, and compassion.

- Increase your self-awareness and notice any discomfort in your body.
- Rub your hands together for 10–20 seconds and set an intention.
- Imagine a ray of deep emerald green emanating from your heart chakra, spreading across your chest, flowing down your arms, into your hands, and out your fingers.
- Place your hands on the body part that is in distress.
- If you can't reach that body part, place your hands on the opposite side of where there is discomfort, and direct the flow of energy to it with your mind and breath.
- Send the body part unconditional love from your heart.
- Feel the energy flow into the body part.
- After several minutes, notice any shifts or changes in the level of discomfort.
- When you feel ready, you can disengage, thank your heart for providing this healing, and continue with your day.

Embodied Exercise

This exercise creates an ongoing practice to give yourself energy and connect with your body.

- Bring your journal and pen.
- Find a space that's quiet and calm, with no distractions.
- Close your eyes and take a couple of deep cleansing breaths.
- Let yourself get comfortable with your feet planted firmly on the floor if you are in a seated position or lying down.
- Breathe in through your nose, down your chest, deep into your belly, and feel your belly expand.
- Take your mind upward to the top of your head.
- In your mind's eye, see yourself rising to the ceiling, then out of your home.
- Climbing higher and higher above your neighborhood, city, province, country, and finally above Earth.
- Then draw your attention to the Universe.
- You may notice a star calling your name, or energetically pulling you to it.
- This is your personal star in the Universe. It is there solely for you.
- See yourself getting closer and closer, then merging inside the star, as if you are returning to your shuttle in space.
- Feel yourself bathed in whatever color(s) of light is connected to your star.
- Feel yourself being energized and bathed in color.

- Ask your star if there is any wisdom it wishes to impart at this time.
- Breathe in any messages, and let them fill every cell in your body. Thank your star for any messages it has provided.
- When you feel ready, envision yourself coming out of the star; trailing behind you is the star's universal life-force energy specific to your healing needs.
- You don't need to know what healing needs to occur. Universal life-force energy has an innate wisdom and will place it wherever it needs to go in your body.
- Start your descent back to Earth.
- See yourself leaving space's atmosphere and coming down to Earth. See your country, then your province, your city, and finally, your home.
- As you return to the room, bring the universal life-force energy down through the top of your head.
- Allow it to flow down into every nook and cranny of your head, neck, shoulders, arms, fingers, chest, stomach, back, butt, thighs, knees, calves, ankles, feet, and toes.
- Let the energy burst forth from your fingers, hands, toes, and feet, and see it encircling your body.
- With every inhale, breathe the universal life-force energy back into your body.
- See it intermingling and permeating every cell, organ, and chakra.
- Now, physically place your hands where you intuitively feel they need to go on your body.
- Alternatively, you can place one hand over your heart chakra, and the other hand over your sacral chakra, which is beneath your belly button. (You could do this nightly as you lie in bed before falling asleep.)

- There is no wrong way to do this, as the universal life-force energy will go wherever it needs to go.
- See the vibrant color(s) of light come down from your star into the top of your head, down your body, and out your hands.
- Feel the deep unconditional love that is emanating universal life-force energy from your star.
- Feel free to move your hands to different parts of your body, or keep them stationary.
- Notice the energy transmission that is taking place from your hands to your body. If your hand is above your body, remember to focus on the space between your hands.
- Do you feel hot or cold, tingling, light pinpricks, or pulling? If not, don't worry. You are still receiving energy.
- You may notice sensations in other parts of your body—where your hands aren't touching. These sensations are normal.
- Take as much time as you like. Ten to 20 minutes a day is exceptionally healing, and helps you connect to your body in a loving nonjudgmental way.
- When you feel you have taken in as much energy as you need, see the energy retreating from your hands, out of your body, and returning to your star for when you need it next.
- Thank your star for providing you with universal life-force energy.
- Feel yourself return to the room, move your fingers and toes, stretch, and gently open your eyes.
- Journal any insights or experiences.

Energy Influences Thoughts and Feelings

Even though you can't see this energy field, it doesn't mean it doesn't exist. Have you ever stepped into a room and felt that something has transpired or is transpiring? There is a reason people say, "You could cut the tension with a knife." The energy is thick and stagnant, and fills the air. If you've ever been in this situation, you may have noticed that your energy and mood changed to match the energy in the room. Suddenly, you are also angry, sad, or anxious, or have a host of other feelings.

Do you know someone you would consider an energy vampire? When you are with this person, is it all about them and what they are going through, with no room for you to talk about yourself? When you leave this person, do you feel drained, sad, or depressed? This person is sucking out all your life energy. You have what they want—happiness, positivity, and energy.

In these situations, check in with yourself to assess whether this energy or emotion is genuinely yours, or if it is someone else's. Ask yourself the following questions:

- How was I feeling or thinking about myself before I saw this person?
- How did I feel, and what kinds of thoughts did I have about myself or them when I was with them?
- Did something specifically happen to me that would have changed my thoughts and feelings?

Suppose you felt positive before you saw the person, and afterward felt negative, and nothing specifically happened to you to change your mood. In that case, you likely picked up that person's negative energy.

Energy Cords

Have you ever heard of energetic cords? They are also known as etheric or ethereal cords or ribbons. Energy cords flow out of you and into other people, animals, places, and even objects. By tapping into other people's energy, you are tapping into them. It helps you to discern how they are feeling, and maybe what they are thinking. Have you ever thought of a friend and then the phone rang and it was them? This phenomenon happens because you tap into each other through energy cords. Energy runs back and forth between you and a person into your physical body, chakras, and energy bodies. The connection with the person, and the strength of the cord, can be the result of living many lifetimes together, or, perhaps, only a short time in this lifetime. Energy cords can attach anywhere on your body.[11] Energy cords are beneficial in the following ways:

- They allow you to connect to people without the need for words.
- You can sense how a person feels emotionally, physically, or mentally without seeing them.
- They are like unbreakable antennae that can reach across the world.
- They fulfill the existential need to *be a part of*, and an inner knowing that you belong.
- They provide energy from others when you are struggling.

Energy Cords

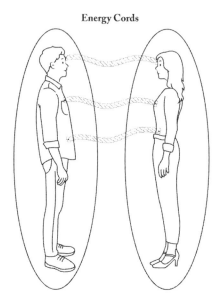

People reach out energetically to you all the time. When someone comes to your mind, they are energetically reaching out to you through the ethereal cord connected to both your bodies. Their need to connect may be because they are lovingly thinking of you, missing you, or there may be something stressful or upsetting happening in their world. When this happens, take a moment to check in energetically with this person with the exercises below.

Embodied Exercise

If you don't have time to sit for several minutes, do the following exercise when someone you know comes to your mind:

- If you need to, go somewhere quiet where you won't be disturbed.
- Take a couple of deep breaths, and center yourself, feeling your feet firmly on the ground.

- Acknowledge the person by saying their name out loud, and let them know you have sensed they are reaching out to you.
- Tell them you only have a couple of minutes at this moment to connect with them.
- In Reiki, you get consent from the person before you send energy. In this instance, they are not present with you to give their consent. You can ask yourself whether or not it's okay to send them energy, and respect whatever response comes up.
- If no comes up, sit in silence for a few minutes, or send some prayers hoping they are well. Speak whatever words come to you in your prayer. There is no right or wrong.
- If yes comes up, send them some energy.
- Alternatively, if you are not sure, ask your guardian angels to connect with their guardian angels to take the energy you are sending to be accepted wherever it needs to go in their body if it is in their best interests.
- Lovingly send them energy through your ethereal cord to them.
- Imagine whatever color comes to your mind. Go with your first instinct.
- See it as a ball of light building inside your body.
- The light source may be coming from a specific chakra. Go with whatever feels right.
- Envision where on your body the ethereal cord is connected to this person.
- See the colored light source pulsing and emitting out through the ethereal cord from the connection point on your body to wherever it connects on the other person's body.

- After a few minutes, tell the person you are now breaking the connection.
- Cross your arms over your chest with your fingers tips on the opposite shoulder. Then move your arms down in a sweeping motion, so your hands rest back down at the sides of your thighs. This motion will break the energetic connection with the person.
- Take a couple of deep breaths and return to what you were doing.
- Later in the day, you may choose to call them or text them to let them know you were thinking of them, and were wondering how they were doing.

Embodied Exercise

If you have more time to spend connecting with this person, you can do the following:

- Find a place to sit where you will not be disturbed.
- Take a couple of deep breaths, center your body, and imagine your feet growing roots deep into Mother Earth.
- Think of the person that has come to your mind.
- Remember to ask for consent as in the above exercise.
- Bring up an image of their face or their whole body.
- You can say in your mind or out loud, "I'm here. How are you? What is going on? Is there anything you need from me?"
- Maybe you get a feeling something is wrong, or you may feel an overall sense of love and joy. Go with whatever feelings come up.

- You can send prayers or words of encouragement, or sit in silence with them.
- Notice how your body feels.
- If you are experiencing pain, tension, or discomfort in a part of your body, ask yourself, "Is this *my* pain in my heart (for example)?"
- You will get a yes or no response. Don't second guess yourself. Accept the first thing that pops into your head as the truth.
- If it is yours, thank your body part for showing up. Tell it you will not forget about it, but you are focusing on this other person right now.
- If it is not yours, ask if this sensation is about the person you are connecting with.
- If yes, place a hand on that body part and lovingly send that body part energy, which will be transmitted through you to the person through the etheric cord.
- You can also send colored light energy as in the above exercise for a more extended period.
- Go with your gut about whatever needs to happen.
- When you feel it is time to end the connection, take a few deep breaths, sense back into your body, feel your feet on the floor, and open your eyes.
- Break the connection by crossing your arms across your body and sweeping them down as in the above exercise.

At first, you may not get any insight, but the more frequently you do this, the more you will get intuitive hits about what might be happening for the person.

Breaking Energy Cords

If you have energy vampires in your life, you may need to dis-connect from them as they are toxic and not likely to change. Ask yourself what this person brings to your life. If the answer is *nothing*, start to disengage. See them less often, and extend the time between meetings. If they question your actions, be as direct as possible without blaming them. They are not able to see how their behavior is affecting others. Let them know that sometimes friends drift apart as they grow in different directions, and you are addressing your own needs, focusing on healing yourself. You will find the perfect words for your situation.

Even after you disengage from them, you may still feel their energy as they continue to reach out to you through their thoughts, texts, or calls. This person is still energetically attached to you through the ethereal cord. When you are ready, cut the energetic cord to stop the negative energy drain on your body. You have to be emotionally prepared to cut ethereal cords as this will sever you from that person. Sometimes people think they are ready to let go of someone, but they are benefiting from having that person in their life. When you sever the ethereal cord, it can leave those who are not fully ready with a sense of loss and emptiness, so be 100 percent sure. You can reconnect cords once they've been cut through new interactions with the person.

First, check in with your brain, and ask yourself, "What will I lose without this person in my life?" If the response is inconse-quential, then you may not be affected by the disconnection. If, however, it is something important like a sense of belonging, and you have no one else in your life to whom you feel connected, then this isn't the time to cut cords. First, you need to ensure other people in your life are meeting your needs, and you feel secure releasing that person.

Second, check in with your heart. What do you experience in your heart when you think about removing this person from your life? Does it feel open and light and peaceful? If not, then it may not be the time to cut cords. Cutting a cord doesn't mean you won't feel sadness for letting them go. Nor does it mean you can't still love them. Acknowledge your sadness, and recognize that letting this person go is in your best interests. Letting toxic relationships go allows for new healthy relationships to come in.

Finally, check in with your body. How does the rest of your body feel when you think about cutting energetic cords with this person, and releasing them from your life? If you experience lightness, relief, relaxation, and less tension, this is validation you are making the right decision. If, however, you experience any pain, discomfort, tension, or upset stomach, then you are not ready to let them go.

If all three—your brain, heart, and body—are in alignment, then you can do the exercise below to cut the etheric cords with this person. Remember, you are doing this with love, not anger or spite. You are releasing them for your mutual best interests.

Embodied Exercise

Below is an exercise to sever ethereal cords with people in your life.

- Find a place where you will not be disturbed. You can either sit or lie down, whichever feels most comfortable.
- Close your eyes. Take a couple of deep cleansing breaths. Feel the air come in through your nose, down your chest, and deep into your belly, and feel it expand.
- Ask out loud or in your mind for Archangel Michael and Archangel Raphael to be present as you cut the etheric cords with this person.
- Archangel Michael protects you from lower energies and negative thoughts. He also provides strength and removes fear. Using his sword, he will cut ethereal cords.
- Archangel Raphael supports us in all areas of our health and healing.
- Envision the person you want to cut cords with, and see them standing in front of you.
- Speak from your heart anything you want them to know, or has been left unsaid.
- Tell them you are grateful for having them be part of your life.
- Tell them what you have learned from them.
- Thank them for being in your life, and that you are releasing them for your mutual highest good.
- See the ethereal cord(s) attached between the two of you.

- Ask Archangel Michael to cut the cord(s) from their roots, and send them to Mother Earth or the Universe for continued energetic support. He has a cobalt-blue aura, so you may see waves of this color as he does this work.
- As you envision Archangel Michael cutting the cords, you may feel a shift in your body, or your body may shiver. These sensations are normal.
- Ask Archangel Raphael to heal all of your energetic bodies, and any blockages associated with this person. Feel those areas where the cords were attached being healed and sealed. He has an emerald-green aura, so you may see this color as he works on healing the areas where you released the cords.
- Afterward, notice your body feel calm and peaceful.
- Thank Archangel Michael and Archangel Raphael for being present and supporting you in this work.
- When you feel ready, take a couple of deep breaths.
- Allow yourself to return to the room slowly, feel your body on the chair, floor, or bed.
- Wiggle your fingers and toes and stretch.
- When you are ready, slowly open your eyes.
- Journal any insights or thoughts.

Energetically Protect Your Boundaries

If you are sensitive to other people's energy, whether they are your friend or not, you need to protect your boundaries energetically. For example, maybe you are a bank teller, or work with the public, and deal with many people daily. These energetic hits leave you vulnerable, and you end up taking on other people's energy. Complete the exercise below in the morning before you leave your home. You may also need to reinforce it several times throughout the day. Notice when your energy starts to wane, or you start to feel emotionally overwhelmed. Your protective barrier has likely come down, and you will need to put it back up.

Embodied Exercise

Here is an exercise to protect your boundaries energetically.

- Take a few moments to center yourself, close your eyes and take a couple of deep breaths.
- If you connect with angels, call on Archangel Michael for support.
- Envision him cocooning you in a bubble of cobalt-blue.
- This energetic boundary will allow you to engage with people, but not take on their negative energy.
- If you don't feel connected to angels, call on the Universe, or your star, to cover you in whatever color comes to your mind. See yourself fully protected and bathed in the color.
- When you are ready, open your eyes and resume your day.

I had a client who would envision herself covered in a magnetic force field that would repel any negative energy but still allow her to connect with people. I thought this was brilliant. Whatever you envision for yourself is what you need. Trust your intuition. There is no right or wrong way to do this. Remember, you are not setting up an energetic boundary that keeps you distant or closed off from people. For example, a brick wall keeps you disconnected from others. Whatever you imagine, allow your heart to be open, and your love, compassion, and spirit will freely emit outward to those you connect with.

Energy Can Create Dis-ease

Are you familiar with Louise Hay's book, *You Can Heal Your Life*? Dis-ease in the body is a manifestation of your limiting beliefs, or what you are struggling with, resulting in physical ailments. Your body is not betraying you. It's talking to you. Your body stores energy from experiences you have not fully processed. Every cell in your body holds your memories.

When you feel pain or discomfort in your body, it is a physical manifestation of something deeper. Connecting with this pain or discomfort allows you to give space for it, and your body will start to release it. Of course, if there is physical pain or disease, it won't magically disappear, nor will you be instantly healed, but it will allow you to work through the stuck emotional energy.

Do not judge or blame your body. Your body is brilliant and wants to have free-flowing healthy Ki. You are living a human existence, and as such, you can have painful experiences that you are incapable of dealing with when they are happening. The body, in turn, stores the negative emotional charge and creates blockages. Along with challenging your limiting or negative beliefs, and changing your mindset to a more truthful and positive outlook, sending yourself Reiki and universal life-force energy can help clear negative blockages before they can manifest as dis-ease.

Clearing Energy

When you feel you have stuck energy in your body, clear the blockages through Reiki, or give yourself energy. Here are some other ways that can support you in a pinch throughout the day:

- Cross your arms over your chest with your fingers tips on the opposite shoulder. Then move your arms down in a sweeping motion, so your hands rest back down at the sides of your thighs. This motion will break any energetic connection with people.

- Using your hands, wipe down your arms, your chest, belly, back, butt, thighs, all the way down to your feet. Imagine you are pulling out any stuck negative energy.

- Wash your hands with water, and imagine any stuck energy being removed from your body as it goes down the drain. Put water on your face and the top of your head.

- Buy a spray to help clear energies or attachments. I purchase from a local company (earthkeepers.ca) that uses crystal essences and pure non-alcoholic therapeutic grade essential oils. Alternatively, you can make your own using one-and-a-half tablespoons of distilled water, one tablespoon of vodka or unscented witch hazel, and 20-24 drops of essential oils. Place it in a small two-ounce spray bottle. Some helpful essential oils include:[12]

  - Cedar—aura cleanser, clears fears, strengthens courage and resolve.
  - Cypress—protection, grounding, purification.
  - Frankincense—protection, cleansing, raises energetic vibrations.
  - Lavender—calming, soothing, relaxing, helps guard against negativity.
  - Lemon—physical and psychic cleanser.
  - Rosemary—protection, clears away negative energies.

- Buy sustainably-harvested sage and smudge your body with the smoke as discussed in Chapter 6. Alternatively, grow your own in your garden or a pot, cut the leaves when fully grown, and hang them to dry before burning them. Use your hands to guide the smoke intuitively toward areas of your body.

Like your body, spaces and rooms can harbor stuck negative energy, especially if there is a lot of clutter, arguing, or unexpressed resentment. Along with decluttering and smudging, you can also use a spray with essential oils to clear rooms.

Benefits of Energy Practices

There are several benefits to utilizing energy practices in your life:

- Quiet the mind.
- Feel more relaxed, calm, and at peace.
- Clear blockages in yourself and your environment.
- Enhance your body's healing capabilities.
- Strengthen your immune system.
- Connect more deeply with your body.
- Aid digestion.
- Release toxins.
- Improve sleep and feel more rested.
- Increase mental, emotional, physical, and spiritual well-being.
- Think clearly.
- Reduce pain and discomfort.
- Reduce stress and anxiety.
- Awaken intuition.
- Balance energy and chakras.
- Promote self-awareness.
- Enhance spiritual connection.
- Increase meditative states.
- Increase positive outlook.
- Increase energy and vitality.

—◊◊◊—

I hope this chapter has enlightened you on the applications and benefits of connecting to your body through energy. When you utilize the mindfulness, grounding, and senses skills you learned in the previous chapters, along with the exercises presented in this chapter, you have the tools to remove energy blockages from your body, set energetic boundaries with others, release negative energy from your environment, and provide yourself universal life-force energy for healing, connection, and embodiment.

—◊◊◊—

Join me in the next chapter on Shamanism—the final chapter in the Reconnection section of this book. I'll discuss what shamanism is, how to use shamanic tools and principles to enhance healing and connect with your body, and how to go beyond yourself to transpersonal levels of awareness and connection.

9

SHAMANISM— AWAKENING THE HEALER WITHIN

*"Humans are a part of creation and shamanism
is our way of connecting with the whole."*

Will Adcock

*"The shaman is a self-realized person.
She discovers the ways of Spirit through her inner awakening."*

Alberto Villoldo

S hamanism is a spiritual practice where the shaman seeks
to be in relationship with the Spirit of all things. Shamans
engage in non-ordinary reality for information and guidance for themselves and others. The same year I got H1N1, I
started my journey in shamanic teachings. The weekend workshops involved rituals and ceremonies that were completely
foreign to me. All religions have rituals and ceremonies, but
they typically don't incorporate the land as a living, breathing
entity. Even though I was completely open to the teachings, and
wanted to learn all I could, I was also cautious and skeptical.

I tend to be somewhat stoic in my expression of feelings. As such, it was challenging to be so vulnerable and open at the beginning of these teachings. On the first weekend, we were in groups of three. Two people witnessed while a third person processed a deep emotional wound. We were all crammed into a small room, with people lying within a couple of feet of each other. One person in the room started screaming out in guttural cries. I thought, "What the hell have I gotten myself into?" I had an impulse to run from the workshop, screaming, never to return. Fortunately, I didn't do that.

Journeying is a central shamanic tool that allows you to connect with the Spirit world in a trance state to draw knowledge from three realms of consciousness for yourself or another person. Later that weekend, we were partnered with someone we didn't know, and instructed to journey for our partner while she journeyed for herself. After I journeyed simultaneously with my partner, we compared what each of us saw. Surprisingly, there were a lot of similarities, some even precisely the same. How could it be that what she was witnessing, I too could see? As discussed in Chapter 7, I tapped into my clairvoyance, clairaudience, clairsentience, and claircognizance. I provided accurate and meaningful information to someone through a journey in my mind, which seemed to come from out of thin air. I was hooked.

Shamanism

Historically, shamans have existed in every culture. When cultures became industrialized, and religion started to centralize rituals and ceremonies they deemed as following God's word, traditional generational teachings were seen as heretical and demonized. Sadly, some of those teachings have been lost. Be honest, when you saw there was a chapter on shamanism, did that bring up a critical bias in you? It's okay if it did. People, who don't know anything about shamanism may perceive that shamans perform voodoo and connect with dark magic. This perception couldn't be further from the truth.

What does it mean to be a shaman? A shaman is a mediator between the spiritual worlds of Heaven and Earth. A shaman is often the healer in the community. They have inherent gifts and abilities to see illness in a person through journeying and other divining tools. Divination uses a specific medium to discern information about the person's past, present, and future. As discussed in Chapter 8, a shaman taps into the energetic blockages that create mental, emotional, or physical dis-ease in the body. If necessary, they perform healing by releasing and resetting the stuck energy. They also provide information to the person about what they saw in the journey. In many indigenous cultures, those gifts come as the result of a near-death experience. Peruvian shamans say you can't become a shaman unless struck by lightning.

More importantly, the shaman is a steward of the land. Shamans work in harmony, and with great respect, for Mother Earth and all she provides. Pachamama is always there for us. She supports us and provides unconditional love. She nourishes us, feeds us, and hydrates us—not only physiologically, but mentally, emotionally, and spiritually. She will take your worries, cares, and wounds and mulch them like compost. You can connect with her and ask her any time for anything. You do everything in your life on her—eat, sleep, live, love, play, and work. In return, all she asks is for your care, respect, and love. Mother Earth breathes life into you.

In Peruvian shamanism, and other indigenous cultures, a plate of food is given to Pachamama first to give thanks for all the abundance she provides. Once Pachamama is fed, people can partake in the meal. Stewardship is about honoring and respecting the land and all living things. Humans are one part of the ecological system. Our responsibility is to take what we need and leave only the smallest footprint on Mother Earth.

"Shamanism is active co-participation with the ways of the land."[1] The land holds an abundant wealth of knowledge. There is no separation between us and the land. It is all the same energy. A shaman's intent is to provide for the well-being of the collective—everyone and everything on this planet.[1]

Why Shamanism?

I had the great privilege of training with José Luis Herrera in Peruvian shamanism from 2010-2012. José is an international speaker, teacher, and facilitator on Peruvian indigenous healing methods. Through his Peruvian lineage, he has over 30 years of experience that he gained through extensive research and apprenticeships with shamans from the desert, jungle, and mountain regions of Peru.[2]

José would impart a series of shamanic teachings at each training weekend, and then we would engage experientially in those teachings as part of our healing journey. The work helped me release emotional wounds I had not fully dealt with. These wounds held me back from connecting fully and openly with people. The training also profoundly changed how I viewed myself in connection with Pachamama, and how the land, with all its abundance, informs me every day. I learned how to pay attention to the messages I received from Pachamama, and all of God's creations. Doing so gave me the ability to connect with my body in a more profound, meaningful way. My body, too, was informing me, but I could not connect with it and hear its messages. Shamanism gave me a different perspective of how I view myself within the world. It also provided tools of co-creation between my physical body and the world around me.

Everything I've discussed in the previous chapters—mindfulness, grounding, senses, and energy—are all required to come together to build a framework for engaging in the shamanic practices I am about to discuss. This chapter on shamanism is about your continual connection to your body through tools and techniques that can provide healing and transformation. It is a practice of communing with your body and the land. Your body is a map of consciousness. Shamanism allows you to tap into this body of knowledge within your intuitive body. It helps you release anything that no longer serves you, creates balance, and awakens your medicine body—returning you to a healed state. Your body is the key to helping you unlock your healed state. This type of connection to your body allows you to move beyond your conditioned responses. Connection is about your awareness and intent as a way of being—a state of being through stillness.[1,3]

Shamanism is also something more rooted. It is a "practical one-on-one relationship with nature."[1] It is the next step in going beyond yourself and your physical body to recognize your connection to everything in this world. All plants, trees, rocks, mountains, waters, animals, and humans are energetically linked. You don't end where your body ends. Your energetic bodies go beyond your physical body. It can be freeing to know your physical body doesn't limit you. It can also be comforting to know you aren't alone in the world.

Please keep an open mind about what I present in this chapter. Some of you may already have knowledge and experiential learning of shamanic or indigenous teachings. For others, this may be entirely foreign territory, and that's okay. The purpose of this chapter is to give you some knowledge and tools about different ways of being, and connecting with yourself, your body, and the physical world around you. Come with open curiosity as you explore the teachings and exercises in this chapter for connecting with yourself and Spirit in its many forms.

Sacred Space

"Sacred space allows us to enter our quiet inner world where healing takes place."[4] When you sit with an intention to work on your healing, creating sacred space is like setting the stage before the curtain goes up. You want all the actors present before the scene begins. Your intent connects you with God. You let Spirit know you are co-creating with it, and calling on its resources from all directions for help. The spirits are there to assist us and support our healing. Taking the time to set sacred space allows you to leave your ordinary world behind so you can sit with the Divine in holy reverence. When you open sacred space, you create a bubble of protection. This protection allows you to feel safe and supported so you can let your barriers down and become informed beyond yourself.[4]

There is no one way to open sacred space. If you are unfamiliar with indigenous teachings about opening space, this will seem foreign. However, I encourage you to do it when engaging in any form of self-healing work, or connecting with your Higher Self and Spirit. You can open sacred space when you journal about emotions you are experiencing and want to process and release. When you co-create with the world around you, open sacred space. Open sacred space when you engage in Reiki, or any other form of energy work, or when you meditate to seek answers to questions. Finally, open sacred space when engaging with the teachings in this chapter.

Dr. Alberto Villoldo on The Four Wind's website created a prayer for opening sacred space. You can find it online by googling it. It can be read by those feeling unsure of what to say on their own. You will invoke the four directions, and Mother Earth and Father Sun, in the following order: south, west, north, east, Mother Earth, and Father Sun. When invoking each direction, stand facing the direction; fan a smudge stick or blow scented water toward the direction. Hold your hand up toward the direction with your palm facing forward while reciting the prayer for that direction. When you call in Mother Earth, place your hand on the ground. When you call in the Father Sun, look up as you direct your prayers there. It is essential after whatever healing work or ceremony you partake in that you close sacred space and thank serpent, jaguar, hummingbird, and eagle to release them back to the four corners of Mother Earth. Finally, thank Pachamama, God or Creator, and other spiritual beings for their ongoing presence and support in your daily life.

You do not need to open sacred space, as noted above, if it doesn't fit your beliefs. You still can, however, open sacred space to whatever your belief system is. What's most important, is setting your intention to do healing work or ceremony. Ask for support and guidance from whatever sentient beings you feel connected with.

You can light a candle, and burn sage or other incense. Then speak whatever words of prayer to invoke the presence of those you wish to be in sacred space with. You can ask for the presence of God, Creator, the Universe, archangels, guardian angels, spirit guides, goddesses, animal guides, or Mother Earth. When you are done, and wish to close sacred space, speak from your heart with love and thank them.

Mesa

"A shaman's *mesa* is a portable altar (where he goes to meet the spirits) or medicine bundle used for healing, ceremony, prayer, and divination."[5] The mesa contents can include anything that provides a spiritual and meaningful connection for you. Some examples include stones from sacred lands, crystals, feathers, pieces of wood, or other artifacts from the shaman's healing journey. "A mesa is the living embodiment of your healing and transformation."[1] You create a transpersonal relationship with your mesa, which transforms your worldview. Transpersonal refers to going beyond yourself to more extraordinary aspects of consciousness, spirituality, psyche, or the Universe. Your mesa is a living embodiment, and symbolic expression, of your connection to the land and the collective.

Power Stones

In Peruvian shamanism, your mesa holds *khuyas* or power stones. You use your khuya to work through wounds that have left you with scarcity in your life, such as aloneness, loneliness, or lack of love, self-love, or abundance. To work through your emotional and physical wounds, go to the land and choose a power stone. Shamanism is about intent. Go to the land with the intent of finding a healing power stone. Go for a walk in the mountains, or down by the river. Be mindful as you walk. Open yourself to the experience of being out in nature. Feel yourself on the land. Follow each footstep. Being in nature to find your power stone is a part of the journey. Use all your senses—sight, smell, sound, taste, and touch. Look around you. Take in the colors and everything you see. What do you smell or hear? Put your hand on trees, plants, rocks, the ground, or in a body of water. Notice how it feels in your body as you connect with Pachamama. What are the sensations flowing through your body? Inhale the fresh air deeply. Let it fill every cell in your body with life-giving energy.

As you explore and connect with Pachamama, you will intuitively be led to your khuya. You will have an intuitive knowing that this is your power stone. Find a place to sit comfortably on the land. Pick up the stone and look at it from all sides and angles. There will be images, shapes, or pictures on the stone that have special meaning and messages specifically for you. Take a couple of deep breaths and hold the stone to your heart. Ask the stone if this is your power healing stone and wait for an answer. You will intuitively get a yes or no response. The answer may come up in your mind, or you may feel the answer in your body. Then, ask the stone if it is willing to leave the land to be with you and help you heal your wounds. Again you will get a yes or no response. If both are yeses, you've found your power stone.

Close your eyes and sit with the power stone in meditation. Ask it for clarity around your healing, or anything it wants to impart to you. Hold the stone in your hands, turning it over and feeling all sides of it. Listen for the response in your internal mind or body. Bring a journal and write down your experience. Nothing may come up at first, and that's okay. However, the more you connect with your body in quiet reflection, the more you will hear your Higher Self speaking to you. In the beginning, people dismiss what comes up as impossible. "This is just my imagination coming up with memories, images, thoughts, feelings, or sensations." It is not your imagination. It is your connection to your Higher Self through God, Source, or the Universe.

Maybe you think this all sounds a little too woo-woo for you. Stones are going to talk to me? Hell, yes! Plants, trees, flowers, rocks, and Mother Earth speak to us all the time. You haven't learned the tools and teachings to listen. I've taken several workshops on how to listen and connect with plants and the medicines they provide. Do not discount the power, energy, and healing that comes from Mother Earth's elements.

Give thanks to Pachamama and the stone for providing abundance and energy to support your healing by providing an offering for Pachamama in return. Many indigenous cultures give back to the land through offerings. In North America, this is often with tobacco. In Peruvian shamanism, Pachamama loves sweets. As such, before you leave on your quest to find your power stone, bring some loose tobacco, sage, or sugar in a small bag to give thanks to Pachamama for all she provides. Blow prayers of thanks into the offering using your breath and words. Speak out loud your gratitude for receiving this power stone for your healing. Infuse your breath from the depths of your belly—exhaling with a forceful *ha* sound. By doing so, you impart your energetic resonance into the offering. Place the offering on the land.

Embodied Exercise

Make it a routine to sit on Mother Earth to connect with her wisdom and healing energy.

- Take a sketch pad, pencils, and pencil crayons with you with the intent of connecting with a specific plant, tree, rock, or body of water.
- Sit comfortably next to the part of nature you want to learn more about and connect with.
- Look at it—sketch in your pad everything you see from all sides and angles. You don't need to be an artist. Don't judge your drawing.
- Touch it—what does it feel like? What sensations do you feel?
- Smell it—does it have a particular smell? Earthy? Woody? Salty?
- Hear it—put your ear to it. Does it have a specific sound?
- Taste it—only if it is safe to do so, and you know it's not poisonous.
- Ask the following questions:

  - What is your essence?
  - What is your personality?
  - What characteristics do you have?
  - What are your uses?
  - What medicine do you provide?
  - Anything else you want me to know about you?

- Write down everything that comes up in your sketch pad or journal.

- When done, thank it for the knowledge and information it has provided you.
- Leave an offering to Pachamama in gratitude for the experience.

Create Your Mesa

Now that you have your first healing power stone, you can create your mesa. A mesa can be extensive with many sacred objects, or it can be one healing stone. The sacred objects are typically wrapped in cloth—forming your medicine bundle. In Peru, this cloth is a colorful textile known as a *mastana*.[5] When you create your mesa, find a unique or meaningful fabric or pouch to hold your healing power stone.

Don't forget about your power stone and mesa. Sit with it, meditate with it, and use it for healing, which I'll discuss shortly. You also need to feed your mesa. You can put sage, tobacco, or flowers in with your medicine bundle. Open your mesa and leave it out on the land at night to be charged and cleansed by Pachamama and the moon.

Altar

An altar, in shamanism, is a place for reverence, reflection, and remembrance. It is a place to connect with your intentions for healing, and bringing forth the life you want to create. It is a place for stillness and turning inward. An altar is a living, breathing reflection of your life. The sacred items you place on it will provide support, guidance, and meaning. It is an anchor to your spiritual path and growth.

Find a place in your home for your altar. Keep it in a place that is not cluttered—a place where you feel calm and peaceful.

Make sure there is enough space in front of the altar so you can sit in silence, meditate, do healing work, and pray.

Find a lower-sized table or stool as your altar, so that when you sit in front of it, you can see and interact with the sacred items. If you are able, place your altar so that you can look out the window when you face it. Seeing out the window allows you to be present with Pachamama, and for your altar to become energetically charged by the sun and moon.

Make your altar inviting. If you have a sacred cloth, place it over the table. Place a candle on your altar and light it every time you sit with your altar. Light sage and smudge, or burn incense. Open sacred space. Place flowers on your altar to feed your intentions and prayers. Below is a list of sacred objects you can place on your altar. It is not an exhaustive list. Choose whatever has meaning for you, for your healing, and your intentions for your future.

- Pictures of yourself, loved ones, or icons.
- Tobacco, sage, sweetgrass, copal, palo santo.
- Agua de florida, rose water, orange blossom.
- Feathers, twigs, stones.
- Khuyas, mesa.
- Crystals.
- Singing bowl, rattles, bells, or drums.
- Figurines to represent spirit guides. For example, a carved bear to represent your spirit animal.
- Artwork.
- Intentions written on pieces of paper.
- Candle.
- Flowers.

As you construct your altar, sit with it, close your eyes, and connect with your heart and ask, "What wants to be here?" You will intuitively know what to add. Every piece you place on your altar will be intentional. Sit with your altar daily. Re-assess your altar. There may be a new theme or intention in your life for a whole new type of altar. If so, clean it, tend to it, and replace the flowers or offerings. Sacred items will come and go as required for your healing needs and intentions.

How to Use Your Khuya for Healing

As I discussed in Chapter 1, we all have wounds from things we have experienced throughout our life. Those wounds, when not processed and healed, reside in our physical and energetic bodies. You stay stuck in the story of your traumas, continue to manifest its energy, and store it as a physical expression in your body. Your woundedness becomes a source of disempowerment.

When you experience trauma, you have soul loss. Soul loss diminishes life-force vitality and strength. It will manifest an energetic woundedness through pain and active scars, or blocks in your energetic bodies or auric field. It will also result in lost qualities for your life—hopes, dreams, promises, or potentials. To prevent further dismemberment in times of intense chaos, you check out. You black out when you experience severe fear, and when you come back to consciousness, you have soul loss. Symptoms of soul loss include:

- Inability to be present in your body.
- Parts of you feel dead, or you numb your feelings.
- Chronic depression (are unable to feel joy).
- Deficient immune system.
- Memory gaps.
- Blackouts.
- Addictions (as a means to alleviate the pain).

- Constant grief and loss.
- Inability to let go.
- Need to fill an internal void (to feel a connection to).
- Difficulty transitioning (can't let go of partners).[1]

You can use your khuya to work through your wounds. When you work through your wounds, you will identify how your body stores your woundedness so you can set it free—not only setting yourself free, but all of your perpetrators too. Healing is about creating a bridge to the soul piece you've lost. By creating a safe space for healing, and working through the wound to release any energetic resonance, you allow the soul piece to return to your body.[1]

If you completed an inventory in Chapter 1, and wrote out all your traumas, wounds, or disturbing experiences, choose one you wish to work on to heal.

Find a quiet space where you can do this work and not be disturbed. Open sacred space. Call in whomever you wish to be present to support your healing. Take out your mesa and power stone. Take several deep breaths, and center yourself to engage in this sacred work. Bring up all the details about this wound you wish to heal. Speak everything you want to release about this situation into the stone. Using your khuya for healing is not a time to be reserved. Cry, yell, scream, and curse your heart out. Don't hold back. You are energetically releasing all of the stored emotion and physical blockages related to this issue.

Take note of the feelings in your body. You may feel physical pain, tension, or discomfort in a specific body location. Feeling discomfort is normal, and, likely, where the wound is stored. Breathe deeply into these parts, and blow out forcefully with a *ha* sound into your stone as many times as you need to feel the energy shift and release. Using counter-clockwise circular motions with the khuya in your palm, rub over the areas on your body where there is discomfort. Wind out all of the stored blocked energy and transfer it into your healing stone.

If there were specific people involved, speak directly to them whatever you need to say. People usually don't get the opportunity to confront their perpetrators, and I don't recommend it. Those who have harmed you don't often own up to the injuries they have caused, whether they participated in their actions consciously or unconsciously. As such, confronting someone can result in re-traumatization, or more harm.

By speaking into your healing stone, you get the opportunity to say what you need to say to release the energy and hurt around this wound. Even though you may have intense anger toward this person, or wish them harm, this is not about attacking them, or asserting some form of revenge. However, you get to call them terrible names, if that will support releasing the feelings and energy you've held onto and stored. Doing so does not energetically send them harm. You are speaking directly into the khuya, which will be placed on Pachamama and released to her.

The release is about how what they did harmed you. Speak out loud how they hurt you—state how this has affected your life, and what you have lost. Throughout the process, breathe deeply into your belly, and exhale out with a *ha* sound into your stone. Take as much time as you need. Emotions and sensations may come in waves. Keep going until you have said everything that needs to be released. When you feel complete, close sacred space and thank those you called to support this healing work.

You will likely feel energetically depleted or tired afterward. Drink lots of water and be kind to yourself. Do not judge or blame yourself for the experience. That is not supportive or helpful. The situation was not something you asked for, and was beyond your control. Forgive yourself for whatever part you played in this trauma or wound. You cannot predict what will happen to you. Sometimes you make choices that lead to situations where you experience harm. Sometimes that harm happens repeatedly with abusive people. It's easy to look back on your past and think, "What if?" or "I shouldn't have been there," or "I should have left them sooner." You are a completely different person now with more knowledge, experience, and personal growth. At the time of the trauma or wounding, you were a less-experienced person, with only the knowledge and abilities you had at the time. If blame comes up, speak those words and feelings into your healing stone.

Next, I'll discuss placing the stone on the land to transmute the negative energy into mental, emotional, physical, and spiritual healing in your body.

Mandala

A mandala is a "symbolic diagram used in the performance of sacred rites and as an instrument of meditation. The mandala represents the Universe. It is a consecrated area that serves as a receptacle for the gods and as a collection point of universal forces."[6] It is like a soul catcher.[1] It is a symbolic microcosm of your world. By creating a mandala, you develop a nonpersonal relationship to the wounds and people involved to help you work through the event in a mythic representation of reality. You feed the people and events to inform you, and allow Spirit to show you lessons and learning. You ask Pachamama, Spirit, and the ancestors of the land to help you.[7]

Take your healing stone and find a place in your yard to leave it on the land. If you don't have a yard, take it to a nearby park where you can visit it for several days. Clear the area of debris. Chose a space that will get both the sun's and moon's rays. Call in all the directions to open sacred space, and call in whomever feels supportive for you.

When you take your healing work out to Pachamama to be worked on and released, you will create a mandala on the ground to represent your world. Take sticks, branches, and twigs to frame your mandala. It can be circular, square, rectangular, or whatever shape you wish. Cross the branches over top of each other as you create the shape to ensure the mandala is closed.

As you stand in front of your mandala, feel into your body and intuitively notice any stuck energy. Take your khuya, and using counter-clockwise circular movements, run the khuya over all the body parts where you feel you are storing stuck energy concerning the wound you are releasing. Imagine you are unwinding the energy of that wound. You can visualize it as a dark cord, chains, smoke, or whatever else comes to mind. Keep moving your khuya over your body until you feel there is nothing left to remove.

When you feel your khuya is fully loaded, sit in front of your mandala. Then reach your hand out with the khuya in your palm. Close your eyes and allow your hand to move over the top of the mandala. Feel into your body and the land, and intuitively gauge where to place your khuya inside the mandala. Provide offerings to Pachamama for the work she is doing to release the energy from the words, feelings, and physical blockages you placed into the healing stone. The offering can be sugar, sage, tobacco, or flowers.

Return to the stone daily for as many days as you feel necessary to release everything about this troubling experience. Take note of your surroundings and the area where you placed your stone. Mother Earth is informing you all the time. Maybe some leaves, twigs, or bugs have shown up close to your stone. Survey the scene and intuitively read into what you see. If your stone is gone, don't panic. It means you've healed the issue when a stone is gone. It has done its job. Find another power stone to work with other wounds to be released.

Sit with your healing stone, pick it up, and notice any more words, feelings, or physical stuck energy. Speak the words that need to be released. Breathe out the wound's emotional and physical energy, and unwind any stuck energy from your body. When complete, place the stone back inside your mandala and feed Pachamama again with an offering. You are *cooking* when you leave the mandala for several days. This process is alchemy. You transform your physical self, and release the energetic matter you placed into the stone to be mulched by Pachamama and transformed into something beautiful.

When you no longer have anything left to say, there are no more troubling feelings, and your physical body feels at peace, then this wound is complete. As in all healing, it can happen in layers. Several years later, another piece you never thought about related to this wound appears. If this happens, you can return to this process to heal whatever has now emerged.

The transformation you will experience from doing this work can be immediate, or happen over time. You may immediately feel lighter, as if a weight has been lifted, or the wound no longer feels troubling or disturbing. Long-term, you may notice you are not the same person—less emotional, happier, more trusting, calmer, or at peace. You may behave differently in relationships. You may feel more authentic, and can be the person you have always wanted to be.

Despacho

During my trip to Peru, we were blessed to learn and engage in daily rituals and ceremonies with the Q'ero shamans. The Q'ero are a Quechua-speaking community that live in the Paucartambo province in the Cusco region of Peru. Throughout the day, we participated in shamanic teachings and traditions from the *pampamesayoq* shamans who work with Mother Earth's energy, and the *altomesayoq* shamans who work with mountain spirits. We went to sacred sites and made three or four prayer bundles—*despachos*—each day.

A despacho is a prayer bundle created with reverence as a gift of thanksgiving, or filled with prayers to support mental, emotional, and physical healing for yourself or others. It is used in a spiritual ceremony to restore balance and harmony in your life, create new possibilities, and establish new ways of being with yourself and the world.

> It establishes a linkage between our three centers of interaction in the *kaypacha* (the physical universe); our *llankay* (our personal power and source of action, located in our solar plexus), our *munay* (the source of our love, located in our heart chakra), and our *yachay* (wisdom, sourced from our foreheads or 'third eye').[7]

When you create a despacho, you build a bridge from your ordinary reality to non-ordinary realms of the Spirit world. You enter into an altered state of consciousness by connecting and aligning with these three energy centers.[8,9]

The despacho is a physical embodiment of offering gratitude to God, Creator, the Universe, or Pachamama and her many life forms. When you create a despacho for Pachamama, it is an act of reciprocity. You give back to the land, and all the nature spirits, for what they provide for you every day. Reciprocity sets a foundation for being in right *ayni,* or right relationship, with Pachamama.

A despacho can also be created with prayers, blessings, and intentions when you have a specific request from Spirit. Have faith that your visions and actions will manifest. You can pray for yourself, your family, community, or country; you can pray to bring peace to a conflict or war, for a disaster like wildfires or pandemics, or all of humanity. As with all prayers, there is no limit.

Among the Quechua-speaking people of the Andes of Peru, Bolivia, and Ecuador, there are 100s of variations of despachos. Despachos are like mandalas. They are beautifully intricate and woven with flowers, seeds, grains, beans, sugar, tobacco, sage, incense, sweets, paper money, and wine, to name but a few things. You choose offerings with specific symbolic meaning and intent to create your despacho. According to Q'ero Elder Don Manuel Q'espi, it is your intention and prayers that "transcends literal and symbolic domains and directly accesses the archetypal and energetic realms."[8] Check out the Center for Shamanic Education and Exchange's short video on the *Q'ero Despacho* for more information and examples of despachos.

Your despacho can be a combination of gratitude and reciprocity to God, Creator, the Universe, Pachamama, archangels, guardian angels, spirit guides, mountain spirits, and animal spirits, and include prayers for healing, or what you wish for in your life. Through a despacho, you set intentions to manifest your reality in the physical Universe. Fill your body with the gratitude you wish to impart into the despacho.

What you put into your prayers and intentions is what you will receive. Engage in this practice with humility and grace, and don't discount the power of this process. Use your whole physical being. Feel the energy in your body. Speak your gratitude and prayers. Feel them coming from the deepest recesses of your spirit and soul. When I say this is a spiritual experience, I am not saying this lightly. Let your inhibitions go. Go deep to the core of your being. The deeper you let go, the deeper you will feel connected to altered states of consciousness and spiritual realms. Be one with the Universe. It's okay if it doesn't feel natural in the beginning. The more despachos you make, the deeper your connection to yourself and this process.

Choose biodegradable items that have specific meaning for you to give gratitude and blessings to Spirit for all it provides in your life. (See the exercise below for a link to potential items and their meanings.) It would be best to resonate with the items you choose according to your intent for the despacho.

Blow prayers into *kintus*—three perfect coca leaves stacked one on top of each other—and then each bundle of kintus is placed in the despacho. As coca leaves are not native to North America, you can use bay leaves. Ensure each bay leaf has no holes or blemishes. As an alternative, you can choose one or several flowers to add prayers and intentions for yourself or others. Use the flower's head, and remove the stems, so it's easier to bundle the despacho when completed.

When you speak the words, say them as if they are already true and have come to fruition. For example, "God, thank you for my perfect healed state. That my mind is clear, and I speak only words of kindness. Thank you to all my like-minded clients who have entrusted me to be a witness in their healing journey. Thank you for my spiritual and financial abundance. Thank you for allowing me to be in right ayni (relationship) with all the people in my life."

As you blow prayers into the kintus, you energetically build the momentum of your intentions. You will feel a vibrational shift in yourself and the energy of the room. "The despacho becomes a living prayer that brings energy shifts and healing."[10] When you have completed your despacho, place your hand over the despacho's center. Move it up or down, or from left to right or right to left. You will feel the energetic vibration you have breathed into the despacho, and a temperature variation. Often, after a completed despacho, I can feel the coolness in my hand when I place it above the despacho.

Embodied Exercise

Below is a step-by-step description of how to create a despacho. Don't let this description limit or hinder you. You can choose to make one however you feel called to do so. It can include one or several items of your choosing. The elements you include don't matter as much as your intent. Check out the end of Alex Stark's article *The Despacho Ceremony* for a list of potential items to include in your despacho, and their meaning (alexstark. com/despacho-ceremonies). Congruently, you can infuse your purpose into each item you choose.

- Collect all the items you wish to include in your despacho.
- You will need a white piece of paper to place your items on, and to wrap them into a bundle once completed.
- You can use wrapping paper, placing your items on the white-sided surface.
- Ensure the paper is big enough to wrap around the items you have chosen to include.
- Keep the items close to the center, and leave the edges to fold them into a bundle.
- You will need string or yarn to tie the despacho bundle once completed.
- Find a quiet place where you will not be disturbed.
- If the weather is nice, sit on Pachamama and feel grounded to her energy.
- Open sacred space, and call in whomever you wish to connect with.
- Gently blow prayers into each item one by one, and then place them in the despacho.

- Speak out loud. Spirit needs to hear your prayers and intentions.

- Speak from your heart whatever words are called for the intent of the despacho.

- You can choose to start with sugar by creating a cross in the center to represent the four directions, and the upper and lower realms, if you feel called to do so.

- Place the items you have prayed into in the despacho in whatever pattern you wish.

- Sit with your despacho once complete. Extend your hands out toward the despacho to impart more gratitude and love. Feel the energy flow from your body, out through your hands and into the despacho.

- Sit quietly with your eyes closed. Allow yourself to receive energy from the despacho, and any messages it wishes to impart to you.

- Once you have placed all your items in the despacho, shape it into a square bundle.

- Start by folding the bottom half of the paper up to the center of the despacho, fold the top half down to overlap the bottom half, and then bring in the right and left sides.

- Wind yarn or string around your despacho bundle. Ensure you don't turn the bundle upside-down; otherwise, you will undo all your prayers.

- Place a flower on top of the bundle securing a bit of the stem under the yarn. Place the head of the flower to point to the top half of your despacho. Always carry your despacho with the top facing out.

- You can either choose to bury your despacho (this will produce slow, steady results), burn it (for swifter transformation), or place it in a body of water (to send your gifts to Spirit).
- If you choose to burn it, turn your back to the fire once you place it in the fire. Do not look at the flames until it has burned down. Turning your back symbolizes non-attachment. Let go, and know Spirit has received your prayers, and is manifesting them.
- Close sacred space.
- If you choose to burn it, do not put water on the fire, let it burn down completely, and bury the ashes once cooled.[9,10]

Fire Ceremonies

Fire ceremonies are an integral part of shamanism and shamanic traditions. They allow you to experience timelessness, connect you with your ancestral lineage, and support shamans to reset their bodies.[1] Indigenous people engage in fire ceremonies as a connection to the land, and to honor the changing of seasons (solstice and equinox) and the moon's cycles—specifically the full moon and new moon.

The winter solstice in the northern hemisphere (December 20 or 21) is a time to turn inward for self-reflection and regeneration. The summer solstice (June 20 or 21) marks the return to light, the light within us, and Christ consciousness. It is a time to celebrate a reconnection to the land, a time for rebirth and growth.

The equinox occurs twice a year—around March 21 and around September 23. During the equinox, the sun is directly above the equator, which results in an equal length of both day and night. Everything is in balance and perfect harmony. It is a reminder to bring balance into your life. For shamans, the spring equinox is a return to life after a cold winter. It is a time of renewal and rebirth—a time for blessing seeds and to awaken the land for planting. The fall equinox is a time to give thanks to Pachamama for the harvest and bounty she provided. It is to honor that Pachamama is preparing for sleep—a type of death.

Fire ceremonies can be another way to release unwanted energies and attachment to things that are troubling you—past wounds, negative thoughts, difficult emotions, fears, or anything that isn't serving your highest self. A fire ceremony to release unwanted energies occurs during a full moon. "By releasing these unwanted energies and old patterns into the fire, you are healing at the soul level."[11] Fire ceremonies can also be used to set positive intentions for your life and prayers of request. A fire ceremony to set intentions occurs during a new moon. You can have a fire ceremony during the cycles of the moon, or the solstice and equinox, but it isn't necessary. You can choose to do a fire ceremony any time you feel a need to release and reset.

Embodied Exercise

Full Moon (Releasing) Ceremony

- Find a quiet space in your home or outside to work on what you wish to release.
- In a seated position, take a couple of deep breaths and close your eyes.
- Ask yourself what you need to release that is no longer serving you.
- Open your eyes and write out or draw whatever comes to mind.
- Create an offering for each item to be released using twigs, flowers, or paper.

- Feel any emotions and blow these into your creation.
- You can also blow emotions and speak into your khuya.
- Now create an offering of gratitude to Pachamama and Spirit for helping you release what is no longer serving you.
- You can bundle together tree branches and flowers with sage or tobacco, or use only one of these items.
- When you feel complete, go outside and start a fire, or inside you can use a wood-burning fireplace, or a special bowl. It doesn't have to be huge.
- Open sacred space, and call in whomever comes to mind—God, Creator, the Universe, archangels, guardian angels, spirit guides, animal guides, or ancestors.
- Speak out loud whatever you are releasing, blowing into each item, and place them one by one into the fire.
- If you used your khuya, wave it over the fire on both sides to release and clear the energy.
- You can also release and reset your body at the fire with your hands.
- Kneel in front of the fire, and use your hands to pull the flames' energy toward your body.
- Using a counter-clockwise circular motion with your hands, rub over your third eye, heart, and belly centers. Then push your hands out toward the fire as you blow out anything you need to release. You can do this as many times as you need for each center.
- Then draw in the fire and, using a clockwise circular motion, infuse the flames into these three energy centers to reset your body.

- When you feel complete, take your bundle of gratitude. Blow in prayers to allow whatever needs to be released, and to help you to return to your healed state. Place this offering into the fire.

- Allow the fire to burn down. Close sacred space, and offer words of gratitude to all those you called into the space to support you.

New Moon (Prayers and Intentions) Ceremony

- This process is the same as above, except you write out or draw your prayers and intentions for the things you would like in your life.

- As with the despacho, speak to those things as if they have already come to fruition. For example, "Thank you for my new partner who treats me, and speaks to me, with respect and kindness, and gives me unconditional love and support."

- It is not necessary to release and reset using fire unless you feel called to do so.

- Know that as your items burn, the smoke is being lifted to Spirit to answer your prayers.

- Walk in faith, as if your prayers are already answered and manifested in your life.

Recapitulation

All shamanic traditions have some form of recapitulation to process one's life. Recapitulation is a technique for retrieving memories and re-living past wounds and trauma(s) using all your senses to release all the stuck thoughts, emotions, body sensations, attachments, and energy. Unprocessed wounds and trauma become stuck or blocked, which drains your life-force energy. It takes energy to keep the memory and emotions of your wounds and trauma(s) alive. Every time you are triggered, you open up the file folder of all your negative past experiences. Unhealed wounds and trauma inform your future behaviors, and keep you stuck. Recapitulation heals trapped negative energy that was left behind after your experiences with others. It is about taking your power and vitality back.

In Peruvian shamanism, you visualize dropping your belly into Pachamama. In this process, you imagine an umbilical cord coming from your belly and going deep into Pachamama. The umbilical cord connects and ties you to Mother Earth. Pachamama provides unconditional love and support, and feeds you her life-giving energy. You then journey in the recapitulation process to past wounds and trauma.

In the exercise below, I will teach you another recapitulation process. Bring up the memory and allow yourself to feel the emotions and body sensations that arise with the memory while breathing and releasing it. Remember, everything you do and experience is stored as energy in your mind, emotions, and body. If you hang onto past wounds and trauma, you continue to relive the hurtful emotions and body sensations over and over again and create unnecessary suffering.

Have you ever heard someone say their life flashed before their eyes during a near-death experience? Or, perhaps, experienced it for yourself? A near-death experience is a natural phenomenon known as a *life review*. This flash of one's memories releases a burst of energy, which transports the person into their next spiritual phase, whatever form that may be. You can use this same energy during the recapitulation process to release harmful experiences, and transform yourself into a healed state.[12,13]

If you didn't do this in Chapter 1, write a list of all your wounds, traumas, disturbing experiences, and the people involved. Instead of doing one wound at a time, you can write out a timeline of the things that happened to you and the people involved at each age. Write out all the significant experiences that affected you for that year of life. Start with conception until time of birth, then each year until you get to your current age.

Yes, this will likely be a lengthy list. There is no need to hurry. You may choose to do one year per recapitulation session. Give yourself plenty of time between sessions to allow your body to shift and feel into its new state of being. You will immediately start to feel lighter and freer, and have more emotional and physical energy return to your body.

For the period between conception and birth, and the first several years of life, you may not have any specific memories for things that transpired, but experiences still happened. You may have heard stories from your parents, siblings, or other relatives that were disturbing. For example, maybe your house was on fire when you were a baby, or maybe your parents lived in a war-torn country while your mom was pregnant with you.

Your body stores the energy of troubling or traumatic situations even if you have no thoughts, emotions, or memories to go with it. Some of you will have vivid memories even as a child in the crib, but not had the language to articulate them. Don't write them off as your imagination; take them as your truth.

You can also do a meditation imagining yourself in those younger years, or during gestation and birth. See if you experience any sense of knowing that something may have happened at the time, or any uncomfortable emotions or body sensations that come up. Write whatever you notice for that period of your life. Use those same thoughts, emotions, and body sensations when you do the recapitulation process for that age.

⸺⸺

I once did a meditation where I had a deep knowing that my mom didn't want me when she was pregnant with me because of several life stressors at the time. I never asked her about this as she may have had no memory of it, or it could have caused harm or suffering for her. My negative belief was, *she didn't want me.* I accessed the feelings of not being wanted to release the blocked energy. In actuality, this was never about me. It was about my mom and her stress at the time. What mother doesn't feel inadequate or incapable of raising a child when they experience stress during pregnancy? Feeling unsure is a typical case of imposter syndrome. You feel like an imposter when you have feelings of inadequacy in whatever area of your life you are experiencing even though you have been successful in that area or similar areas through transferable skills. Also, after the birth, a mother may feel inadequate, and believe they are not doing enough for their baby. Hormones are unstable after birth, making it harder to think clearly; a new mother may experience postpartum depression because of the hormone imbalance.

When you do the recapitulation process using the procedure below, you will bring up all the emotional and physical energy of one experience at a time. You will release the trapped energy of the person who caused you harm that was stuck in your body and energetic field.

As I discussed in Chapter 8, you connect to others through etheric cords. This process is another means of cutting cords with people you have had harmful experiences with. Picture the experience's emotional and physical energy as a bunch of tangled wires that you are hanging onto and dragging around with you needlessly. The recapitulation process allows you to free yourself from these wires and release blocked negative energy.[12,13]

Let yourself feel all the emotions and body sensations to release them. You may feel uncomfortable or drained during the process, but it will shift as you work through it. For those who have traumatic experiences you have never worked through, this process may be too intense and could re-traumatize you. Please seek out counseling with a trauma therapist who can help you safely process and desensitize the experience. It may be several months or years before you feel able to release any lingering stuck negative energy around the trauma through the recapitulation process. Listen to your mind, body, and intuition to discern where you are in your healing, and if you are well enough mentally and emotionally to engage in the recapitulation process.

Embodied Exercise

You may choose to start from the earliest experiences, or with your most recent life events, as they will be more easily recalled.

- Find a quiet space where you will not be disturbed.
- Preferably in darkness so as not to be distracted.
- Cover yourself in a heavy blanket to help contain the energy.
- Close your eyes. Take a couple of deep breaths as you settle into your body, feeling calm and relaxed.
- Vividly bring up the experience or year of life you want to work through.
- Bring up all the colors, people, smells, sights, sounds, tastes, thoughts, emotions, and body sensations of the experience.
- Start with your head facing forward.
- Take a breath in, and turn your head to the left as you exhale.

- Take a deep breath in, and as you slowly turn your head to your right shoulder, picture and draw in the scene, with all the emotional and physical energy attached to it.

- Then, as you exhale, turn your head slowly back to your left shoulder, expelling all the negative thoughts, emotions, sensations, and energy.

- Continue side to side in this process until you feel there is nothing left to release. This back-and-forth action is *fanning* the event.

- Return your head forward. Take a couple of deep breaths to release any lingering energy and allow you to return to your body and the room.

- Wiggle your fingers and toes to feel back into your body.

- You may feel light-headed after a session, or you may feel completely energized. This is normal.

- Feel your feet on the floor, and connect with Mother Earth to become grounded.

- Drink plenty of water to flush out any lingering energetic toxins.

You can do as many recapitulation events as you like in a row. I suggest 15–20 minutes per recapitulation session to start, and leave a minimum of two weeks between sessions. It may take several recapitulation sessions to release all the blocked negative energy from deeper traumas or complex trauma. When you bring up the experience again, and the emotional energy has lessened or disappeared, it means you are releasing. You may no longer visualize the memories, or it may feel like it happened to someone else and not you. You may also experience new clarity or insights about the experience or yourself.[12,13]

In my shamanic teachings, we were fortunate enough to hear José whistle and rattle while we engaged in the recapitulation process. If you would like to enhance your recapitulation experience, you can listen to whistling, rattling, or drumming. The rhythm supports your left and right brain's synchronization and increases alpha and theta waves in the brain.

Alpha waves allow you to be awake, relaxed and calm, to support feelings of well-being and euphoria. Alpha waves are the gateway to your subconscious mind, which houses your emotions, imagination, and intuition.

Theta waves engage your brain between states of wakefulness and drowsiness, and include meditative states. Theta waves are the realm of the subconscious mind. This state supports increased creativity, inspiration, insight, and visualizations. This altered consciousness, or trance state, can bring on shamanic imagery and visual experiences. In this state, you can experience oneness and a deep spiritual connection with the Universe.[14,15,16]

Journey

In shamanism, "part of the soul is free to leave the body."[17] This can occur when you are dreaming or astral traveling. Astral travel or astral projection refers to your ability to have an out-of-body experience. Your soul or consciousness, also known as your astral body, can travel outside of your physical body into the Universe.[18] As discussed earlier in this chapter, a part of your soul can leave due to trauma, known as soul loss. The soul can also leave the body intentionally through a soul flight or shamanic journey.[17]

The shamanic journey is an essential practice used by shamans to connect with the spirit world to provide information and answers to questions for themselves or others in their community. You don't need to be a shaman to utilize this helpful tool to connect with Spirit. Everyone has an innate ability to journey. You only need an open mind and open heart.

In Peruvian shamanism, your physical body and world are organized the same, and represent your overarching cosmology or Universe. There are three levels of *pachas,* or worlds, that represent different spheres of the cosmos. The *hanaqpacha,* or upper world, is also known as the *yachay* (third eye), your vision and intellect. The archetype is *apuchin,* and represents the condor. Apuchin connects you to other light beings in the Universe, and allows you to see things from above, providing you with a different perspective. The *kaypacha* is this world, or the middle world, where all living beings reside. It is also known as *munay* (heart center), which is nonpersonal or unconditional love. The archetype is *chocachinchay,* or rainbow jaguar, and is the bridge between Heaven and Earth. The *ukhupacha* is the lower world or underworld. It is also known as *llankay* (belly or solar plexus), your action or labor and right relationship (ayni) to the land. The archetype is *amaru,* or serpent, and is the creative force of everything. It is the birthing and regeneration of life.[19,20]

When someone engages in a shamanic journey, they may choose which world they wish to journey. What you experience in a journey is as real as your ordinary reality. It is not imaginary. For beginner journeyers, it may be challenging to shut off your critical or skeptical mind. When journeying, try to suspend your critical voice until after the journey has ended. At the beginning of my shamanic teachings, I often believed I was making things up; but as I did more journeying, I recognized there was no way I could have come up with the things I saw. At some point in the journey, you will feel led, and that you are no longer creating. You will feel like an observer. You will experience things outside your realm of knowing. When this happens, Spirit has taken over.[21]

Your only job at this point is to observe and remember. You may see, hear, or feel things, or only have a sense of knowing of what has occurred. As I discussed in Chapter 7, you typically have one or two senses that are the strongest. Some people are more visual, while others may be auditory, sensory, or have an internal knowing. In a journey, everything can be turned upside down. Your strongest sense in your ordinary world may not be your strongest in the spiritual world. Everyone is different in how they experience a journey.

When you come out of the journey, write out everything you experienced. As this is a non-ordinary reality, what you experience will be symbolic. At first, it may appear nonsensical or meaningless, but that is furthest from the truth. As with dreams, you sometimes need to write them out to decipher their meaning and intent. Sometimes the meaning will become more apparent over time. Hence, it is essential to keep a record of everything you experience when you journey.

Undertaking a shamanic journey requires the use of rhythmic sound. In Peruvian shamanism, it is typically through the use of a rattle. In First Nations indigenous cultures, they use a drum known as "riding the drum-horse."[22] The repetitive rhythmic drumming is similar to a galloping horse. The drum and rattle are tools to help transport you from your ordinary reality to non-ordinary or spiritual realities. Hearing the sound of a rattle or drum allows your body and mind to relax, while inducing a trance state. It connects you to the subconscious part of your brain, and puts you in an altered state of consciousness—enhancing your ability to receive shamanic images and visions.

I recommend you listen to a drumming journey that provides a signal to call you back from your deep trance. The drum rhythm will change and slow down near the end to get you out of your altered state, and bring you back into your body. You can search for one online or purchase a CD.

Embodied Exercise

Below are some basic instructions for journeying.

- When you start a journey, have a clear specific intention for your journey.
- It can be a question about something you wish an answer to for your healing, as a means of spiritual growth, or to meet your power or spirit animal.
- Open sacred space.
- Lie down in a comfortable position and, if helpful, cover your eyes with a mask or scarf to block out any light.
- Ensure you are not too cold or too hot, which may distract you from entering a trance state.
- Put on headphones or earbuds and turn on the shamanic drumming.
- Your imagination is the starting point of any journey. Begin by visualizing being in a forest or meadow, and walking down a path. Go with whatever place shows up.
- If you go to the lower world, there will be an opening like a hole in a tree or cave, or entered by diving into a body of water, or another means of entering that world.
- If you go to the upper world, you may climb ladders or trees, or fly on the back of an eagle. Eventually, there will be an opening for ascension.
- If you stay in the middle world, there will still be an opening to another reality.
- Enter the opening.

- You will then find yourself traveling through some sort of tunnel and, eventually, you will come out on the other side.

- When you do, notice your surroundings. Where have you landed? What do you see, hear, feel, and sense? The spiritual realm is not bound by our ordinary reality. You can experience anything.

- Look down at yourself. You may have shape-shifted into an animal or other spiritual being.

- There will be a guide to help you on your journey. It may be an animal, but it can take any form. They usually reveal themselves immediately.

- Say hello. Ask them if they are your journey guide and, if they say yes, tell them your intention for your journey. If they say no, wait until one appears.

- They will take over and lead you to whatever, whomever, or wherever you need, to answer your question for this journey. You are now an observer.

- You may experience several different lands or spiritual realms, or stay in the one you first landed.

- You may meet several different spiritual beings, guardians, or spirit animals.

- If you are seeking answers about your health, you may travel within your body.

- If you are working through emotional wounds, you may meet past abusers or perpetrators, or deceased relatives, to express anger, pain, and you may process grief.

- As a means of spiritual growth, you can meet spiritual teachers who can impart profound, meaningful messages for you, and what it means to live a human existence.

- Thank all the beings you encounter on your journey for whatever knowledge they have imparted to you. Express respect and gratitude.

- When you hear the drum rhythm change, that will be your callback, the signal to return from the journey.

- Thank your guide, and ask them if it's okay to revisit them.

- Return to the tunnel or portal you first emerged from, and allow it to take you back to your starting point.

- Tune back into your surroundings by listening to the sounds in the room.

- Notice your breathing. Take a couple of deep breaths.

- Start to feel back into your body by moving your fingers and toes, and stretching.

- Slowly open your eyes.

- Take your time getting up, and drink some water.

- Journal or draw your experiences immediately, as you are more apt to recall details with greater insight and clarity.

It may be difficult for an individual in longer journeys to return from the spiritual realm. Difficulty returning from a journey is a concern for beginners. If you become skilled at journeying, and can go for long periods, do so with a partner who can call out a keyword to help your mind return to your body to mitigate this potential risk.[17,21,22] If you wish further instruction or teachings before embarking on a journey, check for workshops or mentors in your area.

Andean Research Institute

My mentor, José Luis Herrera, established the Andean Research Institute (andianinstitute.org), a non-profit organization to preserve the culture, medicines, teachings, traditions, and protection of the land of the Andes and Amazon. For those interested in learning more about shamanism, connecting with Peruvian shamanic teachings, volunteering, or donating, please check out their website for more information.

Benefits of Shamanic Practices

The shamanic tools and practices I have discussed in this chapter have several benefits:

- Release and heal unprocessed and stored wounds, traumas, and troubling behaviors.
- Go beyond your body to engage in non-ordinary spiritual realms.
- A more profound connection with your body, yourself, and Spirit.
- Mental, emotional, physical, and spiritual well-being.
- Create balance and harmony in your life.
- Connection and respect for Mother Earth, and all her life forms.
- Recognition of the signs that Pachamama provides.
- Different ways of knowing.

The Disconnected Mountain

I leave you with a short story I wrote during my *Mastery II: Tracking and Divination* shamanic training.

Everyone had heard about the great mountain that overlooked the tiny village. The villagers knew the mountain was full of immense knowledge. They would go there to learn about the world and get answers to all their questions. There was always a line to wait and speak to the mountain. The villagers were so grateful to the mountain for all the knowledge she provided them. They would leave offerings of flowers, drink, and food in gratitude for all she imparted.

However, the mountain felt differently. She envied the villagers. Why you say? She held all of the world's secrets, but she did not feel free.

One day, the youngest girl in the village came to see the mountain. The mountain looked down at the little girl, expecting her to ask a question about the world. Instead, the little girl asked, "How do you know so much about the world?"

The mountain lifted off the top of its snow-capped peak and said, "I have an enormous brain to store all the memories and knowledge of the world through millions of years."

The little girl was thoroughly impressed. Then, she said, "You have so much knowledge, but you look so sad—how come?"

The mountain had to stop and think, and after much deliberation, stated, "You are wise for such a young girl to notice. I am sad because I am always in my head, and have no connection to the rest of my body. I have no limbs to move about in the world. I feel disconnected from my true knowing. I have all the knowledge to impart to you, but no ability to sense my true feelings that reside deep in my caverns."

The little girl looked up quizzically and stated, "But you can see your body, and you can feel your body. You just have to look down from up above those clouds."

The mountain blew away the clouds, and looked down for the first time in centuries, and there was her body. She started to move, and noticed there were trees swaying and rocks falling. There were worn-down paths from where the villagers had come to see her. There was water flowing down from her snow-capped peak. She was awed and amazed that she had forgotten to look down. She had a body, and it was telling her so many things about herself. For the first time, she started truly hearing, seeing, and feeling her body. She finally felt connected, healed, and whole.

She started to cry rivers of joyful tears for the beautiful gift of awareness imparted by this young girl. "Thank you, my child, for bringing me this amazing gift of connection."

The girl smiled and said, "You're welcome," and then she skipped down the mountain path to her home.

—⁓—

In this story, I was the mountain. I lived in my head and felt disconnected from my body. Through my healing and spiritual journey, I reconnected with my body and became embodied. This story also encompasses multiple layers of meaning:

- What it means to be a shaman.
- Respect and gratitude for Pachamama.
- To give back through reciprocity and right ayni.
- Seek wisdom beyond yourself with other spiritual realms.
- Get out of your head.
- Connect and feel your body.
- Sense and feel your feelings.
- Let go of things that no longer serve you.
- Connect with your inner child.
- Recognize that your inner knowing resides within your body.
- Return to your healed state.

—⁓—

If you were a skeptic at the beginning of this chapter, I hope I converted you from being wary to being open to connecting with your body in a more profound, meaningful way, and to go beyond your body to communicate with Spirit in all its forms for self-exploration and healing.

—⁓—

Join me next in the final section of the book. I believe being Your Authentic Self is the most critical piece of the puzzle to connecting with your body, and becoming embodied.

PART III
YOUR
AUTHENTIC SELF

10

YOUR AUTHENTIC SELF—
THERE IS ONLY ONE YOU

"When you stop living your life based on what others think of you, real life begins. At that moment, you will finally see the door of self acceptance opened."

Shannon L. Alder

"You'll never know who you are unless you shed who you pretend to be."

Vironika Tugaleva

Have you ever had an experience that defined the narrative of your life—it became your story?

My narrative and story are about my weight—that I am fat, that it's not okay to be fat, and that said fat needs to be gone for me to be okay, good enough, happy, healthy, accepted, and loved.

I have struggled with my weight my whole life. The size of my body dictated how I saw myself. I learned, at a pretty young age, that it wasn't okay to be fat. When I was approximately eight or nine years old, there was an incident that led to my belief that being overweight is undesirable.

Being Greek, many of my parents' friends owned restaurants. One evening, we were visiting one of those restaurants. I was sitting in the booth with my mom, and she was talking to a woman I believe was her friend. She said she was concerned about my weight. The woman responded that I was young, that it was still baby fat and would eventually fall away on its own.

Kids are like sponges. They absorb everything they hear. They may not be able to process an event entirely, but if it resonates with them as truthful, hurtful, or upsetting, it will be stored in their long-term memory. The subconscious part of the brain will continue to inform them of these beliefs for years to come.

I never spoke up about what they had said about me. I never had a voice back then. I may have even been in shock, not understanding why my mom and this lady would talk about me as if I weren't there. In a nanosecond, without conscious thought, I felt self-conscious. I felt embarrassment and shame about my body. Several negative beliefs took hold that day—*I am not good enough, I am not acceptable, I am a disappointment, I am different, my body is unattractive, being fat is undesirable,* and *I am not lovable.*

Greeks are blunt. They'll say directly to your face what they think about you, especially what they perceive to be your flaws. I've had several of these incidents occur over the years when visiting Greece. Canada, where I grew up, is a country where we breed politeness; directness is considered rude and offensive. Culturally, these two ways of being are on opposite sides of the spectrum, and can cause dissonance or tension between these contradictory behaviors.

My mother, being Greek, learned to speak whatever was on her mind. She grew up believing that being overweight was detrimental and unappealing. She was doing what any mother would. She believed she was getting advice from a friend about what was in her daughter's best interests. She didn't realize this single comment would shape my life's trajectory, diminish my self-esteem, and lead to life-long issues about my value and worth as set forth by others and society.

The Four S's

Why four S's? Why not five or six or ten? I believe self-compassion, self-forgiveness, self-acceptance, and self-love give you the foundation for achieving self-actualization and living authentically. You may be wondering, *What the heck is self-actualization?* To become self-actualized means you realize your full potential by developing your skills, abilities, talents, and gifts, and have appreciation for yourself and your life. When you are self-actualized, you accept yourself fully with all your abilities and limitations. By nurturing your hopes, dreams, creations, self-development, personal growth, and well-being, you realize your full potential and achieve self-fulfillment—you create the life you want!

Self-actualization doesn't occur in a bubble. You achieve it through connection with people, community, animals, nature, and Spirit. The Siksika (Blackfeet Nation) teachings on self-actualization state we arrive on Earth already self-actualized. "We are each born into the world as a spark of divinity, with a great purpose embedded in us."[1] The tribe or community utilizes their knowledge and skills to provide love, care, belonging, and protection to the individual so they can express their gifts and manifest their sacred purpose. Community actualization is achieved when each member of the tribe has their basic needs met and can manifest their purpose. The cycle repeats itself through cultural perpetuity, where knowledge is passed on to continue community actualization, and ensure harmony with the land and all living beings.[1] Find your tribe or community to support you in your self-actualization goals, and help them achieve their own. Re-ignite that spark of divinity and manifest your purpose.

Psychologist Carl Rogers believed that to achieve self-actualization, you must be in a state of congruence. Self-actualization occurs when, who you would like to be (ideal self), is congruent with your actual behavior (self-image).[2] When your ideal self doesn't line up with your self-image, you create discord. Acceptance of who you are, and what you are capable or incapable of doing, allows for harmony and balance with what is. When you can, be, know, and accept yourself fully, you no longer live inauthentically. You have healthy, rational, realistic, and positive thoughts about yourself. You are in touch with, and can express, your emotions. You can trust and connect with your needs and intuition. You can accept yourself and others, and cultivate healthy, loving relationships. Incorporating the four S's into your life is an integral part of becoming self-actualized, and provides the ability to express your authentic self.

Self-Compassion

Have you ever experienced compassion for another human being? Do you know what it is to be compassionate? Compassion is the ability to experience concern and sympathy when someone is suffering, and you desire to help them alleviate their suffering. Compassion can include empathy, but they are two different things. Sympathy is feeling sorrow for another person's misfortune. Empathy is the ability to understand and feel the emotions of another person. Compassion is an expression of your thoughts and feelings along with the desire to help.

Being compassionate with yourself means acknowledging you are suffering and wanting to help yourself. It is not judging or berating yourself when you are unsure, struggling, stressed, overwhelmed, emotionally upset, or have done something you believe to be wrong. It means being kind to yourself. It is speaking to yourself, and about yourself, with empathy, and a desire to find ways to help you move through your suffering.

I notice that clients find it much easier to be compassionate toward others than toward themselves. If you are similar, I want you to think of the experience that is bringing you suffering. Imagine it is happening to a person you love dearly—a spouse, friend, parent, or child. What would you say to them? Would you tell them to suck it up and that they are being ridiculous? That they are stupid or worthless? I highly doubt it. Whatever you would feel, if it were happening to them, is what you need to feel toward yourself. Whatever you would say to them to help make it better, is what you need to speak to yourself.

When you are suffering, feel into those feelings. Don't disregard them. Listen to your thoughts, and speak with kindness toward yourself. Feel the sensations that arise in your body, and support your body's well-being by comforting it, and engaging in self-soothing strategies. These approaches are what it means to be compassionate toward yourself.

Research shows "when we feel compassion, our heart rate slows down, we secrete the 'bonding hormone' oxytocin, and regions of the brain linked to empathy, caregiving, and feelings of pleasure light up, which often results in our wanting to approach and care for other people."[3] When you provide compassion to yourself, you support your body physiologically, and you feel good mentally and emotionally. Here are some benefits to practicing self-compassion:

- Improve your health and well-being.
- Create healthy relationships with yourself and others.
- Feel good and increase happiness.
- Increase the positive effect of the vagus nerve, which slows the heart rate and reduces the risk of heart disease.
- Increase resiliency to stress.

- Lower stress hormones.
- Strengthen immune response.
- Decrease worry.
- Be more open to uncomfortable emotions.
- Improve mental health through positive thinking.
- Increase caregiving behaviors.
- Increase optimism.
- Support better friendships.
- Decrease vindictiveness toward others.
- Increase positive emotions and contentment.
- Higher job satisfaction.
- Increase acts of kindness.
- Decrease feelings of loneliness.[4]

Here are some ways to have more self-compassion:

- Listen and be true to yourself.
- Speak kindly to yourself.
- Compliment yourself daily.
- Forgive yourself. (See next section.)
- Encourage yourself—be your own cheerleader.
- Celebrate your accomplishments.
- Let yourself be imperfect.
- Provide space and acknowledge uncomfortable emotions.
- Nourish your body with whole, healthy foods.
- Support your body through rest and relaxation.
- Engage in alone time for self-reflection, and to re-charge.
- Find balance, and engage in fun, pleasurable activities.
- Connect with supportive uplifting people.
- Disconnect from social media.
- Start a mindfulness or meditative practice.

The more you engage in self-compassion, the more at ease and lighter you will feel in your body and about yourself.

Self-Forgiveness

Self-compassion is the first step toward self-forgiveness. If you can't be compassionate toward yourself, then it will be difficult to forgive yourself. Spend several weeks or months practicing self-compassion, and when you feel ready, work on self-forgiveness.

We all do and say things we wish we hadn't. Many people live with regrets. You may wish you would have made better decisions, and treated people better, but you can't go back in time and change those things. We all make mistakes, but they are not failures. Mistakes provide learning and new insight for better ways of being and engaging in the world. It is how you grow into the person you want to be.

If you are stuck with regrets about things you did, or how you behaved, this results in feelings of anger, guilt, shame, or remorse. It is essential to acknowledge and process your emotions to forgive yourself. If you hold onto these emotions, you beat yourself up over and over again. This endless form of punishment is not supportive, and is debilitating to your mental, emotional, physical, and spiritual well-being. Dense frequencies will be stored in your energetic body, which, if not cleared, can result in disconnection from, and dis-ease in, your body.

Notice if you are stuck in your head and experiencing negative thoughts. Do not be judgmental toward yourself. Remember to be kind and compassionate. Listen to your inner critic. What are you saying about yourself? What limiting or negative beliefs are coming up? Challenge your thoughts and beliefs, and recognize what is factual and accurate about the person you are. If you are struggling to let go, speak the mistake out loud, don't ruminate in silence. By speaking it out loud, you get it out of your head, and help diminish the feelings and burden you may be carrying.

What does it mean to have self-forgiveness? Self-forgiveness is about acknowledging the situation, feeling the uncomfortable emotions, letting them go, and moving on. Forgiving yourself doesn't mean you condone your behavior. It doesn't mean you don't take responsibility for your actions. It means you accept your behavior or the situation, and move past it, without revisiting it repeatedly. There are four R's to self-forgiveness: responsibility, remorse, restoration, and renewal.

When you take *responsibility*, you accept what has happened and show yourself compassion. If you have harmed someone else, take responsibility. If someone else has hurt you, don't berate yourself for not being able to stop it; speak up, or set boundaries. Acknowledge that you did the best you could.

When you take responsibility for your actions, you experience *remorse*, which will bring up normal emotions of guilt and shame. Think of these emotions as a catalyst for positive changes in your behavior. In Chapter 1, I talked about guilt and shame. As a refresher, guilt is felt when an action you took, or didn't take, harmed another person, you *did* something bad. In comparison, you internalize shame—something you say about yourself, a belief you *are* bad. It's normal to feel guilty, but don't dwell on it. Don't internalize it. It does not make you a bad person. Look at your behavior throughout your entire life; don't define yourself by one or two incidents.

When you engage in *restoration*, you make amends with yourself and others. You repair the harm and rebuild trust. Apologize to anyone you've harmed, especially to yourself. When you hurt someone else, whether intentional or unintentional, you also injure yourself. It diminishes your character, and how others see you in the world, and affects your self-esteem—how you view yourself. Say sorry to yourself and mean it.

The process of *renewal* helps you focus on what you learned, and how you want to grow. Ask yourself the following questions:

- What led to my behavior?
- Why do I feel guilty?
- How can I prevent this behavior from occurring again?
- How do I want to be better?[5]

Here are some benefits to practicing self-forgiveness:

- Boost feelings of well-being.
- Improve self-image.
- Increase self-esteem and self-confidence.
- Release perfectionism.
- Decrease depression and anxiety.
- Achieve your goals.
- Increase success.
- Feel fulfilled.
- Increase self-awareness.
- Increase empathy and compassion.
- Create close, meaningful, successful relationships.
- Increase trust.
- Increase positive attitude.
- Increase gratitude.
- Reaffirm values.
- Learn and grow.
- Increase productivity, focus, and concentration.
- Improve cholesterol levels.
- Reduce pain.
- Lower blood pressure.
- Lower risk of heart attack.

By practicing self-forgiveness, you release unhealthy emotional connections with people who have harmed you, or people you have hurt, and heal blocked energy within your body. By bringing your darkness, or shadow side, into the light, you set yourself free.

Embodied Exercise

You can cultivate self-forgiveness by engaging in the Hawaiian Ho'oponopono forgiveness meditation. Ho'oponopono means to *make right*. It supports you to reconnect, deepen, and heal your relationship with yourself.

- Find a quiet space where you will not be disturbed.
- Light a white candle to reflect the light within you. Focus on the flame when you repeat the meditation.
- Take a couple of deep breaths. Imagine you are in a healing circle of light with whomever or whatever situation you are experiencing discomfort with.
- Envision a golden chord of light emanating out from your crown chakra to your Higher Self or guardian angel.
- Envision the same for whomever or whatever you are in the healing circle with.
- Now, envision a golden chord of light from your Higher Self to the other person's Higher Self.
- If you are working on yourself, imagine that aspect of yourself in the healing circle.
- Now envision a golden chord connecting your hearts, and feel the love flowing freely.
- With deep sincerity, say, "I'm sorry," and then "Please forgive me." I'm sorry is about taking responsibility, and please forgive me is helping to restore harmony.

- Then state, "I love you," and then, "Thank you." I love you helps to heal the rift and strengthen the bond between you. Saying thank you expresses gratitude for the opportunity to heal.
- Continue to repeat the four phrases as a prayer or mantra until the negative emotions dissipate and you feel at peace.
- Repeat the Ho'oponopono meditation as often as is necessary to remove negative emotional and physical blockages within yourself and with other people or situations.[6]

Self-Acceptance

Once you have self-compassion and self-forgiveness, you are ready to move on to self-acceptance. What does it mean to have self-acceptance? Self-acceptance means accepting all parts of yourself thoroughly, completely, and unconditionally. When you accept your mental, emotional, and physical attributes, you allow for understanding and recognition of everything you can do, and everything you are incapable of doing—your limitations. Again, do not judge your limitations. They are not negative. They are a part of who you are.

Let's talk about limitations. Maybe you struggle with mental limitations. Cognitive limitations can be genetic due to difficulties during gestation or birth, or because of poverty or trauma. These limitations may include: reduced attention span, difficulty concentrating, reduced ability to absorb and retain information, memory issues, difficulty making decisions, lower IQ scores, or learning disorders. If you struggle with cognitive limitations, there may be ways to support new understanding and tools to help you navigate your limitation. Still, there may be things you are unable to change, and you need to find acceptance of your limitation. Repeatedly berating yourself isn't going to support you, and it causes more harm to your psyche.

Emotional limitations may result in an inability to feel and express emotions, or you may be more sensitive than others, which results in you deeply and intensely feeling your emotions. Being sensitive can be uncomfortable and painful. As such, two things may result. You may completely shut down all your emotions as a means to protect yourself and feel accepted by others, or you may constantly fight with intense emotions, which increases their intensity and presence when you least want them to. Let yourself feel and express your emotions as they arise.

We all have physical limitations. I'm 5'4" and, no matter what I do, I'm never going to be 5'7". Your genes play a big part in shaping your physical characteristics. Sadly, people go to great lengths to change their physical appearance because of a perception of beauty propagated by culture or society. For example, being thin or white-skinned is believed, by many, to be more attractive. By denying your physical attributes, you deny your true self. You deem yourself unworthy based on other people's beliefs. This denial creates suffering and disharmony with yourself and your body. Accept all parts of yourself.

You may not be able to change some things about yourself; some things you can work toward changing, but acceptance needs to begin today—wherever you are currently. People often stop themselves from living their life because they believe they can only do it once something about themselves has changed. For example, "I'll go on a beach vacation once I've lost those last ten pounds," and they end up never going because of how they look. You cannot live in the future; you need to live with *what is* in the present moment.

In Dialectical Behavior Therapy, the term *reality acceptance* means you accept your current reality so as to reduce suffering and increase freedom. One aspect of this is radical acceptance, where you accept the facts of your life totally and completely without fighting against them, or being willful, bitter, or engaging in impulsive or destructive behavior. It is about making a decision to accept what is, and a willingness to participate fully in your life, living it to the fullest.[7]

We are all flawed human beings. Don't compare yourself to anyone else. That person is likely also struggling with limiting and negative beliefs of self. You can never know what another person is going through, or has gone through. Accept yourself now in this moment with all your perceived flaws and abilities. Self-acceptance does not mean you stop growing, or don't work toward achieving your goals, or making yourself better. It is going with the flow and accepting where you are at in this moment in time.

The three areas of focus to increase self-acceptance include self-awareness, self-regulation, and self-transcendence.

Self-awareness is being mindful in the moment about your thoughts, emotions, and body sensations. Take moments throughout the day to check in and notice what you are experiencing. Are you critical of yourself? What is your current emotion? Acknowledge it, name it, and feel it. What sensations are you feeling in your body? Do not ignore, avoid, or suppress your thoughts, emotions, and body sensations. Be mindfully present with everything you experience. Invite in all feelings and sensations. They are part of you. When you increase self-awareness, it supports self-acceptance, and allows you to be okay with what is.

Self-regulation is consciously managing your thoughts, emotions, and behaviors to help you reach your goals. Again, it is imperative to reiterate that you first must recognize, not ignore, your thoughts, feelings, and body sensations. Once you've done this, you can work toward self-regulation. With thoughts, it is about challenging falsehoods and negative beliefs. Instead, state what is truthful and factual about yourself. For example, acknowledge your abilities, gifts, and accomplishments. When dealing with your emotions, name the emotion to acknowledge your experience. Feel the emotions. For example, if you're sad, let yourself cry, then find supportive ways to help soothe your emotions, like deep breathing or meditation. With body sensations, find ways to self-soothe your body, and to reduce the physical sensations. For example, take a hot bath, or wrap yourself in a comforting blanket. Once you can regulate your thoughts, emotions, and body sensations, you can then manage your behaviors—how you act in the world. Behavioral self-regulation is about the ability to act in your best interests compatible with your values.[8] The ability to self-regulate increases self-acceptance because it allows you to recognize you have a choice, and gives you back control over your thoughts, emotions, and behaviors.

Self-transcendence is about "transcending (or rising above) the self and relating to that which is greater than the self."[9] When you become self-transcendent, you rely less on things outside yourself to define who you are. As you rise above yourself and your boundaries, you experience interconnectedness with everything outside of you: nature, your Higher Self, the Universe, or a higher power.[10] There is a sense of oneness and wholeness with all things in the Universe. When you become self-transcendent, you increase self-acceptance by recognizing your life has meaning beyond the physical. Here are some benefits to achieving self-acceptance:

- Ability to realize you are enough as you are.
- Live your life to please yourself.
- Increase happiness.
- Less judgment.
- Increase compassion toward yourself.

- Mental, emotional, and physical well-being.
- Healthier relationships.
- Better self-care.
- Healthier boundaries.
- Expect others to accept you for who you are.
- Increase energy.
- Know yourself better.
- Feel worthy, that you have value.
- Decrease perfectionism.
- Increase problem-solving skills.
- Ability to self-regulate.
- Ability to deal with challenging situations.
- Feel at peace, calm, serene.
- Recognize you have choice.
- Be in control of your life.
- Increase gratitude.
- Increase freedom.
- Less afraid to fail.
- Increase self-esteem.
- Stop seeking approval from others, culture, or society.
- Increase independence.
- Achieve your goals.
- Take more risks, be less fearful.
- See mistakes as learning, not as failure.

Self-Love

Self-compassion, self-forgiveness, and self-acceptance are all acts of self-love. Self-love is loving yourself, not only what you perceive as your good qualities or physical characteristics, but all your differences and imperfections too. Self-love is having respect for your happiness and well-being. It means taking care of yourself and your needs, and not sacrificing your well-being to please others. There are three types of self-love:

1. **Physical**—how you see yourself (self-awareness).
2. **Mental**—how you think of yourself (self-acceptance).
3. **Psychological**—how you treat yourself (self-respect and self-love).[11]

When you can love yourself fully, it positively impacts all areas of your life, including:

- How you make decisions.
- What kind of relationships you choose.
- How you set and maintain healthy boundaries.
- How you speak to yourself and about yourself to others.
- How you cope with problems.
- How you view the world.

Self-love is not derived from things outside yourself. For example, buying new clothes, or getting a new hairdo, isn't going to translate into feelings of self-love. "Self-love is not simply a state of feeling good. It is a state of appreciation for oneself that *grows from actions* that support our physical, psychological, and spiritual growth."[12] Self-love is ever-changing. It grows dynamically through our actions as we mature. It is about acting in ways that increase self-love in your whole being. It is accepting your weaknesses, and your strengths. It is embodying self-compassion, self-forgiveness, and self-acceptance. It focuses on how you want to live your life, and then engage in those ways of being. Here are some questions to ponder that can translate into actions for achieving greater self-love:

- What are your values?
- What is important to you?
- Where do you find personal meaning?

- What is your purpose?
- What is your *why* for being in this life?

In one of Brené Brown's *Unlocking Us* podcasts, she speaks with guest Sonya Renee Taylor. Sonya is the author of *The Body is Not an Apology: The Power of Radical Self-Love*. Sonya states we need to "stop being the host of dis-ease in our body."[13] Here's how I interpret this powerful statement. We create the breeding ground for dis-ease by staying stuck in our story, and recycling the same garbage through our thoughts, emotions, and behaviors. Staying stuck can include:

- Allowing negative self-talk and negative beliefs to poison your system.
- Focusing on negative emotional states.
- Engaging in behaviors that are harmful to you mentally, emotionally, physically, and spiritually.

You can clean up your toxic environment by:

- Speaking words that are kind and nonjudgmental.
- Thinking positively about yourself.
- Deeply feeling and acknowledging positive emotions when they arise.
- Making decisions and taking actions that are only beneficial to your well-being, and in your best interests.

You achieve radical self-love through nurturing, nourishing, and fulfilling yourself. Here are some ways to feel nurtured, nourished, and fulfilled:

- Become mindful of what you think, feel, and want.
- Know who you are and act on this knowledge.
- Become empowered and advocate for yourself.
- Practice self-compassion and kindness toward yourself.

- Speak positively to yourself and about yourself.
- Forgive yourself.
- Accept yourself fully.
- Be true to yourself.
- Live intentionally, with purpose.
- Do something you feel passionate about.
- Write out your dreams and goals.
- Write out your values and what is important to you.
- Acknowledge and celebrate your accomplishments.
- Seek out a mentor, new experiences, or knowledge.
- Volunteer or help someone in your community.
- Focus on meeting your needs.
- Choose supportive and meaningful relationships.
- Find your tribe.
- Hang out with uplifting and positive people.
- Spend time with a pet, or get a pet, and receive uncon-ditional love.
- Set and maintain healthy boundaries.
- Say no to things that don't support you.
- Protect yourself.
- Put yourself first.
- Prioritize your time.
- Unplug from technology and social media.
- Journal your thoughts, emotions, and experiences.
- Meditate or pray daily.
- Practice deep breathing.
- Create a gratitude journal.
- Create a vision board.
- Read books that support your growth.
- Listen to and connect with your body through the tools provided in this book.

- Get plenty of sleep.
- Take naps and breaks as needed.
- Eat healthy, life-affirming foods.
- Explore intimate relationships and sexual pleasure.
- Engage in some form of exercise.
- Listen to music, sing, and dance.
- Have fun, play, and create.
- Spend time in nature.
- Get a manicure, pedicure, or massage.
- Go on a retreat or vacation.[12,14]

This list is by no means exhaustive. I hope it sparks some ways for you to engage with your life to increase feelings of self-love. Here are some benefits to achieving self-love:

- Increase self-compassion.
- Increase empathy and compassion for others.
- Acceptance of self and your life circumstances.
- Forgiveness of self and others.
- Take responsibility for your actions.
- Increase empowerment, resiliency, and agency.
- Feel more in control.
- Greater clarity and insight.
- Growth and self-actualization.
- Choose yourself first.
- Self-respect.
- No longer seek approval, or compare self to others.
- Live your life authentically.
- Life satisfaction.
- Increase success.
- Increase feelings of fulfillment.

- Mental, emotional, physical, and spiritual well-being.
- Ability to express your thoughts and opinions easily.
- Focus on the positive.
- Increase happiness.
- Make decisions that are in your best interests.
- Enjoy being alone with yourself.
- Lower stress.
- Decrease illness.
- Choose to nourish your body with sleep, food, water, and exercise.
- Feel comfortable in your body.
- Be embodied.
- Increase motivation to achieve your goals.
- Increase self-confidence, self-esteem, and self-worth.
- Increase socialization.
- Healthier relationships.
- Ability to deal with difficult situations.
- Ability to embrace your hardships.
- Think optimistically.
- Increase creativity.

Self-love does not happen overnight. It comes with time, and engaging consistently with the practices mentioned in this chapter.

Embodied Exercise

Practice the exercise below for 10–15 minutes each day, for a week or longer, to increase feelings of self-love. I find this exercise to be more soothing and revealing with no overhead lights on. You can light a candle, or do this exercise at dusk before complete darkness sets in.

- Find a place where you can either sit or stand in front of a mirror.
- Face the mirror. Get as close to the mirror as you can without straining yourself.
- Shake out any tension, and let yourself sink into the floor.
- Take in a couple of deep breaths. Inhale through your nose, deep into your belly, and exhale out any tension or nervousness about looking at yourself.
- Look directly deep into your eyes, as if you're peering past them.
- Become grounded with Pachamama to feel supported and receive unconditional love.
- Imagine a golden chord of light emanating out of your belly, and reaching deep into the core of Pachamama.
- Imagine Pachamama's magnum, her life-giving blood, coming up through the golden chord of light into your belly, and filling every pore, every cell of your body with unconditional love.
- Keep breathing and feeling unconditional love.
- Now, imagine a golden chord of light emanating from your crown chakra, and reaching out to the cosmos to connect with Source, and you receiving unconditional love from God, Creator, or the Universe in return.
- Imagine the purest brightest color of white coming down from Source through the golden cord into the top of your head, and filling every pore and cell of your body with unconditional love.
- Keep looking directly into your eyes, and keep breathing and feeling unconditional love.

- Imagine the red and white light co-mingling throughout your body, and filling your heart.
- Say the following phrases out loud slowly and with conviction: *I am loved. I am worthy of love. I deserve to be loved. I am love. I love and accept all parts of me.*
- If any thoughts come up, state *a thought* in your head. Then bring yourself back to focusing on your eyes and the words you are speaking.
- Keep repeating these words as much as you need to. Add any other words of love and acceptance toward yourself.
- The longer you do this, and the dimmer the room is, your face and body will become blurred, soften, or disappear altogether.
- When you are ready to end, thank Pachamama and Source for the unconditional love.
- Slowly return to the room, wiggle your fingers and toes, and stretch your body.
- Journal about your experience. Write out how you feel about yourself and your body, and any insights or messages from Source.

Finding Your Authentic Self

To be authentic means to be genuine. To live your life authentically means you do so without reservation, criticism, or excuses. God created only one of you in the world. Even if you are an identical twin, there will be parts of your personality, dreams, and goals that are different. You are unique. You are a culmination of your characteristics, personality, tastes, abilities, knowledge, gifts, and experiences. It would be a shame to hide parts or all of you because you fear fitting in, being ridiculed, or not accepted.

We all have a deep longing to be accepted and feel we belong, but if you can't accept and love yourself and your offerings to the world, you are cheating others of your knowledge, expertise, and gifts. Break the mold. Break out of the box that's holding you back from living authentically, and join the world of the living—shine brightly with all you have to offer. When you do, you will start to seek out and gravitate toward like-minded people who see and accept you for who you are, and appreciate what you have to offer. For example, if you love creating miniature dolls, then take a course, or connect online with other people who enjoy the same hobby. If you like to dress in flashy colors, then do it. Hold your head up high when you walk out in the world. Feel confident and proud to be your true self.

People are hungry for honesty and authenticity when connecting and building relationships with others. You can intuitively sense a facade and disingenuous person immediately, even if you don't consciously realize it. This is off-putting. When you don't present yourself authentically, others will disengage from you. Putting on a veneer to please others will prove detrimental in the long run. If you can't be truthful and authentic, people will not feel they can trust you. Trust is achieved through complementary revelations. Intimacy (into me see) is achieved through comparable mutual sharing of experiences. If you are open and vulnerable in your sharing, the other person will match you, and also share their vulnerability. If you hold back, the other person is likely to hold back in the same way. They won't feel safe to be truthful and authentic with you. People want realness!

Embodied Exercise

Start a journal to learn more about your true self. Below are some questions to explore. (Some of these you may have completed in Chapter 3 in the exercise under Change Your Mindset.)

- What were you like as a child? Were you social and talkative, or quiet and reflective? Did you have lots of friends or only a few? What did you like to do? What brought you joy?

- What were you like around 18 years old? What were your hopes and dreams? What did you expect for your future?

- What type of person are you? What are your characteristics? As a reminder, check out my article, *What Kind of a Person Are You?*[15] There you will find a list of over 600 personality characteristics. Ask friends and family about the type of person you are. Is this person different from your own perception of yourself, or your child or early adult self? If yes, why? When and why did you change?

- What do you value? For example, honesty, hard work, or spirituality. What are your beliefs? For example, religion, spirituality, or philosophies about life. What is important to you about the type of person you want to be, or expect in others, and the life you want to lead?

- What are your successes, accomplishments, and gifts? What do you do well? What are your strengths, weaknesses, or limitations?

- What do you like about your current job, or being at home? What do you dislike about it? Is this what you thought you'd do with your life? If not, why? When and why did it change?

- What currently brings you joy outside of your work and family? What are your hobbies and interests? What are you passionate about and could speak about for hours?

You don't have to complete all these questions to know your true self. Keep adding to this list as you learn more about yourself.

To live from a place of authenticity, you need to know yourself well. Along with the exercises in this chapter, this book's tools and techniques will help you connect with yourself and your body. The exercises will help you know more about the person you are, the person you want to be, and what matters to you—your true self. Through self-awareness, self-reflection, prayer, mindfulness, and meditation, you can connect with your inner light and Higher Self to seek out answers and clarity. You will embody what it means to be authentically you and engage authentically with others and the world. Here are some ways you can do this:

- Be vulnerable in your interactions and relationships by communicating openly.
- Speak your truth by using your voice and words to express yourself.
- Reveal different parts of yourself, for example, your values, interests, or beliefs to those who love, honor, and accept you.

- Let your inner light be your guide by connecting with your Higher Self through prayer, meditation, or quiet self-reflection.
- Set and maintain healthy boundaries.
- Let go of patterns, behaviors, and relationships that no longer serve you.
- Let go of judgment—be kind and compassionate to yourself and others.
- Love, accept, and care for yourself, and your ability to love, care for, and be of service to others will be strengthened.
- Choose love over fear—allow love to flow through happiness, joy, contentment, and peace.
- Be creative, open your mind, and expand your thinking—there are no limits.
- Live courageously—take risks and be open to new experiences.
- Let down your walls, and open your heart to give and receive the love you deserve.
- Connect with your intuition, inner knowing, or Higher Self to guide you.
- Tap into your strengths to experience joy and empower you to live the life you want.
- Prioritize yourself, and engage in daily self-care practices.
- Connect with your gifts and purpose to find meaning in your life.
- Find balance in your life by engaging in different hobbies, interests, and leisure activities.
- Free your spirit creatively through song, breath, dance, movement, play, music, art, and emotional expression.
- Notice how the Universe and Source are gently guiding your path of synchronicities.

- Practice gratitude by seeking out the light, joy, love, kindness, beauty, and goodness in all of your experiences.
- Connect with Spirit, Source, the Universe, God, or Creator for self-transcendence.
- Celebrate and honor yourself and your life.
- Live your highest self by being authentic in all areas of your life, with no exceptions.
- Live each day to the fullest.[16]

Please choose one or several of these practices. Do them for several weeks or months until they become fully ingrained in your natural way of being. Keep increasing and adding more of these practices. Before you know it, you will know your true self and engage with the world more authentically.

I wanted to leave you with this one last thought about the importance of living authentically. If I had the power to change you into anything you wanted to be—your personality, appearance, or vocation—would you take it? I recently read the book *Song of Heyoehkah* by Hyemeyohsts Storm. The characters are on a vision quest to seek meaning, harmony, and balance with themselves and their world through indigenous *medicine ways*. The protagonist, Dancing Tree, is asked if he would like to be transformed into a handsome man who could sway women. He excitedly asks if they could give that to him. Rose Bush responds, "Of course…But it would destroy forever our beautiful son Dancing Tree! Would you will your own death for that?"[17] Dancing tree is confused by it causing his death. Silver Comb replies, "Because you would die the same as if we were to drive your lance through your heart. You would no longer be yourself!"[17]

Don't cause your death. Embrace all of the things that make you uniquely you. There is no one like you—with your experiences, knowledge, gifts, and talents. You are here in this body, living this life for a reason. Remember your Divine spark and great purpose. Don't toss it away by trying to be someone else, or something you are not. The world would suffer a significant loss for not experiencing the beauty of your authentic self.

Sharing Your Journey

As you begin to explore and engage in your journey of self-awareness, self-acceptance, self-love, self-development, self-growth, and spirituality, it can be challenging, draining, exciting, and extremely rewarding. You may want to go out and tell your friends or family all the things you are doing to better yourself, or as a means of getting their support. This is a time to be discerning about who you speak to about what you are doing, and the changes you are making. If you have experienced a person to be abusive, critical, or unsupportive in the past, they are not the person to disclose to. They may feel threatened and their own insecurities and feelings of low self-worth may be triggered. They may be fearful of you changing and leaving them behind. They may be uneducated, and not understand why you are choosing such alternative approaches. People are fearful of what they don't understand.

If you are taking courses, workshops, or retreats, seek out other group members who are sharing a similar experience; they are more likely to understand what you are going through. Alternatively, seek out other like-minded individuals who are open to having deeper philosophical and meaningful conversations about working on themselves and creating new ways of being in the world.

Sometimes it's best to keep your experiences close to the heart. When you speak to others about the profound changes you are making, or experiences you are having, they might not get it. You would be diminishing the magnificence and meaning of your experience. By speaking about it, you are energetically releasing its magical properties out into the world. Keep it precious. Bring it forward in your memory often. Revel in the emotional quality and physical sensations thinking about your journey brings up in your body. Sit in silence with it. Embody it. Your journey is a gift. Cherish it and protect it as you would a newborn baby. When you are ready to emerge from your cocoon, people will experience your transformation and wonder how you got there. Maybe then, if they ask, you'll share your insights, but only if it feels right.

Putting It All Together

The fact you read this book means, somewhere in your life, you became disconnected from your body, and your whole, perfect, complete, unique, and authentic self. You have likely experienced several wounds and traumas that created your narrative, which shaped and defined how you view yourself, treat yourself, and behave in the world.

Connecting to your body, and becoming embodied, means you first need to understand how you have disconnected from your body, as outlined in the Disconnection section. Becoming embodied means acknowledging your wounds and traumas, and processing and healing them. It is acknowledging where you have lacked boundaries in your life, and setting healthy boundaries. It is realizing your negative thoughts, limiting or negative beliefs, and cognitive distortions, and changing the words you speak to yourself, the words you speak to others about yourself, and speaking up for yourself. It is recognizing the ways you have either ignored, repressed, or stuffed down uncomfortable emotions, or have felt overwhelmed by intense emotions, and, instead, acknowledge, name, and feel all your emotions.

In the Reconnection section, I talked about how to reconnect with your body and physically feel into your body through Mindfulness, Grounding, Senses, Energy, and Shamanism. These chapters give you the knowledge, tools, and ways of being to help you connect with your body physically and spiritually, and become embodied. Keep returning to the exercises in these chapters to deepen your relationship and connection with your body.

The exercises in the book are not only about healing and clearing the ways you disconnected from your body, but engaging in new ways of being and behaviors. It's also engaging in the numerous ways to reconnect with your body by integrating the knowledge, tools, and ways of being discussed in the chapters in the Reconnection section. Finally, and most importantly, when you live a life of compassion, forgiveness, acceptance, and love of self, there is a complete integration to being embodied, and living your authentic self.

—⁓—

I wish you well on your journey of self-discovery, connection with your body, and embodiment.

With Blessings,

Vicky xo

IN GRATITUDE

*"Cultivate the habit of being grateful for every good thing
that comes to you, and to give thanks continuously.
And because all things have contributed to your advancement,
you should include all things in your gratitude."*

Ralph Waldo Emerson

This book could not have been written without all the teachers, mentors, family members, friends, and clients along the way who provided guidance, support, teachings, lessons, growth, healing, and new ways of being and connecting with the world.

To Karine Schipper, my friend and Reiki teacher, thank you for supporting me on my healing journey, leading me to my life's purpose, teaching me Reiki, and for always being there when I needed support or new understanding. Your wisdom, gifts, and friendship have been a blessing. You are a beautiful soul.

To José Luis Herrera, thank you for bringing the teachings of Peruvian shamanism to my part of the world. These teachings allowed me to heal past wounds, release stuck emotions, and, more importantly, experience a new connection with myself and Pachamama. Your knowledge, presence, and grounding energy made these teachings more deeply embedded in my psyche.

To Cindi Johnston, thank you for including me in Earth Traditions, and steering me toward the Peruvian shamanism workshops. You opened up a whole new world that was missing in my life. Thank you for providing a reference letter that supported me in getting into my Master's program, and for all you continue to do for the collective.

To my shaman sisters and treasured friends, Carolyn Boston and Tammy Kremer, I feel so blessed that we met on this shamanic journey. Thank you for all the support, encouragement, and spiritual nourishment. For holding space and making me feel safe to be vulnerable when tears needed to flow, and for challenging me to continue to grow and release the things that no longer serve me. Thank you for all the travel, adventures, hikes, golf games, dinners, and movie dates. Thanks for all the laughs, and putting up with my hyper-competitive nature during our game nights. You both embody what it means to be a friend.

To my graduate school mate, colleague, and wonderful friend, Carissa Karner, I feel so blessed that we connected at school and have continued to grow our friendship. Thank you for always being there with kindness, support, and words of encouragement. Thank you for your insights to help me with my book title. I am in awe with your drive to get out of your comfort zone and find new ways to expand your business. You are my inspiration, and helped to lead the way for me to achieve my goals.

To my friend Stephanie Hrehirchuk, thank you for meeting with me over three years ago to provide your knowledge and insight, and to hear about my thoughts on writing a book. Thank you for the initial day of mind mapping to flesh out the chapters for the book, for offering writing workshops and courses that kept me on track, and for providing ongoing knowledge, support, and encouragement. I love that we met while doing our Reiki Master training, and that all these years later, you led the way by writing your own books, and guided me through the process during mine. I am forever grateful.

To my dear friend, Constadina Zarokostas-Vasiliades, thank you for taking the time out of your hectic life to do a first read through, and provide copy and content edits. Thank you for the supportive feedback and encouragement. Your insights and knowledge of the material helped to fill in some of the missing gaps, and to ensure I provided accurate information. Thank you for steering me to Karine when I needed to support my body's healing after contracting H1N1. Who knew where all of that would lead?

To my mom, Aspasia, thank you for showing me the importance of compassion, selfless giving, and strength in diplomacy. For your unconditional love, always being there for Chris and me with whatever we needed, and for all the amazing dinners. The love for your children and grandchildren is incomparable.

To my dad, George, thank you for showing me the importance of family and hard work. You have always been there to help out and support me, Chris, or your friends with whatever task needed to be done. No job was ever too small. Whatever you did, you did freely with love for the benefit of Chris and me.

To my brother, Chris, and sister-in-law, Leah, thank you for your support and encouragement in all my business endeavors. To my beautiful and kind-hearted niece, Alexa, and intelligent and fun-loving nephews, Evan, Stefan, and Adrian, thank you for bringing such joy to my life. I love seeing your personalities shine, and seeing where your purpose and journey take you.

To my editor, Maraya Loza-Koxahn, for your thoroughness, thoughtfulness, and insight that made this book shine.

A big shout out and thank you to Irina Bondarev, Tianne Cao, Despina Karouzos, Joyce Lang, and Youla Paikos for being the first guinea pigs to read my book. Your feedback was helpful to know I was providing content that was supportive, informative, and engaging.

To God, my guardian angels, archangels, ascended masters, star nations, spirit guides, animal guides, and Pachamama, thank you for supporting me on my journey and helping me realize my purpose in this lifetime. For the signs and serendipities that let me know you are there and leading me in the right direction. With deep love and gratitude for all you have done and continue to do behind the scenes.

ENDNOTES

Introduction

1   Roubekas, V. (2017). My journey. https://
    psychotherapycalgary.com/about/my-journey
2   Garden Goddess. (2018). Pachamama.
    http://www.thegoddessgarden.com/
    pachamama/#:~:targetText=Pachamama%20is%20a%20
    fertility%20goddess,as%20Gaia%20and%20Mother%20Earth.

Chapter 1—Trauma

1   Roubekas, V. (2017). Anxiety. https://psychotherapycalgary.
    com/anxiety
2   Carter, R. (2014). The human brain book: An illustrated guide
    to its structure, function, and disorders (2nd ed.). New York,
    NY: DK Publishing.
3   Luman Learning. (n.d.). Functions of the autonomic nervous
    system. https://courses.lumenlearning.com/boundless-ap/
    chapter/functions-of-the-autonomic-nervous-system
4   Marich, J. (n.d.). Reptilian brain of survival and
    mammalian brain. https://www.gracepointwellness.
    org/109-post-traumatic-stress-disorder/article/55760-reptil
    ian-brain-of-survival-and-mammalian-brain
5   Braive. (2016). The fight flight freeze response. https://www.
    youtube.com/watch?v=jEHwB1PG_-Q

6   Higgins, B. (2019). The body's language of stress. https://
     www.youtube.com/watch?v=NR54K_Sm88k

7   Bracha, H. S. (2004). Freeze, flight, fight, fright, faint:
     Adaptationist perspectives on the acute stress response
     spectrum. CNS Spectrums, 9(9), 679-685.

8   Hedva, B. (2021). E-mail correspondence.

9   Bhandari, S. (2020). Dissociative identity disorder (multiple
     personality disorder). https://www.webmd.com/mental-health/
     dissociative-identity-disorder-multiple-personality-disorder

10   Virzi, J. (2020). Fawning: The fourth trauma response
     we don't talk about. https://finance.yahoo.com/news/
     fawning-fourth-trauma-response-dont-202416242.html

11   Walker, P. (n.d.). The 4Fs: A trauma typology
     in complex PTSD. http://pete-walker.com/
     fourFs_TraumaTypologyComplexPTSD.
     htm?utm_source=yahoo&utm_medium=referral&utm_
     campaign=in-text-link

12   Finch, S. D. (2019). 7 subtle signs your trauma response is to
     'fawn'. https://letsqueerthingsup.com/2019/07/06/7-subtle-sig
     ns-your-trauma-response-is-to-fawn

13   Hedva, B. (2013). Betrayal, trust and forgiveness: A guide to
     emotional healing and self-renewal (3rd ed). Bonners Ferry,
     ID: Wynword Press.

14   Hase, M., Balmaceda, U. M., Ostacoli, L., Liebermann, P., &
     Hofmann, A. (2017). The AIP model of EMDR therapy and
     pathogenic memories. Frontiers in Psychology, 8, 1578-1585.

15   Waddington, C. H. (1942). Endeavour, 1, 18–20.

16   Brav, J. (n.d.). Clearing ancestral baggage. https://www.
     radiantwholenesshealing.com/clearing-ancestral-baggage

17   Pearlman, L. A. & Saakvitne, K. W. (1995). Trauma and the
     therapist: Countertransference and vicarious traumatization
     in psychotherapy with incest survivors. New York, NY: W. W.
     Norton.

18   McCann, I. L. & Pearlman, L. A. (1990). Psychological
     trauma and the adult survivor. New York, NY: Brunner/Mazel.

19   Ladd, L. (2021). Trauma responses. https://www.youtube.
     com/watch?v=mhYgDN6HNyE

20 Gill, L. (2017). Understanding and working with the window of tolerance. https://www.attachment-and-trauma-treatment-centre-for-healing.com/blogs/understanding-and-working-with-the-window-of-tolerance

21 Linehan, M. M. (2015). DBT skills training handouts and worksheets (2nd ed.). New York, NY: The Guildford Press.

22 Bugental, J. F. T. (1987). The art of the psychotherapist. New York, NY: Norton.

Chapter 2—Boundaries

1 Chesak, J. (2018). The no BS guide to protecting your emotional space. https://www.healthline.com/health/mental-health/set-boundaries

2 What is a boundary? (n.d.). Handout provided at Calgary Communities Against Sexual Abuse.

3 Lancer, D. (2018). What are personal boundaries? How do I get some? https://psychcentral.com/lib/what-are-personal-boundaries-how-do-i-get-some

4 Boundaries. (n.d.). Handout provided at Calgary Communities Against Sexual Abuse.

5 Sexual Assault Support Center for Waterloo Region. (2004). Signs of healthy/unhealthy boundaries. http://www.sascwr.org/files/www/resources_pdfs/incest/Signs_of_healthyunhealthy_boundaries.pdf

6 Wright, A. (2008). Psychological properties of colors. http://www.colour-affects.co.uk/psychological-properties-of-colours

Chapter 3—Thoughts

1 Sasson, R. (n.d.). How many thoughts does your mind think in one hour? https://www.successconsciousness.com/blog/inner-peace/how-many-thoughts-does-your-mind-think-in-one-hour

2 Radwan, M. F. (n.d.). Limiting beliefs. https://www.2knowmyself.com/false_beliefs/limiting_beliefs

3   Radwan, M. F. (n.d.). How limiting beliefs
    are created. https://www.2knowmyself.com/
    how_limiting_beliefs_are_created

4   Psychology Tools. (n.d.). EMDR cognitions. https://www.
    psychologytools.com/worksheet/emdr-cognitions

5   Grohol, J. M. (2019). 15 common cognitive
    distortions. https://psychcentral.com/
    lib/15-common-cognitive-distortions

6   Living Well. (2003). Cleaning up stinkin' thinking (August
    issue).

7   Grohol, J. M. (2018). 10 proven methods for fixing
    cognitive distortions. https://psychcentral.com/lib/
    fixing-cognitive-distortions

8   Harteneck, P. (n.d.). 5 ways to stop your racing
    thoughts. https://www.psychologytoday.com/ca/blog/
    women-s-mental-health-matters/201604/5-ways-stop-your-r
    acing-thoughts

9   Lazarus, R. S. (1982). Thoughts on the relations between
    emotion and cognition. American Psychologist, 37(9),
    1019-1024.

10 Van Dijk, S. (2012). Calming the emotional storm: Using
    Dialectical Behavior Therapy skills to manage your
    emotions & balance your life. Oakland, CA: New Harbinger
    Publications, Inc.

11 Lynne, N. (2018). The teachings of Hermes
    Trismegistus and the 7 hermetic principles. https://
    www.foragingforfreedom.com/single-post/2018/07/24/
    The-Teachings-of-Hermes-Trismegistus-an
    d-the-7-Hermetic-Principles

12 Positive Magnet Energy. (2014). What does it mean
    "As within, so without. As above, so below?" https://
    positivemagnetenergy.wordpress.com/2014/10/28/
    quote-as-within-so-without-as-above-so-below

13 Huff Oberlin, K. (2017). As within so without, as
    above so below. https://holistic-connections.net/
    as-within-so-without-as-above-so-below

14 Roubekas, V. (2021). What kind of a person are you? https://psychotherapycalgary.com/2021/01/25/personality-characteristics

15 Emoto, M. (2004). The hidden messages in water. Hillsboro, OR: Beyond Words Publishing, Inc.

Chapter 4—Emotions

1   Cannon, W. B. (1927). The James-Lange theory of emotions: A critical examination and an alternative theory. The American Journal of Psychology, 39(1/4), 106-124.

2   Van Dijk, S. (2012). Calming the emotional storm: Using Dialectical Behavior Therapy skills to manage your emotions & balance your life. Oakland, CA: New Harbinger Publications, Inc.

3   Myers, D. G. & Dewall, C. N. (2015). Psychology (11th ed.). New York, NY: Worth.

4   Cherry, K. (2020). Understanding the Cannon-Bard theory of emotion. https://www.verywellmind.com/what-is-the-cannon-bard-theory-2794965

5   Schachter, S. & Singer, J. (1962). Cognitive, social, and physiological determinants of emotional state. Psychological Review, 69(5), 379–399.

6   Shiel, W. C. Jr. (n.d.). Medical definition of sensorium. https://www.medicinenet.com/script/main/art.asp?articlekey=15732

7   Shaman Durek. (2019). Spirit hacking: Shamanic keys to reclaim your personal power, transform yourself, and light up the world. New York, NY: St. Martin's Essentials.

8   Lynne, N. (2018). The teachings of Hermes Trismegistus and the 7 hermetic principles. https://www.foragingforfreedom.com/single-post/2018/07/24/The-Teachings-of-Hermes-Trismegistus-and-the-7-Hermetic-Principles

9   Linehan, M. M. (2015). DBT skills training handouts and worksheets (2nd ed.). New York, NY: The Guildford Press.

10 Wegner, D. M., Schneider, D. J., Carter, S. R., & White, T. L.
    (1987). Paradoxical effects of thought suppression. Journal of
    Personality and Social Psychology, 53(1), 5.
11 Jeffrey, S. (n.d.). A definitive guide to Jungian shadow work:
    How to get to know and integrate your dark side. https://
    scottjeffrey.com/shadow-work
12 Othon, J. E. (n.d.). Carl June and the shadow: The ultimate
    guide to the human dark side. https://highexistence.com/
    carl-jung-shadow-guide-unconscious
13 Rosenberg, J. (2016). Emotional mastery: The gifted
    wisdom of unpleasant feelings. https://www.youtube.com/
    watch?v=EKy19WzkPxE
14 Galor, S. (2011). The benefits of emotional expression.
    https://drsharongalor.wordpress.com/2011/12/19/
    the-benefits-of-emotional-expression

Chapter 5—Mindfulness

1   Lumen. (n.d.). What is consciousness? https://
    courses.lumenlearning.com/wsu-sandbox/chapter/
    what-is-consciousness
2   Wikipedia. (2020). Self-awareness. https://en.wikipedia.org/
    wiki/Self-awareness
3   Wikipedia. (2020). Proprioception. https://en.wikipedia.org/
    wiki/Proprioception
4   Wikipedia. (2020). Interoception. https://en.wikipedia.org/
    wiki/Interoception
5   Stanford Encyclopedia of Philosophy. (2015). Bodily
    awareness. https://plato.stanford.edu/entries/bodily-awareness
6   Google Dictionary. (n.d.). Mindfulness. https://www.google.
    ca/search?q=definition+of+mindfulness&source=lmns&bih=6
    25&biw=1366&hl=en&sa=X&ved=2ahUKEwi-i7nI77LuAhU
    xJjQIHdrfBEEQ_AUoAHoECAEQAA
7   Linehan, M. M. (2015). DBT skills training handouts and
    worksheets (2nd ed.). New York, NY: The Guildford Press.
8   Van Dijk, S. (2012). Calming the emotional storm: Using
    Dialectical Behavior Therapy skills to manage your

emotions & balance your life. Oakland, CA: New Harbinger Publications, Inc.

9   Word Sense Dictionary. (n.d.). Meditari. https://www.
     wordsense.eu/meditari

10   Dienstmann, G. (n.d.) A history of meditation (a 5,000 year
     timeline). https://liveanddare.com/history-of-meditation

11   Hurley, K. (2020). 5 common myths about meditation,
     debunked. https://www.wellandgood.com/
     goal-of-meditation-misconceptions

12   Alidina, S. & Marshall, J. J. (2021). Types of mindfulness
     meditation. https://www.dummies.com/religion/spirituality/
     types-of-mindfulness-meditation

13   McAndrew, P. (n.d.). Chanting the chakra sounds and
     the nervous system. https://www.evolutionvt.com/
     chanting-the-chakra

14   Nayak, B. (2020). Health benefits of om chanting. https://
     www.drbrahma.com/health-benefits-of-chanting-om

15   Bumgardner, W. (2020). Walking a labyrinth as
     spiritual exercise. https://www.verywellfit.com/
     walking-the-labyrinth-3435825

16   One Light Many Windows. (2010). Mandalas, labyrinth and
     mazes. https://culturalsymbolism.wordpress.com/2010/12/28/
     mandalas-labyrinth-and-mazes

17   Wikipedia. (2021). Qigong. https://en.wikipedia.org/wiki/
     Qigong

18   Wikipedia. (2021) Sacred dance. https://en.wikipedia.org/
     wiki/Sacred_dance#Christianity

19   Wikipedia. (2021). Ecstatic dance. https://en.wikipedia.org/
     wiki/Ecstatic_dance

20   Simpson, M. J. (2016).Powwow dances. https://www.
     thecanadianencyclopedia.ca/en/article/powwow-dances

21   Tribal Trade. (n.d.). Pow-wow dance: Styles, teachings
     and meanings. https://tribaltradeco.com/blogs/teachings/
     pow-wow-dance-styles-teachings-and-meanings

22   Palermo, E. (2015). What is tai chi? https://www.livescience.
     com/38063-tai-chi.html

23 Achanta, R. (2020). A brief history of yoga. https://www. stylecraze.com/articles/a-brief-history-of-yoga

24 Realize the Truth. (2018). What is self-realization? https://airatmaninravi.medium.com/ what-is-self-realization-7702eaab42b1

25 Basavaraddi, I. V. (2015). Yoga: Its origin, history and development. https://www.mea.gov.in/ search-result.htm?25096/Yoga:_su_origen,_historia_y_ desarrollo#:~:text=Introduction%20%3AYoga%20is%20 essentially%20a,harmony%20between%20mind%20 and%20body.&text=The%20word%20'Yoga'%20is%20 derived,'%20or%20'to%20unite'.

26 Walk In Love. (2020). 10 verses about being still. https:// walkinlove.com/blogs/walk-in-love/10-verses-about-being- still#:~:text=%2B%20Psalm%2046%3A10%20He%20 says,need%20only%20to%20be%20still.

27 Chopra, D. (2013). 5 steps to harness the power of intention. https://www.mindbodygreen.com/0-9603/5-steps-to- harness-the-power-of-intention.html

28 Ireland, T. (2014). What does mindfulness meditation do to your brain? https://blogs.scientificamerican.com/guest-blog/ what-does-mindfulness-meditation-do-to-your-brain

29 Joshi, M. (2017). How does mindfulness affect the brain? https://www.bupa.co.uk/newsroom/ourviews/ mindfulness-my-brain

30 Davis, D. M. & Hayes, J. A. (2012). What are the benefits of mindfulness? https://www.apa.org/monitor/2012/07-08/ ce-corner

Chapter 6—Grounding

1   Claytor, K. (2021). What does it mean to be centered? https:// kaseyclaytor.com/2020/04/what-does-it-mean-to-be-centered

2   Raab, D. (2020). What is centering? What is grounding? https://www.psychologytoday. com/ca/blog/the-empowerment-diary/202002/ what-is-centering-what-is-grounding#:~:text=Individuals%20

who%20are%20centered%20are,in%20the%20decisions%20
we%20make.

3   Wonderopolis. (n.d.). How many cells are in the human body?
    https://wonderopolis.org/wonder/how-many-cells-are-in-th
    e-human-body

4   Brady, D. (2017). Health benefits of grounding
    (earthing). https://www.fibrofix.com/blogs/news/
    health-benefits-of-grounding-earthing

5   The Miracle of Essential Oils. (2016). 5 grounding essential
    oil recipes & 15 best essential oils for grounding. https://www.
    themiracleofessentialoils.com/grounding-essential-oil-recipes

6   Clarke, J. (n.d.). Soothe your nervous system with 2-to-1
    breathing. https://yogainternational.com/article/view/
    soothe-your-nervous-system-with-2-to-1-breathing

7   Rifkin, R. (2017). How shallow breathing affects your
    whole body. https://www.headspace.com/blog/2017/08/15/
    shallow-breathing-whole-body

8   Hedva, B. (2015). Embodied awareness. Embodied Awareness
    Training Workbook. Calgary, Canada: (n.p.).

9   CrystalBenefits. (n.d.). 12 crystals that aid grounding
    and make you feel positive. https://crystalbenefits.com/
    crystals-that-aid-grounding

10 Earthing Canada. (2017). Finding your centre: Grounded
    meditation techniques. https://earthingcanada.ca/
    grounding-meditation-techniques

11 Indigenous Corporate Training. (2017). A
    definition of smudging. https://www.ictinc.ca/
    blog/a-definition-of-smudging

12 Patterson, S. (2019). 8 reasons you should try smudging &
    why you should do it at home. https://www.naturallivingideas.
    com/smudging

13 Wilson, D. R. (2019). 11 benefits of burning sage, how to
    get started, and more. https://www.healthline.com/health/
    benefits-of-burning-sage

14 Evolation Yoga. (n.d.). Why we Om when opening and
    closing a yoga class. http://www.evolationyogaatlanta.com/
    why-we-om-when-opening-closing-a-yoga-class

15 Estrada, J. (2018). Incorporate hand mudras into your meditation practice to level up your life. https://www.wellandgood.com/good-advice/hand-mudras

16 Northrope, C. (2016). 10 health reasons to start drumming: The health benefits of beating your own drum. https://www.drnorthrup.com/health-benefits-drumming

17 Dangeli, J. (2018). Tibetan singing bowls: The ancient brain entrainment methodology for healing and meditation. https://jevondangeli.com/tibetan-singing-bowls-the-ancient-brain-entrainment-methodology-for-healing-and-meditation

18 Santos-Longhurst, A. (2018). Music as therapy: The uses and benefits of sound healing. https://www.healthline.com/health/sound-healing

19 Saotome, M. (1989). The principles of Aikido. Boston, MA: Shambhala.

20 Westbrook, A., & Ratti, O. (1970). Aikido and the dynamic sphere. Tokyo, Japan: Charles E. Tuttle Company. pp. 16-96.

21 Sun Bear & Wabun. (1992). The medicine wheel: Earth astrology. New York, NY: Fireside.

22 India Parenting. (n.d.). The earth element personality (bhoomi). https://www.indiaparenting.com/starsigns/499_4566/the-earth-element-personality-bhoomi.html

23 India Parenting. (n.d.). The air element personality (vaayu). https://www.indiaparenting.com/starsigns/499_4565/the-air-element-personality-vaayu.html

24 India Parenting. (n.d.). The fire element personality (agni). https://www.indiaparenting.com/starsigns/499_4567/the-fire-element-personality-agni.html

25 India Parenting. (n.d.). The water element personality (jal). https://www.indiaparenting.com/starsigns/499_4568/the-water-element-personality-jal.html

Chapter 7—Senses

1   Star Institute. (n.d.). Your 8 senses. https://www.spdstar.org/basic/your-8-senses

2   Bradford, A. (2017). The five (and more) senses. https://www.livescience.com/60752-human-senses.html

3   Pasco. (n.d.). Sound waves. https://www.pasco.com/products/guides/sound-waves#:~:text=There%20are%20many%20different%20types,%2C%20loud%2C%20noise%20and%20music.

4   Natural Park Service. (2018). Understanding sound. https://www.nps.gov/subjects/sound/understandingsound.htm#:~:text=The%20units%20of%20frequency%20are,Hz%20are%20known%20as%20ultrasound.

5   Kumar, K. (n.d.). What are the ten basic smells? https://www.medicinenet.com/what_are_the_ten_basic_smells/article.htm

6   Study. (n.d.). Chemoreceptors: Definition, location & function. https://study.com/academy/lesson/chemoreceptors-definition-location-function.html

7   Quizlet. (n.d.). 5 types of sensory receptors. https://quizlet.com/39127979/5-types-of-sensory-receptors-flash-cards

8   Lynne, N. (2018). The teachings of Hermes Trismegistus and the 7 hermetic principles. https://www.foragingforfreedom.com/single-post/2018/07/24/The-Teachings-of-Hermes-Trismegistus-an d-the-7-Hermetic-Principles

9   MacCoun, C. (2008). On becoming an alchemist: A guide for the modern magician. Boston, MA: Trumpeter Books.

10 Dörfler, V., & Ackermann, F. (2012). Understanding intuition: The case for two forms of intuition. Management Learning, 43(5), 545-564.

11 Virtue, D. (2011). The angel therapy handbook. Carlsbad, CA: Hay House, Inc.

12 Virtue, D. (2007). How to hear your angels. Carlsbad, CA: Hay House, Inc.

13 Rice, K. M. (2020). 4 main types of intuition. https://rawandritual.com/bloghome/fourtypesofintuition

14 Radford, B. (2013). Channeling & spirit guides: Voices from within, not beyond. https://www.livescience.com/38561-channeling.html

Chapter 8—Energy

1   Feynman, R., Leighton, R., & Sands, M. (1964). The Feynman lectures on physics, vol. 3. California Institute of Technology. http://www.feynmanlectures.caltech.edu/III_01.html
2   Anando. (n.d.). The new science: We are made up of energy not matter. http://www.lifetrainings.com/We-are-made-of-Energy-not-Matter.html
3   Milo, R., & Phillips, R. (n.d.). What is the power consumption of the cell? http://book.bionumbers.org/what-is-the-power-consumption-of-a-cell
4   Honervogt, T. (2008). The complete Reiki tutor: A structured course to achieve professional expertise. London, UK: Octopus Publishing Group Ltd.
5   Pathfinder Ewing, J. (2008). Reiki shamanism: A guide to out-of-body healing. Findhorn, Scotland: Findhorn Press.
6   Lubeck, W, Petter, F. A., & Rand, W. L. (2002). The spirit of Reiki. Twin Lakes, WI: Lotus Press.
7   Schipper, K. (n.d.). Reiki: The Usui system of natural healing first degree manual. Calgary, Canada: (n.p.).
8   Zarokostas-Vasiliades, C. (2021). Editorial comments.
9   Conn, K. J. (2019). The seven major chakras. https://www.learnreligions.com/seven-major-chakras-1729254
10 Dynamo House. (n.d.). Chakras. Melbourne, Australia: Dynamo House Pty. Ltd.
11 MacLennan, C. (2016). What are etheric cords? https://www.blissfullight.com/blogs/energy-healing-blog/what-are-etheric-cords
12 Natasha (2019). DIY aura cleansing spray for clearing negative energy. https://natashalh.com/diy-aura-cleansing-spray

Chapter 9—Shamanism

1   Herrera, J. L. (2010). Cosmology I.
2   Rainbow Jaguar Institute of Alberta. (2017). https://www.facebook.com/RainbowJaguarAlberta/

posts/master-peruvian-shaman-jose-luis-herrer
a-offers-for-the-first-time-in-santa-cruz/1537766439578415

3 Herrera, J. L. (2012). Mastery II: Tracking and divination.

4 Villoldo, A. (2000). Shaman, healer, sage: How to heal
yourself and others with the energy medicine of the Americas.
New York, NY: Harmony Books.

5 Villoldo, A. (2016). What is a shaman's mesa? https://
thefourwinds.com/blog/shamanism/what-is-a-shamans-mesa

6 Encyclopaedia Britannica. (n.d.). Mandala. https://www.
britannica.com/topic/mandala-diagram

7 Herrera, J. L. (2010). Cosmology II.

8 Beeler, M. (2016). Despacho ceremony with Peruvian shaman
José Luis Herrera. http://www.pachakuti.pe/news/2016/10/8/
despacho-ceremony-with-peruvian-shaman-jose-luis-herrera

9 Sol, M. (n.d.). Despacho ceremony: How to practice the
ancient shamanic art of manifestation. https://lonerwolf.com/
despacho

10 Villoldo, A. (2016). What is a despacho? https://
thefourwinds.com/blog/shamanism/what-is-a-despacho

11 Shaman Sisters. (2014). How to perform a fire
ceremony. https://shamansisters.com/blogs/blo
g/18544775-how-to-perform-a-fire-ceremony

12 Shamans Cave. (n.d.). The recapitulation exercise. https://
www.shamanscave.com/self-healing/the-recapitulation

13 McMahon, R. (2016). Recapitulation: Release your past
and reclaim trapped energy. https://www.youtube.com/
watch?v=JGB2YUt1110

14 Northrope, C. (2016). 10 health reasons to start drumming:
The health benefits of beating your own drum. https://www.
drnorthrup.com/health-benefits-drumming

15 Konopacki, M., & Madison, G. (2018). EEG responses to
shamanic drumming: Does the suggestion of trance state
moderate the strength of frequency components? Journal of
Sleep and Sleep Disorder Research, 1(2), 16-25.

16 Kotsos, T. (n.d.). Brain waves and the deeper states of
consciousness. https://www.mind-your-reality.com/brain_
waves.html

17 Shaman Links. (n.d.). The shamanic journey. https://www.shamanlinks.net/shaman-info/about-shamanism/the-shamanic-journey

18 Wikipedia. (2020). Astral projection. https://en.wikipedia.org/wiki/Astral_projection

19 Bath, J. (2010). Peruvian shamanic teachings.

20 O'Neill, P. (2014). Glossary of terminology of the shamanic & ceremonial traditions of the Inca medicine lineage. http://www.incaglossary.org/intro.html

21 Starnes, G. (2010). The shamanic journey. https://www.youtube.com/watch?v=hU1_eM39Y3I

22 Serr, S. (2020). The shamanic journey. http://www.shamanism-101.com/Shamanic_Journey.html

Chapter 10—Your Authentic Self

1   Ravilochan, T. (2021). Maslow got it wrong. https://gatherfor.medium.com/maslow-got-it-wrong-ae45d6217a8c

2   Prera, A. (2020). Self-actualization. https://www.simplypsychology.org/self-actualization.html

3   Greater Good Magazine. (2020). What is compassion? https://greatergood.berkeley.edu/topic/compassion/definition

4   Good Magazine. (2020). Why practice it? https://greatergood.berkeley.edu/topic/compassion/definitio n#why-practice-compassion

5   Cherry, K. (2020). Taking the steps to forgive yourself. https://www.verywellmind.com/how-to-forgive-yourself-4583819#:~:text=Forgiveness%20is%20often%20defined%20as,you%20believe%20has%20wronged%20you.&text=1%EF%BB%BF%20Learn%20more%20about,at%20forgiving%20your%20own%20mistakes

6   Stiles, K. G. (2020). Ho'oponopono Hawaiian forgiveness meditation. https://www.pureplantessentials.com/products/hooponopono-hawaiian-forgiveness-meditation-by-kg-stiles

7   Linehan, M. M. (2015). DBT skills training handouts and worksheets (2nd ed.). New York, NY: The Guildford Press.

8 Ackerman, C. E. (2020). What is self-regulation? https://positivepsychology.com/self-regulation

9 Ackerman, C. E. (2020). What is self-transcendence? https://positivepsychology.com/self-transcendence

10 Pillay, S. (2016). Greater self-acceptance improves emotional well-being. https://www.health.harvard.edu/blog/greater-self-acceptance-improves-emotional-well-201605169546

11 Healthy Me Pa. (2018). 4 benefits of self-love and why it's important. https://www.healthymepa.com/2018/05/15/4-benefits-self-love-important

12 Khoshaba, D. (2012). A seven-step prescription for self-love. https://www.psychologytoday.com/ca/blog/get-hardy/201203/seven-step-prescription-self-love

13 Brown, B. (2020). Unlocking us podcast with Sonya Renee Taylor. https://brenebrown.com/podcast/brene-with-sonya-renee-taylor-on-the-body-is-not-an-apology

14 FC Wellness Company Ltd. (n.d.). 60 ideas for self-care and self-nurturing. https://www.fcwellnesscompanyltd.com/60-ideas-for-self-care-and-self-nurturing.html

15 Roubekas, V. (2021). What kind of a person are you? https://psychotherapycalgary.com/2021/01/25/personality-characteristics

16 Marter, J. (2017). 15 ways to live authentically and amazingly. https://www.huffpost.com/entry/15-ways-to-live-authentically-and-amaingly_b_6649610

17 Storm, H. (1981). Song of Heyoehkah. New York, NY: Ballentine Books.

ABOUT THE AUTHOR

Vicky Roubekas has a Master of Arts in Counseling Psychology from the Institute of Transpersonal Psychology. She is a psychologist, coach, author, and speaker who helps women connect with their body so they live a life of ease, joy, and authenticity. She has a private practice in Calgary, Canada where she sees clients in person and online. Vicky is trained in Eye Movement Desensitization and Reprocessing (EMDR). She is a Certified Hakomi Therapist, a mindfulness-based somatic therapy. She is a Certified Embodied Awareness Facilitator, offering spiritually-directed therapy. She is a ThetaHealing™ practitioner. Vicky is a Peruvian Shaman Practitioner and Reiki Master. She lives with her dog, Koko, and cat, Naia.

Connect with Vicky at **VickyRoubekas.com**.
Find her on Instagram **@vickyroubekas**.

CONGRATULATIONS FOR READING THE BOOK!

NEED MORE SUPPORT ON YOUR *EMBODIED* JOURNEY?

The best way to connect with your body and create a new way of being is to take action. You started that through the *Embodied* exercises in this book. Your next step to implementing lasting change is to take the *Embodied* online course or enroll in *Embodied* coaching.

Everyone who completes the online course or engages in the coaching program will receive more tools and personal one-on-one and group support to connect with their body and become fully *Embodied*.

ARE YOU READY TO GET STARTED?

JOIN TODAY AT VICKYROUBEKAS.COM

YOUR NEXT STEPS WITH
EMBODIED

 Sign Up for a Free *Embodied* Meditation

 Enroll in the *Embodied* Online Course

 Sign Up for *Embodied* Coaching

 Subscribe to the Vicky Roubekas
YouTube Channel

VICKYROUBEKAS.COM

WISH THE *EMBODIED* EXERCISES WERE
AVAILABLE IN AUDIO?

GREAT NEWS—THEY ARE!

PURCHASE THEM NOW AT

VICKYROUBEKAS.COM

Manufactured by Amazon.ca
Bolton, ON

28957545R00238